EASY LIVIN'
LOW-CALORIE
MICROWAVE
COOKING

Also by the author:
Easy Livin' Microwave Cooking
Easy Livin' Microwave Cooking for the Holidays

EASY LIVIN'
LOW-CALORIE
MICROWAVE
COOKING

· ❄ ·

KAREN KANGAS DWYER

· ST. MARTIN'S PRESS   NEW YORK ·

NOTE

· ❄ ·

The reader should consult with a physician before undertaking any diet or exercise program. This is especially important if the reader has any medical condition or is taking any medications that might be affected by diet or exercise.

The recipes contained herein are the result of the author's research and experience. Neither the publisher nor the author makes any warranty, express or implied, with respect to this book or its contents, and neither is or shall be liable for any claims arising from use of or reliance on this book.

EASY LIVIN' LOW-CALORIE MICROWAVE COOKING. Copyright © 1990 by Karen Kangas Dwyer. All rights reserved. Printed in the United States of America. No part of this book may be used or reproduced in any manner whatsoever without written permission except in the case of brief quotations embodied in critical articles or reviews. For information, address St. Martin's Press, 175 Fifth Avenue, New York, N.Y. 10010.

Nutritional Analysis by Marsha Viers, registered dietitian and president of the Nebraska Dietetic Association (1989), and Shelly Oestmann, registered dietitian.

Library of Congress Cataloging-in-Publication Data

Dwyer, Karen.
  Easy livin' low-calorie microwave cooking/Karen Kangas Dwyer.
    p.   cm.
  ISBN 0-312-03821-6
  1. Low-calorie diet—Recipes. 2. Microwave cookery. I. Title.
RM222.2.D88 1990
641.5'635—dc20   89-24142
                                      CIP

10 9 8 7 6

I dedicate this book to all those who, like myself, have struggled with dieting and fad diets, and who have concluded that healthy eating is not a diet for a period of time but rather a way of life.

This book is my attempt to make healthy low-calorie, low-cholesterol, and low-sodium foods easy to prepare and easy to enjoy for even a novice cook.

I also dedicate this book to my best friend since our college days together, Michelle Jewell Tilts, whose constant encouragement has helped me stick to new eating habits and pursue many other difficult challenges.

Finally, I dedicate this book to my mother, Fern Miller, whose struggle with high cholesterol and high blood pressure has made me more aware of the dangers associated with these problems and the urgency of finding a realistic solution through altered eating habits.

CONTENTS

— · ❄ · —

INTRODUCTION

1

— · ❄ · —

THE MICROWAVE OVEN IS PERFECT FOR LOW-CALORIE
HEALTHY COOKING

5

— · ❄ · —

ANSWERS TO BASIC MICROWAVE QUESTIONS

7

— · ❄ · —

NUTRITIONAL ANALYSIS

19

— · ❄ · —

APPETIZERS AND BEVERAGES

29

— · ❄ · —

BREADS AND MUFFINS

41

— · ❄ · —

DESSERTS, BARS, AND CAKES

55

— · ❄ · —

EGGS AND BREAKFAST FOODS

89

— · ❄ · —

FISH

107

— · ❄ · —

MEATS AND MAIN DISHES

139

· ❋ ·

POULTRY

177

· ❋ ·

PASTA, RICE, AND CASSEROLES

229

· ❋ ·

SAUCES, SEASONINGS, DRESSINGS, AND PRESERVES

241

· ❋ ·

SOUPS AND SANDWICHES

257

· ❋ ·

VEGETABLES, SALADS, AND ACCOMPANIMENTS

285

· ❋ ·

SUBSTITUTIONS AND EQUIVALENTS

333

· ❋ ·

INDEX

337

· ❋ ·

HARD-TO-FIND MICROWAVE AIDS

355

· ❋ ·

ABOUT THE AUTHOR

359

· ❋ ·

INTRODUCTION

·❄·

As soon as I hit twenty, I began to gain weight. Assured that it could be attributed to college life—including dorm food and late-night pizza—I was certain those extra pounds would roll off as soon as I was into my first teaching job.

After one year of teaching high school home economics—including at least one daily foods class of brownies, cookies, French toast, cream puffs or éclairs, along with judging over three hundred foods at the county fair (I tasted all of them)—I found those extra twenty pounds were not just rolling off.

By my mid-twenties I was quite familiar with not only low-carbohydrate diets and quick weight loss fad diets, but also the all-fruit diet, the liquid protein diet, and the grapefruit-and-broccoli diet (it was two days on this one and a late night of schoolwork that eventually led me to consume every leftover in the classroom refrigerator).

Finally, I took the advice of a *Reader's Digest* article on dieting sensibly for a lifetime. I cut down on white flour, white sugar, fat, and red meat, and began to lose weight slowly. By my late twenties I was down twenty pounds and back to my precollege weight.

During this time I acquired my first microwave oven, so microwave cooking and lowering the fat and calorie content of foods seemed to work together beautifully. I developed an array of delicious low-calorie microwave recipes for my own enjoyment. It was actually a game I loved to play—I'd look at a recipe and plan how I could take out most of the fat, sugar, and calories yet still have it taste delicious.

But then I met my husband Larry! Our two-year courtship included dinners out, dinner and a show, dinner theater, football games and dinner, Sunday brunches after church, and lots of lunches at beautiful Omaha restaurants.

You guessed it—ten unwanted pounds and clothes that wouldn't fit. I enrolled in Weight Loss Clinic, then in Diet Center, then in Weight Watchers. Of course I always ate "off" those diets on the weekends. Finally I lost the ten pounds one week before I marched down the aisle to say "I do."

After three months of carefree eating, including daily four- and five-course meals, Larry had gained thirty pounds and I had gained back those same ten pounds. A few months later, a family physician advised us both to lose some weight.

I began to cook those same delicious low-calorie recipes for Larry and me that I once cooked for just myself. In less than a year we were both back to our normal weight and physically felt better than ever.

Now people often say to me, "Oh, I bet you never diet!" I simply respond, "No, I never diet; low-calorie eating is a way of life for me."

I still love to microwave especially rich and calorie-laden foods for special occasions, holidays, or dinner parties. But on an everyday basis, I try to follow the guidelines of the American Heart Association, which recommends limiting fat, cholesterol, sodium, and fatty red meat while eating daily:

- 6 ounces or less of lean poultry, meat, and seafood (or equivalent protein in dried beans, peas, or nuts)

- 2 servings of low-fat milk products (1 serving = 8 ounces milk, ½ cup cottage cheese, etc.)

- 3 servings fresh fruit or juice (1 serving = 1 medium-size fruit or ½ cup juice)

- 3 servings of vegetables (1 serving = ½ to 1 cup raw or cooked)

- servings of low-fat, high-fiber breads, cereals, or pasta to fit an individual calorie plan (1 serving = 1 ounce/slice bread, ½ cup rice, pasta, or cereal)

However, the purpose of this book is not to recommend a diet for you. Your doctor or dietitian will do that.

I hope that the recipes in this book will be a help and inspiration to you. You can make delicious foods with a minimum of preparation time, from common household ingredients, that are low in calories, low in cholesterol, and low in sodium.

Happy Healthy Microwaving,
Karen

THE MICROWAVE
OVEN IS PERFECT
FOR LOW-CALORIE
HEALTHY
COOKING

———— · ❄ · ————

The microwave oven is perfect for cooking low-calorie, low-fat, low-cholesterol, and low-sodium recipes.

• Since foods made in the microwave cook in approximately one-fourth the time required for the conventional stove-top method, they will retain more of the natural flavors and will therefore *taste more satisfying* without the addition of butter, salt, or MSG. Microwaved foods even are apt to have a *more appetizing appearance,* because they often retain their color, shape, and texture more than conventionally cooked foods do.

• Microwaved foods, because of their shortened cooking time, *retain their full nutritional value,* which is often lost in long conventional cooking. In addition, fresh or frozen vegetables retain their water-soluble vitamins since microwave cooking requires little or no water.

• *Fats* (with their substantial calories) *can easily be reduced or omitted* from most microwave recipes—foods can be microwaved without the butter or shortening needed for stove-top cooking or frying. Microwaved meats and poultry also lose more of their fat when microwaved on a roasting rack than when fried or broiled.

• Because one or more family members may be on a diet that requires restricted or special foods, the microwave oven will make preparing a single food or entree *simple and fast*. Little clean-up is needed because foods can be prepared, microwaved, and served in the same dish.

What better time than now to try low-calorie cooking, especially when the microwave oven helps the food look and taste so good?

ANSWERS TO BASIC MICROWAVE QUESTIONS

❄

WHAT ARE MICROWAVES AND HOW DOES THE MICROWAVE OVEN WORK?

Microwaves are simply electromagnetic waves—similiar to radio waves, only shorter. They are nonionizing, unlike X rays, and do not produce any harmful buildup.

Microwaves penetrate food and cause the liquid molecules in the food to vibrate approximately 2.5 billion times per second. To illustrate how this works, rub your hands together very quickly. You will notice that the friction produces heat. During microwave cooking the water molecules, vibrating at 2.5 billion times per second, create friction. This friction produces heat that, in turn, causes the food to actually cook itself.

Microwaves are produced in every microwave oven in the same way.

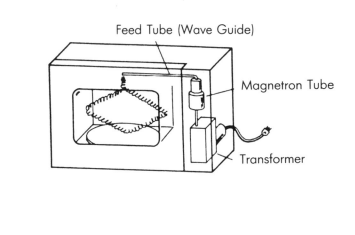

Feed Tube (Wave Guide)

Magnetron Tube

Transformer

The power cord conducts electricity to a transformer. The transformer converts low-voltage electricity into high-voltage electricity to empower the magnetron tube. The magnetron tube produces microwave energy and directs it down a feed tube into the microwave oven. The microwaves bounce off the acrylic-covered metal interior of the oven. Remember these three principles:

1. **Microwaves are reflected by metal.**
2. **Microwaves pass through glass, paper, wood, and plastic products.**
3. **Microwaves are attracted to water, fat, and sugar.**

WHAT IS STANDING TIME?

Standing time is one of the most important principles in microwaving cooking. It refers to the time immediately after the microwave oven has shut off.

Standing time is the time that the food continues to cook while the vibrating molecules slow down from the microwaving vibrations of 2.5 billion times per second. The microwave oven is shut off. No microwaves are in the food—but the food is still cooking!

Standing time is part of the recipe's cooking time. Most recipes will say something like this: Microwave 10 minutes and let stand 3 minutes. The total cooking time of the food is really 13 minutes.

WHAT UTENSILS OR DISHES SHOULD I USE
IN MY MICROWAVE OVEN?

Remember that microwaves pass through glass, paper, wood, and plastic. Therefore, you may:

- Use any paper products: paper cups for hot beverages, paper plates, paper towels, waxed paper, and so on.

- Use any dishwasher-safe plastic containers: plastic bottles, plastic wrap, Styrofoam cups, or boil-in bags. *Do not use soft plastics* (for example, Tupperware storage containers, unless labeled for microwave use, and so on), which often melt from hot fat or sugar.

- Use any heatproof glass (such as Corning Ware, Fire King, ceramics, china, and pottery) that is safe for microwave cooking. *Do not use fine china, lead crystal, or glass trimmed with metal.*

- Use wooden utensils or straw baskets for short-term heating only. Use toothpicks instead of metal skewers. Do not use wooden platters or cutting boards for long-term cooking. When the water evaporates from the wood after microwaving, the wooden piece will crack.

Remember that microwaves are reflected by metal. Therefore:

- Do not use metal utensils, except as specified for a convection microwave oven. Many new microwave ovens allow for the use of small amounts of foil to shield corners of foods, but *check your oven's instruction manual* (see page 15 for tips on shielding with foil).

HOW CAN I KNOW IF A PIECE OF COOKWARE IS MICROWAVE-SAFE?

For cookware that is not labeled "microwave-safe," the following test will determine if a pan, plate, dish, and so on, is microwave-safe.

MICROWAVE COOKWARE TEST

Fill a custard cup or glass measuring cup with 1 cup of warm water. Place the cookware in question next to the cup of water. (Do not allow the two to touch.) Microwave for 1 to 1½ minutes at HIGH (100%). The water should become very hot. If the adjacent dish is safe for microwaving, it will remain cool. If the dish becomes warm, *do not* use it in your microwave; it is absorbing the microwaves and probably contains metal or metallic paint.

WHAT SHAPES OF DISHES AND FOODS WORK BEST FOR MICROWAVING?

Ring-shape or round dishes work best for microwaving because the microwaves can penetrate the food evenly from all sides.

Ring-shaped dishes and foods allow the microwaves to reach the center of foods. Therefore, the center of the food cooks as quickly as the sides and bottoms cook.

Whenever possible, shape foods such as hamburgers and meat loaf into a ring or doughnut shape.

Arrange food such as drumsticks or asparagus in the oven so that the thicker edges are on the outside and the thin, delicate ends are on the inside.

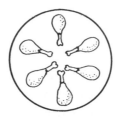
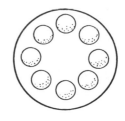

Chicken Drumsticks   Muffins or Custard cups or Appetizers

WHEN SHOULD FOODS BE COVERED IN THE MICROWAVE?

Food should be covered when the recipe recommends it or when moisture or steam should be retained in cooking, as with vegetables or casseroles.

- *Cover tightly* means to use a matching lid or plastic wrap. *Cover with vented plastic wrap* means to cover tightly with plastic wrap but leave a small edge turned back for a vent so the plastic doesn't split and so a burst of steam does not burn your hand.

- *Cover loosely* means to use waxed paper, a paper towel, or a paper napkin. Moisture and steam must escape from breads and meats to prevent sogginess. Use waxed paper when a sticky food may stick to a paper towel.

- *Microwave uncovered* means the food needs drying rather than moisture, heats quickly, and usually will not spatter.

HOW DO I KNOW WHETHER TO USE THE LONGEST OR THE SHORTEST AMOUNT OF TIME LISTED IN A MICROWAVE RECIPE?

Microwave ovens can be purchased in different sizes with varying wattages, so a range of cooking times is always listed for each microwave recipe.

- 700-watt ovens cook the fastest. Use the shortest amount of time.

- 650/600-watt ovens cook quickly, but not as fast as 700-watt ovens. Use a time in the middle of the range of the cooking times listed.

- 400/500-watt ovens are compact microwave ovens and therefore cook more slowly than midsize ovens. Use the longest cooking time listed. (Compact ovens often need one-eighth to one-quarter more time than a general microwave recipe recommends. Follow the compact microwave instructions when listed. See additional tips on page 14.)

SHOULD I "ROTATE," OR TURN, THE DISH WHEN MICROWAVING?

The ability of microwave ovens to cook evenly has improved greatly during the past five to ten years. Still, some microwave ovens have poor cooking patterns. Often all parts of the oven do not receive the same amount of microwaves. The food will be cooked well on one side, undercooked in the center, and overcooked on the other side.

- If you notice the food does not cook evenly in your oven, rotate the dish one-quarter turn halfway through the cooking time of most recipes (or as directed) to ensure even cooking.

• If your microwave has a turntable, rotating the food may not be necessary.

WHICH POWER LEVEL SHOULD I USE?

Just as you would not cook all of your foods in a conventional oven at 500° F., so, too, you should not microwave all foods at HIGH (100%).

The various (and lower) power levels cycle the microwave energy on and off to allow for slower and more even cooking. (This allows time for the heat to spread to the cooler and uncooked areas.)

Although many microwave manufacturers have tried to standardize the names of the different power levels, varying power-level names abound. Some microwave ovens even use percentages instead of names for the power levels. The following chart lists the various names used for the different power levels and the percentage of microwave energy associated with each.

VARIABLE POWER LEVELS CHART

NAME OF POWER LEVEL	% OF POWER	FOODS THAT COOK BEST AT THIS POWER LEVEL
HIGH or FULL POWER	100%	Small amount of food that cooks quickly; candies, beverages, and vegetables.
MEDIUM HIGH or ROAST	70%	All foods that are to be reheated; eggs, appetizers, and soups.
MEDIUM or SIMMER or BAKE	50%	Stews, some cakes, yeast breads, and quiches.
DEFROST or MEDIUM LOW	30%	All foods that are to be defrosted, cakes, quick breads, cheesecakes, and tough meats.
LOW or WARM	10%	Butter and cream cheese and all foods that need to be softened or kept warm.

ARE THERE ANY SPECIFIC ADJUSTMENTS TO MAKE WHEN USING A COMPACT MICROWAVE OVEN (400 TO 500 WATTS) IN THESE RECIPES?

Some of the recipes have compact microwave oven variations and instructions. Here are a few additional tips to keep in mind:

• Cooking at HIGH (100%) power in a 500-watt oven is similar to cooking at MEDIUM HIGH (70%) in a 700-watt oven.

• Therefore, *compact oven owners should use one power level higher than most (600- to 700-watt) recipes indicate.* For example, if a recipe recommends cooking at DEFROST (30%), use MEDIUM (50%); if it recommends MEDIUM (50%), use MEDIUM HIGH (70%); if it recommends MEDIUM HIGH (70%), use HIGH (100%).

• If a recipe recommends cooking at HIGH (100%), add about one-eighth to one-quarter more time than is recommended.

WHAT CAN I DO IF MY MICROWAVE OVEN HAS ONLY ONE POWER LEVEL?

You can reduce the power level HIGH (100%) to MEDIUM HIGH (70%) by placing a custard cup filled with 1 cup of water in the back of your microwave oven. The water will attract some of the microwaves and produce the effect of lowering the power level. While this method does not always work perfectly, many people have found it helpful.

In compact ovens (500 watts), you can successfully substitute HIGH (100%) power for MEDIUM HIGH (70%) power because the wattages are equivalent.

WHAT ARE "SENSITIVE FOODS"?

Sensitive foods are foods that pop, curdle, or dry out when cooked at HIGH (100%), such as eggs, cheese, mayonnaise, yogurt, sour cream, mushrooms, or kidney beans. Any food containing these ingredients should be microwaved at MEDIUM HIGH (70%) or lower for any lengthy cooking.

WHAT IS SHIELDING?

Shielding means to cover corners of square or rectangular baking dishes and bony pieces and edges of food with aluminum foil. This will prevent these areas from overcooking during microwaving.

- Never cover with foil more than one-quarter of the food you are microwaving.

- Never allow the foil to touch the sides of the oven.

Most microwave ovens manufactured since 1980 are built with specially protected magnetron tubes that allow for the use of small amounts of metal without damage to the tube.

- Read the instruction book that comes with your microwave oven to determine if you can use foil in it. Check under "poultry" for details, as manufacturers often recommend shielding turkey wings and legs during microwaving.

WARNING: DO NOT USE FOIL UNLESS YOUR MANUFACTURER'S INSTRUCTION BOOK RECOMMENDS IT.

Shielding Tips

For rectangular or square dishes:

- Use four 1½-inch to 2-inch squares or triangles of aluminum foil to cover corners of food and pan (shiny side down)

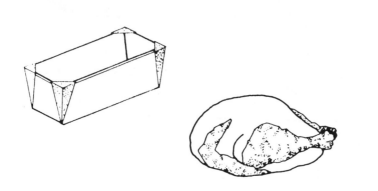

to prevent them from overcooking and hardening while microwaving. Remove foil during the last 2 to 3 minutes of microwaving time for cakes, breads, and bars.

For small or bony pieces of meat or poultry:

• Wrap aluminum foil (shiny side on the inside) around those pieces to prevent them from overcooking and drying out. Most meat and poultry pieces need shielding during only the first half of the cooking time.

HOW DO I USE A TEMPERATURE PROBE?

A temperature probe is the heat-sensing accessory that comes with many microwave ovens. When the probe is attached to the microwave oven and programmed, the oven will automatically shut off when the internal temperature of the food reaches the temperature you programmed.

To work accurately, the probe must be inserted two-thirds of the way into the center of the food. Do not allow it to touch the bone or the fatty layer of the food.

After inserting the probe into the food, program both the temperature and the power level on your microwave oven. (Many recipes list temperatures so you can use your probe.) During standing time your food will usually rise 10 to 15 degrees more, so temperatures to which you set your probe

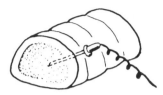

will be lower than those used with a conventional meat thermometer.

The probe will not work for microwaving candy syrups because it programs only to 200° F.

DO I NEED TO USE A TEMPERATURE PROBE?

Recipes in this cookbook sometimes list both cooking time and temperature so you can use your probe if you like. However, it is not necessary. Using a probe can be helpful when microwaving meat or poultry or when internal temperature accuracy is important to avoid overcooking the food.

WHAT IS COMBINATION COOKING?

Combination cooking refers to the use of both your conventional and microwave oven in a recipe. It can cut the cooking time for some foods by up to 50 percent. In combination cooking, many recipes are started in the conventional oven to ensure browning and then transferred to the microwave oven to speed cooking.

WHAT IS A CONVECTION MICROWAVE OVEN?

A convection microwave is a convection oven and a microwave oven. Convection cooking uses fan-forced hot air. In a convection oven, a high-speed fan circulates hot air throughout the oven cavity. The moving air surrounds the food and quickly seals in the juices.

In convection microwaving, the microwaves cycle on and off with this fan-forced hot air, producing traditionally browned and crisped foods in half the time of a regular conventional oven.

Some convection microwave recipes are included in this cookbook along with adaptations for combining your regular oven with your microwave oven to produce similar results.

WHICH CONVECTION MICROWAVE OVEN SETTING SHOULD I USE?

Convection microwave ovens use different terms for oven settings. Each convection recipe in this book gives possible names of settings on your microwave oven. (For example: Low-Mix Bake 350° F. on one oven is about the same as Code 2 on another or Combination 2 on still another.)

NUTRITIONAL
ANALYSIS

——————— · ❄ · ———————

Each recipe in this book includes a nutritional analysis that tells you the amount of calories, carbohydrates, fat, protein, dietary fiber (although dietary fiber values for some foods have not been established), cholesterol, sodium, and diabetic exchanges per individual serving.*

The nutritional analysis is given to assist you in planning and preparing meals to fit your diet plan. To obtain the nutritional analysis figures, the following assumptions were made:

- When two ingredient choices in a recipe are given, for example, 1 teaspoon fructose or ½ packet sugar substitute), the nutritional analysis was calculated using the first choice (1 teaspoon fructose).

- All garnishes or foods listed as optional are included in the

....

* This nutritional analysis information was obtained from the computer software program "Nutritionist #2" with an updated data base. All decimal figures were rounded off to the nearest whole number. The diabetic exchanges were calculated separately by hand, based on the nutritional recommendations in the Exchange List for Meal Planning (1986), developed by the American Diabetic Association and the American Dietetic Association in Cooperation with the U.S. Department of Health, Education, and Welfare.

nutritional analysis figures. Any suggestions recommended in the Tips or Variations are *not* included.

- For meat, poultry, and fish recipes, the nutritional analysis was calculated using the edible portion, trimmed of visible fat.

- When a range of weight or measurement is given (for example, 2 to 2½ pounds acorn squash), the nutritional analysis was calculated using the lesser weight.

- Since some alcohol calories evaporate when heated, the nutritional analysis reflects this reduction.

- When an asterisk (*) follows an ingredient, the nutritional analysis was calculated using the low-sodium products.

CALORIES AND DAILY REQUIREMENTS

A calorie—the amount of heat required to raise the temperature of one kilogram of water one degree centigrade—is the unit used to measure the energy-producing value of food. We must have food, and therefore calories, to move, work, live, and breathe. However, if we take in more calories than we need, the body will neatly (or not so neatly) store the excess in the form of fat. Therefore, it is important to balance our daily calorie intake with the energy we expend to avoid weight gain.

Daily calorie requirements vary with each person, depending on the amount of exercise you do and the rate of your basal metabolism (the rate at which the body uses calories when it is at rest). You can calculate the approximate number of calories you need each day to maintain your weight by multiplying your current weight by 14 (women) or 16 (men). (This approximation is for people who get moderate exercise.)

To maintain a healthful weight-reduction program, many physicians and dietitians recommend losing only one to two pounds per week. On the average, one pound of stored fat contains 3,500 calories, so to lose one pound per week you will need to expend 500 more calories than you take in each day. To lose two pounds, you will need to expend 1,000 more calories than you take in daily.

Reducing your daily calorie intake to fewer than 1,000 calories can be harmful and will not supply the body with proper nutrition. In addition, some research has shown that a very low calorie intake may cause the body to adapt to the new level and use fewer calories for daily activities. It is far better to lose weight with a combination of diet and exercise than to cut your calorie intake below 1,000.

To help you fit the foods into your diet plan, calories for every recipe in this cookbook are given in the nutritional analysis. Be sure to consult your physician before beginning any weight-reduction plan to determine the calorie intake and diet that are best for your health.

CARBOHYDRATES

There are two kinds of carbohydrates: simple and complex. Simple carbohydrates are simple sugar units, such as glucose, maltose, fructose, and sucrose (including table sugar, honey, brown sugar, molasses, corn syrup, maple syrup, and other natural sweeteners), that the body absorbs quickly. Simple carbohydrates are often called "empty calories" because they provide only short bursts of energy and contain few vitamins and minerals.

Long chains of simple sugar units are called complex carbohydrates, which include starch and cellulose. They are digested slowly and provide the body with a steady source of energy. In addition, many complex carbohydrates (such as whole-grain breads, cereals, rice, and pasta, as well as dried beans, peas, and lentils) are good sources of vitamins, minerals, and dietary fiber.

The U.S. Recommended Daily Allowance (RDA) of carbohydrates is 300 grams. To help you calculate your daily carbohydrate intake, the nutritional analysis lists grams of carbohydrates for each recipe.

FATS

Fats store energy and the essential fat-soluble vitamins A, D, E, and K. One gram of fat supplies twice as many calories (9) as a gram of protein (4) or carbohydrate (4). The number of calories in fat remains the same whether the fat is of vegetable or animal origin. Dietary fat comes in three forms: saturated, monounsaturated, and polyunsaturated.

Saturated fats come primarily from animal sources and are usually solid at room temperature. They have been linked to elevated blood cholesterol, and a diet high in saturated fats may contribute to heart disease. Animal sources of saturated fats include butter, lard, cheese, whole milk, meats, and poultry. Vegetable sources include cocoa butter, coconut oil, and palm oil.

Monounsaturated and polyunsaturated fats come primarily from plant sources and are liquid at room temperature. Research has shown that they can help lower blood cholesterol. Sources of monounsaturated fats include peanut oil and olive oil. Sources of polyunsaturated fats include corn oil, safflower oil, sunflower oil, soybean oil, cottonseed oil, and polyunsaturated margarine.

Although we need some fat daily, excess intake of fat has been linked to certain cancers (colon, breast, prostate, ovarian, pancreatic, and lung) as well as weight gain and its resulting problems. The American Heart Association recommends that Americans consume no more than 30 percent of their daily calories from fat. (At present, most Americans consume about 40 percent of their daily calories from fat.) Saturated fats should make up 10 percent or less of this daily calorie intake.

The recipes in this cookbook use monounsaturated and polyunsaturated fats whenever possible. The nutritional analysis lists the milligrams of fat in each recipe to help you calculate your daily fat intake and stay within recommended guidelines.

PROTEIN

Proteins (chains of amino acids) are essential for a variety of biological functions, including growth, maintenance, and repair of body tissues. Protein actually helps the body produce antibodies to combat disease and hormones to regulate body processes. Excess protein, however, is stored as fat.

Protein is obtained from animal sources (meat, poultry, fish, eggs, dairy products) and plant sources (dried beans and peas, cereals, whole grains, soybean products, seeds, nuts). The U.S. RDA of protein for adults and children is about 45 grams, which is not difficult to obtain.

One ounce of meat, poultry, or fish (or ½ cup cooked dried beans or peas, 1 egg, or ¼-cup egg substitute) contains about 8 grams of protein. Eating just 6 ounces of meat, poultry, or fish (or equivalent of eggs or dried beans) will provide enough protein to meet the U.S. RDA (6 ounces × 8 grams = 48 grams of protein).

To help you calculate your daily protein intake and stay within the recommended guidelines, the nutritional analysis of each recipe lists grams of protein for individual servings.

DIETARY FIBER

Dietary fiber comes from plant sources and includes those substances that the body cannot digest. There are two main types of dietary fiber: soluble and insoluble. Soluble fiber includes pectins and gums (found in oat bran, navy beans, lentils, split peas, carrots, sweet potatoes, apples, and citrus fruits), and has been found to help prevent and treat heart disease by lowering blood cholesterol. Soluble fiber also has been shown to help stabilize blood sugars in diabetics.

Insoluble fiber (found in wheat bran, whole-wheat breads, nuts, seeds, popcorn, unpeeled fruits, and vegetables) speeds the passage of wastes through the intestines. It helps prevent constipation and diverticular disease, and has been linked to the prevention of some types of cancer.

Dietary fiber measurements are given in the nutritional

analysis of recipes in this book for bread items and some of the fruit and vegetable dishes. The dietary fiber content of some foods is not yet available. In such cases, the dietary fiber category in the nutritional analysis is marked N/A (not available).

Keep in mind that the National Cancer Institute recommends eating 20 to 30 grams of dietary fiber per day.

CHOLESTEROL

Cholesterol is a waxy, white, powdery substance, invisible to the naked eye, that is found in every animal cell and animal food source, including egg yolks. The body uses cholesterol to produce cell walls and hormones.

The body manufactures cholesterol and also obtains it from food. Medical studies have linked excessive amounts of cholesterol in the blood to the increased risk of heart disease. Recent research has also shown that if you lower your cholesterol level, you can help reduce the risk of heart disease and even reduce the effects of narrowing blood vessels caused by cholesterol buildup. The National Heart, Lung and Blood Institute reports that about half of all Americans have elevated (total) blood cholesterol levels of more than 200 milligrams per deciliter and urges every adult to ask for cholesterol information as part of a physical examination.

The American Heart Association recommends that cholesterol intake should be about 100 milligrams per 1,000 calories consumed daily—and should never exceed 300 milligrams daily, no matter how many calories you eat. For example, if an average woman eats 1,800 calories per day, her daily cholesterol intake should be about 180 milligrams; if an average man eats 2,300 calories per day, his cholesterol intake should be no more than 230 milligrams.

Many of the recipes in this cookbook are lower in cholesterol than similar conventionally cooked foods. The nutritional analysis lists the milligrams of cholesterol in each recipe to help you plan your diet and stay within the guidelines set by your doctor and the American Heart Association.

SODIUM

Sodium is a mineral that the body needs to stay healthy: It helps balance the water in your body. According to the American Heart Association, the average American consumes about 4,000 to 5,000 milligrams of sodium daily, which is one and one-half to five times too much. It recommends that Americans should stay within an adequate sodium range of 1,000 to 3,000 milligrams per day (one level teaspoon of salt contains 2,132 milligrams of sodium). Diets high in sodium have been linked to high blood pressure or hypertension, which can lead to heart attacks and strokes. All recipes in this book are low or reduced in sodium to help you stay within these guidelines. The nutritional analysis of each recipe provides milligrams of sodium for individual servings.

If you are on a sodium-restricted diet be sure to use unsalted or low-sodium products.

DIABETIC EXCHANGES*

Many diets, especially diabetic diets, are based on food choices a person can make at each meal or snack. These food choices, called exchanges, have been grouped into six lists as part of a guide developed by the American Dietetic Association and the American Diabetic Association, called Exchange Lists for Meal Planning (1986).

The six lists group foods that contain similar amounts of carbohydrates, protein, fat, and calories. A person on a specified diet can use these lists to help control nutrient and calorie intake according to the food plan. Any food on a list can be exchanged for any other food on the same list.

The following chart shows the six exchange lists, the amount of nutrients and calories in one serving, and examples of foods (per one serving) on each list.

. . . .

*In this cookbook, the diabetic exchanges are approximate calculations. Please note that the meats used in many of the recipes (such as white fish or skinned chicken breasts) are even lower in fat than the lean-meat exchange and are therefore lower in calories than the lean-meat exchange indicates on the lists.

EXCHANGE LISTS

EXCHANGE LIST	CARBOHYDRATE (GRAMS)	PROTEIN (GRAMS)	FAT (GRAMS)	CALORIES
Starch/Bread ½ cup cereal grain or pasta or 1 ounce bread (¾ cup ready-to-eat unsweetened cereals, ½ cup cooked cereal, ⅓ cup cooked rice, ⅓ cup cooked dried beans/peas/lentils, 1 3-ounce baked potato, 1 slice whole wheat bread, 1 6-inch tortilla, ½ hamburger bun, 3 cups popped popcorn)	15	3	trace	80
Meat 1 ounce lean, medium-fat, or high-fat meat or protein substitute				
Lean Meat (1 ounce any lean ham, veal chop, skinless chicken thigh, or fresh or frozen fish, ¼ cup cottage cheese, 2 tablespoons grated Parmesan cheese, 3 egg whites, ¼ cup egg substitute)	—	7	3	55
Medium-fat Meat Also omit ½ fat exchange. (1 ounce ground beef, beef roast, liver, pork chops, veal cutlets, chicken with skin, tuna in oil, mozzarella cheese, or diet cheeses, 1 egg, 4 ounces tofu)	—	7	5	75
High-fat Meat Also omit 1 fat exchange (1 ounce of corned beef, spare ribs, pork sausage, fried fish, or bologna; 1 tablespoon peanut butter)	—	7	8	100
Vegetable ½ cup cooked vegetables/juice or 1 cup raw vegetables (½ medium artichoke, 1 cup raw carrots, onions, spinach, tomato, zucchini	5	2	—	25
Fruit ½ cup fresh fruit or juice; ¼ cup dried fruit (1 apple, ½ grapefruit, ¾ cup mandarin oranges, 1 small pear, 1 cup raspberries, 3 prunes, ½ cup orange juice)	15	—.	—	60

EXCHANGE LIST	CARBOHYDRATE (GRAMS)	PROTEIN (GRAMS)	FAT (GRAMS)	CALORIES
Milk				
1 cup milk, ½ cup evaporated milk; 8 ounces yogurt				
Skim Milk	12	8	trace	90
(1 cup 1% milk or low-fat buttermilk or ½ cup nonfat dry milk or 8 ounces plain nonfat yogurt)				
Low-fat Milk	12	8	5	120
(1 cup 2% milk or 8 ounces plain low-fat yogurt)				
Whole Milk	12	8	8	150
(1 cup whole milk; 8 ounces plain yogurt)				
Fat				
Unsaturated Fat	—	—	5	45
(1 teaspoon margarine or mayonnaise; 1 tablespoon diet margarine or reduced-calorie mayonnaise; 1 teaspoon oil (corn, cottonseed, sunflower, safflower, soybean, olive), 2 whole pecans, 1 tablespoon salad dressing)				
Saturated Fat	—	—	5	45
(1 teaspoon butter, 2 tablespoons coconut, 2 tablespoons sour cream, 1 tablespoon cream cheese)				
Free Foods				
Contain less than 20 calories (bouillon, fat-free broth, coffee, sugar-free gelatin, sugar substitute, vinegar, 1 tablespoon catsup, seasonings)				

THE SURGEON GENERAL'S REPORT REAFFIRMS THE NEED TO REDUCE CALORIES, CHOLESTEROL, AND SODIUM

In 1988 the Surgeon General for the first time in history made recommendations to the American public about nutritious and healthy eating. He wrote that diet plays an important role in five out of ten leading causes of death in Americans. Sixty-eight percent of all deaths in the United

States are related to heart disease, cancer, stroke, diabetes, and atherosclerosis.

His report exhorts us to:

- Achieve and maintain a desirable body weight by limiting calorie-rich foods (high in fat and sugar) in our diets, minimizing consumption of alcohol (no more than two drinks per day), and increasing energy expenditure through regular exercise.

- Reduce our intake of fats, especially saturated fats, and increase our intake of complex carbohydrates and fiber.

- Reduce sodium intake by limiting the use of sodium at the table and in food preparation as well as by choosing foods low in sodium.

APPETIZERS AND BEVERAGES

GENERAL TIPS FOR MICROWAVING
APPETIZERS

- Mix dips and spreads in advance. Heat and spread on canapés, crackers, and breads just before serving.

- Choose crackers and breads that are sturdy and crisp so they don't become soggy when microwaved with spreads on them.

- Microwave crackers and breads on at least two layers of paper towels. The towels absorb the moisture and keep the crackers crisp.

- Use HIGH (100%) power for microwaving most small appetizers.

- Use MEDIUM HIGH (70%) power for microwaving all appetizers and dips that contain cheese, cream cheese, sour cream, yogurt, mayonnaise, or mushrooms, because these are sensitive ingredients that can curdle or dry out.

GENERAL TIPS FOR MICROWAVING BEVERAGES

- Microwave most beverages at HIGH (100%) power until boiling.

- Watch milk beverages closely as they boil over easily when microwaved.

LOW-CAL TOMATO COCKTAIL (NONALCOHOLIC)

· · · · ·

A delicious appetizer beverage, especially on a cold day.

46-ounce can (6 cups) tomato juice*
2 teaspoons beef bouillon granules,* dissolved in 1½ cups hot water
2 teaspoons Worcester-shire sauce

½ teaspoon onion powder
1 tablespoon lemon juice
8 cloves and 1 lemon, thinly sliced (into 8 slices), to garnish

1. Combine all ingredients except cloves and lemon slices in a 2-quart microwave-safe glass bowl.
2. Microwave for 11 to 14 minutes at HIGH (100%), until hot (160° F.). Pour into mugs.
3. Place a clove in the center of each lemon slice. Garnish each cocktail with clove-studded lemon slice before serving.

Yield: 10 servings

——————— · ❄ · ———————

* Use no-salt-added variety for lowest sodium value, if desired.

Variation: Cloves can be omitted, if desired. Simply garnish with the thin lemon slices.

Nutritional Analysis per ¾-Cup Serving

Calories: 31   Fiber: N/A
Carbohydrate: 7   Cholesterol: 0 mg
Fat: Trace   Sodium: 31 mg
Protein: 1   Diabetic exchanges:
                                          Vegetable: 1.5

TIPS
·······

These are three of my favorite low-calorie nonalcoholic beverages. I especially like to serve them to my guests with appetizers.

NONALCOHOLIC BEVERAGES
· · · · ·

No need to microwave these beverages, but they make nice accompaniments to microwaved meals.

·················· SPARKLING ROSÉ ····················

12 ounces reduced-calorie   12 ounces diet lemon-lime
   cranapple juice   soda

·················· MOCK CHAMPAGNE ····················

12 ounces apple cider   12 ounces diet ginger ale
   (made without sugar)

·················· CITRUS COOLER ····················

1 cup unsweetened   16 ounces diet ginger ale
   grapefruit juice or   2 teaspoons lime juice
   orange juice

1. Thoroughly chill all ingredients.
2. Choose four long-stem beverage glasses.

3. Combine ingredients for chosen beverage. Fill each glass with ¾ cup (6 ounces) of each beverage. Serve immediately.

Yield: 4 servings (6 ounces each)

———————— · ❄ · ————————

Nutritional Analysis per ¾-Cup Serving

	Rosé	Champagne	Cooler
Calories:	20	41	37
Carbohydrate:	5	10 g	9 g
Fat:	0 g	0 g	0 g
Protein:	0 g	0 g	0 g
Fiber:	N/A	N/A	N/A
Cholesterol:	0 mg	0 mg	0 mg
Sodium:	3 mg	34 mg	41 mg
Diabetic exchanges:	Free	Fruit: 0.5	Fruit: 0.5

COFFEE OLÉ

———————— · · · · · ————————

4 cups water
4 teaspoons instant
  decaffeinated coffee,
  Postum, or Cafix
½ teaspoon ground
  cardamom

¼ teaspoon almond extract
¼ teaspoon vanilla extract
½ packet sugar substitute
  (equivalent to 1
  teaspoon sugar),
  optional

1. Combine water, coffee, and cardamom in a 4-quart microwave-safe glass bowl. Microwave for 8 to 9 minutes at HIGH (100%), or until hot.
2. Stir in extracts and sugar substitute. Pour into mugs or serving pot. Serve immediately.

Yield: 4 cups (8 ounces each)

———————— · ❄ · ————————

WARM CITRUS APPETIZER

· · · · ·

1 cup unsweetened
  pineapple juice
1½ cups low-calorie
  cranberry juice
1½ cups hot water
3 cups unsweetened
  orange juice

1½ tablespoons lemon
  juice
Orange slices to garnish,
  optional

1. Combine all ingredients in a 2-quart bowl.
2. Microwave for 11 to 12 minutes at HIGH (100%), until hot (160° F). Serve in glass mugs garnished with a thin orange slice, if desired.

Yield: 8 to 10 servings (6 to 7 ounces each)

──────── · ❄ · ────────

CALIFORNIA STUFFED MUSHROOMS

TIPS
· · · · · · · · ·

10 medium mushrooms (approximately 6 ounces), cleaned

½ cup low-fat cottage cheese

½ teaspoon beef bouillon granules*

½ teaspoon dried chives

¼ teaspoon Worcestershire sauce

Although California Stuffed Mushrooms do not need to be micro-waved, they are delicious served before any of the microwaved entrees.

1. Remove stems from mushrooms; set caps aside. Discard stems or store for another use.
2. Using a food processor or blender, process cottage cheese, bouillon granules, chives, and Worcestershire sauce until smooth. Stuff each mushroom cap with cheese mixture. Place on serving tray and refrigerate until serving time.

Yield: 10 stuffed mushrooms

Nutritional Analysis per Serving (1 Mushroom)

Calories: 15

Carbohydrate: 1 g

Fat: Trace

Protein: 2 g

Fiber: N/A

Cholesterol: 1 mg

Sodium: 56 mg

Diabetic exchanges: Free

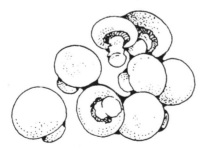

*Use unsalted variety for lowest sodium value, if desired.

Choose an avocado that is heavy and free of bruised or dark spots. It will most likely be unripe. (A ripe avocado will yield to pressure when pressed with your fingertips.) To ripen, put in a brown paper bag and leave at room temperature for one day.

If you're in a hurry, microwave an unripened avocado for 1 minute at HIGH (100%) to soften.

Avocados contain vitamins A and C and niacin, as well as potassium and 2 grams of protein. However, they also contain unsaturated fat, so you may want to limit them to an occasional treat.

LOW-CALORIE GUACAMOLE DIP

──── · · · · · ────

Serve with assorted fresh vegetables or wheat wafers.

¼ cup chopped green or yellow onion
1 small clove garlic, minced, or ¼ teaspoon garlic powder
¼ cup chopped fresh parsley

1 ripe avocado, halved and pitted
1 cup (8 ounces) low-fat cottage cheese
1 tablespoon fresh lime juice

1. In a small microwave-safe bowl or custard cup, combine the onion, garlic, and parsley. Microwave for 1½ to 2 minutes at HIGH (100%), until vegetables are softened. Set aside.
2. Scoop out avocado pulp and discard skin. Combine pulp, cottage cheese, lime juice, and cooked vegetables in a food processor or blender. Process 20 seconds or until smooth. Cover and refrigerate until serving time.

Yield: 2 cups

──────── · ❄ · ────────

Nutritional Analysis per 2-Tablespoon Serving

Calories 20
Carbohydrate: 1 g
Fat: 1 g
Protein: 1 g
Fiber: N/A
Cholesterol: 1 mg

Sodium: 32 mg
Diabetic exchanges:
Free for under 2 tablespoons
Over 2 tablespoons, fat: 0.5

MOCK MARINATED HERRING

—————— · · · · · ——————

A perfect low-calorie treat for herring lovers.

2 tablespoons water
1 cup coarsely chopped
   celery (about 2 stalks)
2 medium onions, thinly
   sliced and separated into
   rings
1 small eggplant, peeled
   and cut into strips 4
   inches long by 1 inch
   wide

1 cup plain nonfat yogurt
4 teaspoons lemon juice
½ packet sugar substitute
   (equivalent to 1
   teaspoon sugar)
Dash ground cloves
Dash salt substitute
1 small bay leaf

TIPS
....

Try serving Mock Marinated Herring with assorted whole wheat crackers or green pepper and other sliced vegetables.

1. Combine water, celery, onion, and eggplant in a 2-quart microwave-safe casserole. Cover with vented plastic wrap. Microwave for 8 to 10 minutes at HIGH (100%), or until vegetables are tender but not mushy, stirring twice. Drain and discard liquid. Cool completely.
2. Combine remaining ingredients in a mixing bowl; gently toss with cooled vegetables. Refrigerate at least 2 hours, or until serving time. Remove bay leaf before serving.

Yield: 3½ cups

—————— · ❄ · ——————

Nutritional Analysis per 3-Tablespoon Serving

Calories: 12
Carbohydrate: 2 g
Fat: Trace
Protein: 1 g

Fiber: N/A
Cholesterol: Trace
Sodium: 15 mg
Diabetic exchanges: Free

TIPS

Neufchâtel cheese is a perfect substitute for the cream cheese used in traditional dips. Neufchâtel contains 30 fewer calories per ounce than cream cheese.

······················· CHEESE BALL ·······················

2 packages (8 ounces each) Neufchâtel cheese or low-fat cream cheese
2 tablespoons green onion, diced very fine

8-ounce can crushed pineapple in juice, drained well

······················· COATING ·······················

1 tablespoon dried parsley
½ cup unsalted sunflower seeds

1. Microwave Neufchâtel cheese in a 2-quart microwave-safe bowl for 1 to 1½ minutes at MEDIUM HIGH (70%) to soften. Beat onion and drained pineapple into the cheese using a spoon or electric mixer. Chill slightly and form into a ball.
2. Combine coating ingredients. Roll cheese ball into coating. Cover and refrigerate until serving time. Serve with assorted melba toast rounds, wheat crackers, or vegetables.

Yield: 30 servings

——————— · ❄ · ———————

Nutritional Analysis per 2-Tablespoon Serving

Calories: 56	Cholesterol: 12 mg
Carbohydrate: 2 g	Sodium: 61 mg
Fat: 5 g	Diabetic exchanges:
Protein: 2 g	Lean meat: 0.25
Fat: N/A	For fat: 0.75

SPINACH DIP IN RYE BREAD

TIPS

1 round loaf crusty rye
   bread
2 packages (10 ounces
   each) frozen chopped
   spinach
8-ounce package
   Neufchâtel cheese
1 cup (8 ounces) plain
   nonfat yogurt

½ cup reduced-calorie
   mayonnaise
¼ cup finely chopped
   green onion
1 teaspoon Seasoned Salt
   Substitute #1 (see page
   244) or store-bought
   alternative
Dash nutmeg

TIPS

If spinach packages
are wrapped in foil, re-
move foil before mi-
crowaving.

1. Cut a 2-inch slice from top of bread. Cut a circle 1½ inches from outer edge of crust. Remove center, leaving at least 2 inches of bread on bottom. Cut leftover bread (center and top pieces) into cubes for dipping. Store all in a plastic bag until serving time.

2. Microwave spinach in packages on a paper towel for 9 to 10 minutes at HIGH (100%), or until thawed. Drain well. Pat spinach with a paper towel to remove moisture. Set aside.

3. Microwave Neufchâtel cheese in a 2-quart microwave-safe bowl for 1 to 1½ minutes at MEDIUM HIGH (70%) to soften. Mix in yogurt, mayonnaise, onion, Seasoned Salt Substitute, nutmeg, and drained spinach.

4. At serving time, spoon spinach-cheese filling into pre-pared bread loaf. Place on paper plate lined with two paper towels. Microwave for 1½ to 2 minutes at MEDIUM HIGH (70%), or until bread is warm. Serve with bread cubes and/or sliced fresh vegetables on a serving tray.

Yield: 16 servings

ZUCCHINI-STUFFED MUSHROOMS

18 medium (1½-inch)
mushrooms
(approximately 12
ounces), cleaned
1 green onion, thinly
sliced to equal 2
tablespoons
1 teaspoon reduced-calorie
margarine*

1 small zucchini, cleaned
and shredded to equal 1
cup
¼ cup grated low-fat
Parmesan cheese
Dash paprika to garnish,
optional

1. Remove stems from mushrooms. Set caps aside. Chop
   stems.
2. Combine stems, onion, and margarine in a 1-quart microwave-safe casserole. Microwave covered with wax paper for
   2 to 3 minutes at HIGH (100%), or until vegetables are
   tender. Stir in zucchini. Cover again. Microwave for 2 to
   3 minutes longer at HIGH (100%), or until zucchini is
   tender. Stir in Parmesan cheese.
3. Spoon zucchini mixture into mushroom caps. Arrange 9
   caps in a circular fashion on a pie plate or a paper plate.
   Microwave for 2 to 2½ minutes at MEDIUM HIGH
   (70%), or until heated through.† (Rotate plate halfway

....
*Use unsalted variety for lowest sodium values, if desired.
†**Compacts:** Use HIGH (100%) instead of MEDIUM HIGH (70%) in step
#3.

through cooking time if necessary for even cooking.) Garnish with paprika, if desired. Repeat with remaining caps. Transfer to a serving tray and serve immediately.

Yield: 18 mushrooms

———————— · ❄ · ————————

Nutritional Analysis per Serving (2 Stuffed Mushrooms)

Calories: 27

Carbohydrate: 2 g

Fat: 2 g

Protein: 2 g

Fiber: N/A

Cholesterol: 2 mg

Sodium: 56 mg

Diabetic exchanges:
  Vegetable: 1

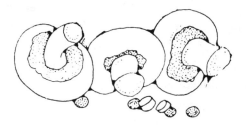

BREADS AND MUFFINS

· ❄ ·

GENERAL TIPS FOR MICROWAVING QUICK BREADS AND MUFFINS

- Microwaved breads do not brown. To create an attractive appearance, brush the top with milk and sprinkle with one of the following before microwaving:
    cracker crumbs
    cinnamon and fructose or sugar
    Parmesan cheese and/or poppy seeds
    oatmeal, cornmeal, or crushed cereal

- Microwave muffin batter in two paper liners (one will absorb the moisture) for 25 to 30 seconds at HIGH (100%). For six muffins, microwave for about 2½ minutes at HIGH (100%).

- For bread, always use a microwave-safe bread or tube pan that has been greased with oil (or sprayed with vegetable coating) and dusted with sugar. *Do not dust with flour* because the bread will stick and be difficult to remove from the pan.

- If the bottom of microwaved bread tends not to cook in your microwave oven, place the bread pan on an inverted pie plate so microwaves can easily reach the bottom. Do not use a rack.

- When using a microwave loaf pan, shield edges 1 to 1½ inches with foil to prevent ends and corners from overcooking before the center is done. Remove foil for the last half of the microwaving time. Do not use foil shielding if your owner's manual does not recommend it.

- As a rule of thumb, microwave quick breads for 7 to 9 minutes at MEDIUM HIGH (70%). Let stand 5 minutes.

- If you are using delicate ingredients such as cheese, cream cheese, or large amounts of fruit in a quick bread recipe, microwave for 9 minutes at MEDIUM (50%) and then again for 2 to 5 minutes at HIGH (100%). Let stand 5 minutes.

- Bread is done when a toothpick inserted near the center comes out clean.

GENERAL TIPS FOR MICROWAVING YEAST BREADS

- To proof or quickly "raise" dough, cover with plastic wrap. Microwave for 1 minute at MEDIUM (50%). Let rest 10 to 15 minutes. Repeat one to two times. Uncover before baking.

- Microwave yeast breads for 10 to 13 minutes at MEDIUM (50%) with edges shielded 1 to 1½ inches. Remove foil for the last half of cooking time. Microwave two loaves for 13 to 16 minutes at MEDIUM (50%) with edges shielded as directed above. *Do not* use foil shielding if your owner's manual does not recommend it.

GENERAL TIP FOR DEFROSTING BREADS

• To defrost a loaf of frozen bread or package of buns, rolls, or English muffins, remove twist tie and slide two layers of paper towels under loaf or buns to prevent sogginess. Leave plastic bag open at one end.

For a 1-pound loaf of bread or eight buns, or twelve rolls, or six English muffins, microwave for 3 to 3½ minutes at DEFROST (30%). Let stand 3 minutes.

For a 1½-pound loaf, microwave for about 3½ to 4 minutes at DEFROST (30%). Let stand 3 minutes. Or you can microwave for 50 to 75 seconds at HIGH (100%) and let stand 5 minutes.

For two pieces of bread, one doughnut, or a roll, microwave for 35 to 45 seconds at DEFROST (30%).

GENERAL TIP FOR REHEATING BREADS

• To reheat bread or rolls, always wrap them in paper towels to prevent sogginess. (You can reheat them in a paper-towel–lined straw basket, if desired.)

For one loaf of bread or eight rolls/muffins, microwave for 1 to 1½ minutes at MEDIUM HIGH (70%).

For four rolls, muffins, or bagels, microwave for about 25 to 35 seconds at MEDIUM HIGH (70%).

For one roll, muffin, or bagel, microwave for 10 to 15 seconds at HIGH (100%).

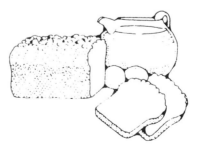

LOW-CALORIE BRAN MUFFINS

—————— · · · · · ——————

No flour in this recipe; for diet food, they taste great!

1 small zucchini, unpeeled, washed and grated to equal ½ cup
1 large Red or Golden Delicious apple, unpeeled, washed, cored, and grated to equal 1 cup
1 teaspoon vanilla
½ cup **Egg Substitute** (see page 91) or Egg Beaters or 2 large eggs
½ teaspoon ground nutmeg
1 teaspoon ground cinnamon
½ teaspoon baking soda
1 teaspoon baking powder
1 teaspoon lemon juice
8 packets sugar substitute or ⅓ cup sugar
1 cup unprocessed wheat bran, uncooked

1. In a food processor bowl, blender container, or mixing bowl combine all ingredients except bran.
2. Add bran and blend well.
3. Spoon batter into microwave-safe muffin cups (or a microwave muffin pan) or custard cups lined with 2 paper cupcake liners each. Fill each ½ to ⅔ full.
4. Microwave for 3½ minutes at MEDIUM (50%).
5. Microwave for 1 to 2 minutes at HIGH (100%) to finish cooking. (Muffins will be very moist.) Remove the outside liner on each muffin and cool.

Yield: 10 to 12 muffins

—————— · ❄ · ——————

Nutritional Analysis per Muffin

Calories: 52
Carbohydrate: 7 g
Fat: 2 g
Protein: 3 g

Fiber: 1 g
Cholesterol: Trace
Sodium: 81 mg
Diabetic exchanges:
Bread: 0.5

I created this recipe while trying to lose a few pounds on a very low-calorie diet. No flour! No sugar! The zucchini and apple provide bulk. I found them quite tasty when I was trying to live without bread and butter.

BLENDER APPLE–OAT BRAN MUFFINS

·········· MUFFIN BATTER ··········

⅓ cup frozen apple juice concentrate, slightly thawed
¼ cup skim milk
1 egg white
1 tablespoon vegetable oil
2 tablespoons granulated sugar or brown sugar, packed

1 cup plus 2 tablespoons oat bran, uncooked
1 teaspoon baking powder
½ teaspoon ground cinnamon

·········· FRUIT ··········

½ large Red Delicious apple, unpeeled, cored and chopped

1 tablespoon raisins, optional

1. Place, in order listed, all muffin batter ingredients in a food processor or blender. Process until well blended. Stir in chopped apple, and raisins, if desired.
2. Line six 6-ounce microwave-safe custard cups with 2 paper cupcake liners each. Fill each ¾ full with batter. Arrange in circle fashion in microwave oven.
3. Microwave 6 for 3 to 3½ minutes at HIGH (100%), or until a toothpick inserted in the center comes out clean, rearranging cups halfway through cooking time. Remove the outside liner on each muffin and cool on a cooling rack.

Yield: 6 muffins

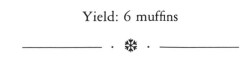

Variations: For 12 muffins, double the ingredients. Proceed as directed. Microwave only 6 muffins at a time.

For 1 muffin, microwave for 30 to 40 seconds at HIGH (100%).

For 2 muffins, microwave for 1 to 1½ minutes at HIGH (100%).

Nutritional Analysis per Muffin

Calories: 109
Carbohydrate: 17 g
Fat: 4 g
Protein: 4 g
Fiber: 2 g

Cholesterol: Trace
Sodium: 71 mg
Diabetic exchanges:
  Bread: 1
  Fat: 0.5

STRAWBERRY–OAT BRAN MUFFINS

1 cup plus 2 tablespoons
  oat bran, uncooked
¼ cup brown sugar,
  packed
1 teaspoon baking powder
1 tablespoon vegetable oil
1 egg white, slightly
  beaten

¼ cup skim milk
½ cup frozen unsweetened
  strawberries and juice,
  slightly thawed
1 drop red food coloring,
  optional

1. Place all ingredients in a food processor, blender, or mixing bowl. Process, beat, or mix until well blended.
2. Line six 6-ounce microwave-safe custard cups with 2 paper cupcake liners each. Fill each ¾ full with batter. Arrange in circle fashion in the microwave oven.
3. Microwave 6 for 3 to 3½ minutes at HIGH (100%), or until a toothpick inserted in the center comes out clean, rearranging halfway through cooking time. Remove the outer liner on each muffin and cool.

Yield: 6 muffins

· ❄ ·

TIPS

If some batter is left over after filling custard cups in step #2, fill one more cup. However, do not microwave more than six at a time. See Variations.

To enhance the appearance of the muffins, sprinkle with cinnamon and sugar. (Mix 2 teaspoons sugar and ½ teaspoon cinnamon in a small bowl. Sprinkle lightly over six muffins immediately after microwaving.)

High in oat bran (soluble fiber), which can help lower blood cholesterol, Strawberry Oat Bran Muffins have no flour and are low in calories.

Variations: For 12 muffins, double ingredients. Proceed as directed. Microwave only 6 muffins at a time.

For 1 muffin, microwave for 35 to 45 seconds at HIGH (100%).

For 2 muffins, microwave for 1 to 1½ minutes at HIGH (100%).

Nutritional Analysis per Muffin

Calories: 118	Cholesterol: Trace
Carbohydrate: 21 g	Sodium: 74 mg
Fat: 4 g	Diabetic exchanges:
Protein: 4 g	Bread: 1.25
Fiber: 2	Fat: 0.5

MELBA TOAST

· · · · ·

6 very thin slices whole
  wheat bread, cut in half

Place bread in 2 layers of paper towels in microwave oven. Microwave for 3 to 4 minutes at HIGH (100%), turning over once. Let stand at least 2 minutes.

Yield: 12 pieces

· ❋ ·

Nutritional Analysis per Piece

Calories: 35	Fiber: N/A
Carbohydrate: 8 g	Cholesterol: 0 g
Fat: 1 g	Sodium: 80 mg
Protein: 2 g	Diabetic exchanges:
	Bread: 0.5

HIGH-FIBER APPLE-BRAN MUFFINS

— — — · · · · · — — —

Use your convection microwave or your conventional range.

···················· MUFFINS ·····················

2¼ cups high-fiber bran
   cereal (cold cereal)

1¼ cups skim milk

2 tablespoons vegetable oil

¼ cup Egg Substitute (see
   page 91) or Egg Beaters
   or 1 large egg

¼ cup brown sugar,
   packed

3 teaspoons baking
   powder

1¼ cups whole wheat
   flour

1 large Red Delicious
   apple, cored and
   coarsely chopped

½ cup raisins

················ TOPPING (OPTIONAL) ····················

⅓ cup whole wheat flour

3 tablespoons white sugar

3 tablespoons brown
   sugar, packed

½ teaspoon ground
   cinnamon

⅓ cup regular
   polyunsaturated
   margarine, softened

1. Using a food processor, blender, or electric mixer and bowl, combine cereal, milk, vegetable oil, and Egg Substitute. Process a few seconds until well blended. Add the brown sugar and baking powder; process again until well mixed. Blend in flour; fold in apple and raisins.

2. Pour batter into 15 microwave-safe muffin cups (in muffin pans) or custard cups that have been sprayed with vegetable coating.

3. For optional topping: Using a food processor or pastry blender, mix topping ingredients until crumbly. Sprinkle each muffin with the topping.

4. **For convection microwave:** Low-Mix Bake at 400°F (or Combination 2 or Code 2) for 20 minutes for 1 pan or 25

TIPS
········

These high-fiber bran muffins have been a special help to family members of mine who must be on high-fiber diets. Each muffin provides 8 grams of dietary fiber.

Don't worry if you don't have a convection microwave. This recipe works just as well using your conventional oven.

Three convection microwave settings are listed. Choose the one that corresponds with the power setting on your convection microwave oven.

To reheat these muffins, microwave for 10 to 15 seconds per muffin at MEDIUM HIGH (70%). For example, 6 muffins will take 60 to 90 seconds at MEDIUM HIGH (70%). If your microwave oven does not have MEDIUM HIGH (70%) power, microwave for 10 seconds per muffin at HIGH (100%).

I like to use All Bran Extra Fiber cereal in this recipe.

minutes for 2 pans (using the raised rack). Let stand for 10 minutes. Invert and cool.

For regular (conventional) oven: Preheat your oven to 400° F. Bake for 25 to 30 minutes. Let stand for 5 minutes. Invert and cool.

Yield: 15 muffins

————— · ❊ · —————

Nutritional Analysis per Muffin, Without Topping

Calories: 141   Cholesterol: Trace
Carbohydrate: 28 g   Sodium: 164 mg
Fat: 4 g   Diabetic exchanges:
Protein: 4 g   Bread: 1.5
Fiber: 4 g   Fat: 0.5

CRANBERRY – OAT BRAN BREAD

TIPS

1 cup raw cranberries (see tip, page 301)

½ cup oat bran, uncooked

¾ cup whole wheat flour

¾ cup all-purpose flour

¼ teaspoon ground allspice

½ teaspoon baking soda

1 teaspoon baking powder

2 teaspoons grated orange peel

¼ cup brown sugar, packed

¼ cup granulated sugar

3 medium egg whites, slightly beaten

½ cup unsweetened orange juice

¼ cup vegetable oil

2 tablespoons chopped walnuts

1. Using a food processor or blender, coarsely chop cranberries. Set aside.
2. Using a food processor or electric mixer and bowl, combine bran, flours, allspice, baking soda, baking powder, orange peel and sugars until blended. Add egg whites, orange juice, and vegetable oil. Process until thoroughly mixed. Fold in chopped cranberries and walnuts. Pour into a 9 × 5-inch glass or microwave-safe loaf pan that has been sprayed with vegetable coating.
3. Place on an inverted saucer in the microwave oven. Microwave for 5 minutes at MEDIUM (50%). Rotate pan ½ turn. Microwave for 3½ to 4 minutes at HIGH (100%) (see tip at left for doneness). Let stand 5 to 10 minutes. Loosen sides with a knife and invert onto a rack to cool.

Yield: 1 loaf

Nutritional Analysis Per Slice (¹/₁₆ Loaf)

Calories: 117

Carbohydrate: 17 g

Fat: 4 g

Protein: 3 g

Fiber: Trace

Cholesterol: 0 mg

Sodium: 57 mg

Diabetic exchanges:

Bread: 1.25

Fat: 0.25

TIPS

To check bread for doneness, insert a toothpick into center of bread. It will come out clean when bread is done. The top of the bread may still look moist, but it will dry out when cooled.

Freeze cranberries before chopping, as they will maintain a better texture.

Oat bran supplies protein and the B vitamin thiamine. It is also very filling, which may make Cranberry–Oat Bran Bread helpful to those on reducing diets.

TIPS

To add more fiber to the recipe, I often use 5 cups of whole wheat flour instead of the white, wheat, and rye flour mixture.

This delicious breakfast bread tastes best sliced and then toasted.

See page 15 for tips on shielding corners with foil.

*This no-knead bread is made to be sliced and toasted.
It's delicious!*

1½ cups all-purpose flour
3 cups whole wheat flour
½ cup rye flour
⅓ cup granulated sugar or brown sugar, packed
1 teaspoon salt, optional
½ teaspoon baking soda
2 packages dry yeast
2½ cups skim milk
1 cup raisins
Cornmeal to dust pan and garnish

1. Set aside 1 cup of the all-purpose flour. Using a food processor or electric mixer and bowl, combine the remaining 4 cups of flours, sugar, optional salt, baking soda, and yeast.
2. Microwave milk in a 1-quart microwave-safe bowl for 3 minutes at HIGH (100%) or until 130° F. Add slowly to dry mixture, beating well.
3. Beat in remaining 1 cup of flour. Fold in raisins.
4. Pour into 2 glass or microwave-safe 9 by 5-inch loaf pans that have been greased and dusted with cornmeal.
5. Allow dough to rise, covered, 40 to 50 minutes in a warm place. For speed rise, microwave for 1 minute at MEDIUM (50%) covered with plastic wrap. Let stand 10 minutes. Microwave again for 1 minute at MEDIUM (50%). Let stand 10 minutes.
6. Uncover. Sprinkle lightly with cornmeal. Microwave each loaf with corners shielded for 6 minutes at MEDIUM HIGH (70%).† Remove foil shielding and microwave again for 2 to 2½ minutes at MEDIUM HIGH (70%). (Rotate dish once if necessary for even cooking.)
7. Let stand 5 minutes before removing from pans.

Yield: 2 loaves

†**Compacts:** Microwave for 5 minutes at HIGH (100%). Remove foil shielding and microwave again for 2 to 3 minutes at HIGH (100%) in step #6.

Variations: Omit raisins or substitute dates.

Substitute all white flour or wheat flour or any flours to make 5 cups total.

Nutritional Analysis per ½-Inch Slice

Calories: 93	Cholesterol: Trace
Carbohydrate: 20 g	Sodium: 103 mg
Fat: Trace	Diabetic exchanges:
Protein: 4 g	Bread: 1
Fiber: N/A	Fruit: 0.25

SLIM CORN BREAD

· · · · ·

· · · · · · · · · · · CORN BREAD · · · · · · · · · · ·

5 tablespoons vegetable oil
3 tablespoons sugar
2 large egg whites
¾ cup nonfat buttermilk
1 cup flour

¾ cup cornmeal
1½ teaspoons baking powder
½ teaspoon baking soda
Dash salt, optional

· · · · · · · · · · · TOPPING · · · · · · · · · · ·

2 tablespoons crushed cornflakes

1. Using an electric mixer and bowl or food processor, beat oil, sugar, egg whites, and buttermilk until blended. In a mixing bowl, mix remaining dry cornbread ingredients; beat into buttermilk mixture until smooth.
2. Pour batter into a microwave ring pan that has been sprayed with vegetable coating and dusted with crushed cornflake topping. Place on an inverted saucer in the microwave oven. Let stand 5 minutes.

If a microwave ring pan is not available, create your own: Place a custard cup, open end up, in the center of an 8-inch or 9-inch round microwave-safe baking dish.

Slim Corn Bread is very moist after microwaving. It will dry out and resemble traditional corn bread in a few hours.

Instead of crushed cornflakes, you can dust the ring pan with 1 tablespoon cornmeal in step #2.

3. Microwave for 5½ to 7 minutes at MEDIUM HIGH (70%), or until top is no longer doughy.† (Rotate pan once if necessary for even cooking.) Let stand 5 minutes. Invert onto serving plate. Cut into wedges.

Yield: one 10-inch ring

———————— · ❋ · ————————

Nutritional Analysis per Serving (¹⁄₁₂ Ring)	
Calories: 137	Cholesterol: 1 mg
Carbohydrate: 18 g	Sodium: 102 mg
Fat: 6 g	Diabetic exchanges:
Protein: 3 g	Fat: 1.25
Fiber: N/A	Bread: 1

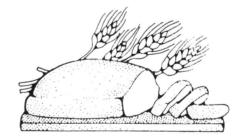

....
† **Compacts:** Microwave at HIGH (100%) instead of MEDIUM HIGH (70%) in step #3.

DRY BREAD CRUMBS

——————— · · · · · ———————

4 slices high-fiber reduced-
    calorie whole wheat or
    white bread (fresh)

Place bread on 2 layers of paper towels in the microwave oven. Microwave for 3 to 4 minutes at HIGH (100%), turning over once. Let stand at least 2 minutes; crumble.

Yield: 1 cup dry bread crumbs

——————— · ❄ · ———————

Nutritional Analysis per 1 Cup Bread Crumbs

Calories: 160	Fiber: 8 g
Carbohydrate: 28 g	Cholesterol: 0 mg
Fat: 1 g	Sodium: 420 mg
Protein: 8 g	Diabetic exchanges:
	Bread: 2

TIPS
· · · · · · · ·

Because many recipes call for dry bread crumbs, you can quickly make your own following these simple instructions.

Use a food processor to help crumble the bread crumbs after microwaving, if desired.

For Seasoned Bread Crumbs, see page 243.

DESSERTS, BARS, AND CAKES

· ❄ ·

GENERAL TIPS FOR MICROWAVING BAKED GOODS

- Bars and cakes do not brown in a microwave oven, so take advantage of this and make those with fruit or carob chips.

- Use any microwave-safe round or square dish. Round dishes work best, especially those with a center tube, because they produce the most even cooking results. When possible, use a microwave bundt or tube pan, which helps the micro-waves penetrate and bake the center thoroughly.

- You can get a tube pan effect by inserting a drinking glass upright into the center of a microwave-safe mixing bowl. Mix, insert the glass, and bake in the same dish.

- Always spray a cake or bar dish with vegetable coating and then dust lightly with sugar. *Do not use flour* for dusting. The bars will stick to the dish if you do.

- Fill a cake or bar pan only two-thirds full, as microwaved cakes and bars rise more than conventionally baked ones.

- Cake or bars are done when a toothpick inserted near the center comes out clean. A few moist spots may appear on top after cooking, but these will evaporate during standing time. If the center starts to sink, microwave the product 1 to 2 minutes longer.

- Place the baking dish on an inverted saucer or pie plate while microwaving if you find that the bottom of your baked goods do not cook completely.

- Always shield corners of square dishes with foil to prevent hardened corners when using HIGH (100%) power (see page 15).

- Decrease water and other liquids by 1 tablespoon per cup in most recipes when converting from a conventional to a microwave recipe.

GENERAL TIPS FOR MICROWAVING PIES AND DESSERTS

- Microwave cookie crumb crusts on MEDIUM HIGH (70%) to set them quickly.

- Transfer commercial frozen pie crusts while frozen from foil pans to glass or microwave-safe pie pans.

- For single-crust pies, bake the pie crust first before adding the filling.

- Microwave pumpkin or custard pies (because of their "sensitive ingredients") at MEDIUM (50%).

- Pudding mixes can be cooked on HIGH (100%) because stabilizers prevent curdling.

- Custard-type desserts with eggs do curdle easily, so they should be cooked on MEDIUM (50%) or MEDIUM HIGH (70%).

- Reheat single servings of pie or dessert by microwaving for 30 to 40 seconds at MEDIUM HIGH (70%) per slice or serving.

GENERAL TIPS FOR MICROWAVING DRIED FRUITS

- Dried fruits become stewed fruits by microwaving 1 cup fruit with ½ cup water for 3 to 5 minutes at HIGH (100%) until boiling. Let stand covered for 30 minutes.

- To plump dried fruit (raisins, prunes, apricots, and so on), add 2 tablespoons hot water to 1 cup dried fruit in a small microwave-safe bowl. Microwave for 40 to 60 seconds at HIGH (100%). Let stand one minute.

TIPS
....

Carob powder, similar to cocoa in appearance and taste, can be purchased in the health food section of your grocery store and substituted for cocoa in most recipes. It contains one-tenth the amount of fat, four times the calcium, and none of the caffeine of chocolate or cocoa.

See the shielding tips (page 15) for information on shielding corners. If you cannot use foil strips in your microwave oven, lower the power setting to MEDIUM HIGH (70%) and increase the total cooking time to 10 to 11 minutes in step #3.

CAROB AND OAT BRAN CAKE BROWNIES

——————— · · · · · ———————

Nutritious oat bran takes the place of flour in this recipe.

⅓ cup reduced-calorie margarine*

¼ cup carob powder†

½ cup brown sugar, packed

½ cup hot water

1 cup oat bran, uncooked

½ teaspoon baking powder

2 large egg whites, slightly beaten

⅓ cup nonfat plain or vanilla yogurt

½ teaspoon chocolate or vanilla flavoring

Dash powdered sugar to garnish, optional

1. Microwave margarine and carob powder in a 2-quart microwave-safe bowl for 30 seconds at HIGH (100%). Blend in brown sugar and hot water. Stir in bran and baking powder until well blended. Stir in egg whites, yogurt, and flavoring.

2. Spread into an 8-inch square microwave-safe pan that has been sprayed with vegetable coating and lightly dusted with sugar. Shield corners with foil.

....

*Use unsalted variety for lowest sodium value, if desired.
†Cocoa powder can be substituted for the carob powder, but be sure to consider the extra fat content in your diet.

3. Microwave for 6 minutes at HIGH (100%). Remove foil shielding and rotate pan. Microwave for 2 to 3 minutes at HIGH (100%), or until center is almost done. Cover with plastic wrap and let stand 10 minutes. Cool, cut into bars, and place on a serving dish. Sprinkle with powdered sugar to garnish, if desired.

Yield: 20 brownies

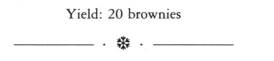

Variation: For Carob Raisin or Date Brownies, add ½ cup raisins or chopped unsweetened dates with the flavoring in step #1.

Nutritional Analysis per 2- × 1½-Inch Bar

Calories: 53   Cholesterol: Trace
Carbohydrate: 9 g   Sodium: 19 mg
Fat: 2 g   Diabetic exchanges:
Protein: 1 g   Bread: 0.5
Fiber: 1 g   Fat: 0.25

OAT BRAN–DATE BARS

⅔ cup water
2 teaspoons lemon juice
1½ cups chopped dates
¼ cup reduced-calorie
    margarine*
¼ cup brown sugar,
    packed

¾ cup unsifted flour
½ cup oat bran, uncooked
½ cup quick rolled oats
¼ teaspoon baking soda
¼ cup (2 ounces) frozen
    apple juice concentrate,
    slightly thawed

....

*Use unsalted variety for lowest sodium value, if desired.

1. Combine water, lemon juice, and dates in a 1-quart microwave-safe bowl. Microwave uncovered, for 4 to 5 minutes at HIGH (100%), or until thickened. Set aside.
2. Using a food processor or electric mixer and bowl, combine margarine and brown sugar until creamy. Add flour, oat bran, oats, baking soda, and apple juice concentrate. Process or mix until crumbly. Using the back of a spoon, pat ¾ of mixture into an ungreased 8-inch square glass baking dish.
3. Microwave for 3 to 4 minutes at HIGH (100%), or until mixture is puffy. Pour thickened dates over cooked oat mixture and spread evenly. Set aside.
4. Spread remaining crumbly oat mixture on a paper plate. Microwave for 1 to 1½ minutes at HIGH (100%),† or until puffed. Using a spoon, crumble mixture and sprinkle over date layer.
5. Microwave for 2 to 3 minutes at MEDIUM HIGH (70%), or until bubbly.† Let stand to cool.

Yield: 20 bars

——————— · ❄ · ———————

Variation: For Date Bars, omit oat bran and apple juice, increase brown sugar to ½ cup total. Proceed as directed.

Nutritional Analysis per 2- × 1½-Inch Bar

Calories: 93   Cholesterol: 0 mg
Carbohydrate: 19 g   Sodium: 32 mg
Fat: 1.6 g   Diabetic exchanges:
Protein: 2 g   Bread: 0.75
Fiber: 1 g   Fruit: 0.5

. . . .

†**Compacts:** Microwave for same time at HIGH instead of MEDIUM HIGH (70%) in step #5.

CINNAMON APPLE BARS

————————— · · · · · —————————

1¼ cups oat bran, uncooked

¼ cup all-purpose flour

¼ teaspoon baking soda

1 teaspoon ground cinnamon

¾ cup (6 ounces) frozen apple juice concentrate, slightly thawed

2 large egg whites, slightly beaten

⅓ cup reduced calorie margarine*

1 teaspoon vanilla or burnt sugar flavoring

¼ cup chopped apple and/or ¼ cup raisins

Use a sweet apple such as Red or Golden Delicious for best results.

1. Combine all ingredients except apple and/or raisins in a food processor or mixing bowl. Process or beat with electric mixer until well blended. Stir in chopped apple and/or raisins.

2. Spread into an 8-inch square microwave-safe pan that has been sprayed with vegetable shortening and lightly dusted with sugar. Microwave for 11 to 12 minutes at MEDIUM HIGH (70%), or until center is no longer doughy. Cool completely. Cut into bars and serve.

Yield: 20 bars

————————— · ❄ · —————————

Nutritional Analysis per 2- × 1½-Inch Bar

Calories: 56

Carbohydrate: 9 g

Fat: 2 g

Protein: 2 g

Fiber: 1 g

Cholesterol: 0 g

Sodium: 10 mg

Diabetic exchanges:

Bread: 0.5

Fruit: 0.25

· ·

*Use unsalted variety for lowest sodium value, if desired.

For a special treat, serve slices topped with 2 tablespoons Fast Raspberry, Strawberry, or Blueberry Sauce (see page 64) or decorate top of cheesecake with fresh raspberries and mint leaves before serving.

To drain cottage cheese, place in a colander and press with a spoon, allowing excess liquid to drain off. (For some brands there may be only a few teaspoons excess liquid.)

Regular cheesecake has about 100 calories *more* per slice.

Save 50 additional calories by making your own yogurt cream cheese and substituting it for 8 ounces cream cheese. To make yogurt cheese: Place 16 ounces plain nonfat yogurt (no gelatin added) in a coffee-filter-lined strainer over a bowl. Refrigerate overnight. Discard whey in bowl.

BLENDER RED-RASPBERRY CHEESECAKE (OR BLUEBERRY OR STRAWBERRY CHEESECAKE)

⸻⸻ . . . . . ⸻⸻

············ RASPBERRY-CHEESE FILLING ···············

8-ounce package of Neufchâtel cheese

2 cups (16 ounces) low-fat cottage cheese, drained

½ cup Egg Substitute (see page 91) or Egg Beaters or 2 large eggs

½ cup sugar or 12 to 14 packets sugar substitute

3 teaspoons cornstarch dissolved in 2 tablespoons skim milk

1 cup fresh or frozen red raspberries, cleaned and stems removed

2 drops red food coloring, optional

························· CRUST ····················

9-inch Low-Cal Graham Cracker Crust (see page 82), cooled

1. Unwrap Neufchâtel cheese and place in a 2-quart microwave-safe bowl. Microwave for 40 to 60 seconds at MEDIUM HIGH (70%), or until softened.
2. Using a food processor, blender, or electric mixer and bowl, combine cheese and remaining filling ingredients until blended. Pour filling back into 2-quart bowl.
3. Microwave for 7 to 8 minutes at HIGH (100%), or until very hot, stirring twice.
4. Pour filling into cooled crust. Microwave for 5 to 7 minutes at MEDIUM HIGH (70%),† or until almost set (center will jiggle slightly). Let cool. Refrigerate at least 4 hours.

Yield: one 9-inch cheesecake

⸻⸻ · ❄ · ⸻⸻

†**Compacts:** Microwave at HIGH (100%) for the same length of time indicated in step #4.

Variation: Substitute 1 cup fresh or frozen blueberries or sliced strawberries for the raspberries.

Nutritional Analysis per Serving (¹/₁₀ Cheesecake)

Calories: 167
Carbohydrate: 13 g
Fat: 8 g
Protein: 10 g
Fiber: N/A
Cholesterol: 22 mg

Sodium: 304 mg
Diabetic exchanges:
  Bread: .5
  Fat: .75
  Fruit: .25
  Lean meat: 1.25

EASY BLENDER CHEESECAKE

· · · · ·

.... FILLING ....

1½ cups (12 ounces) low-
  fat cottage cheese,
  slightly drained
1 cup (8 ounces) low-fat
  vanilla or plain yogurt
2 teaspoons cornstarch
  dissolved in 1
  tablespoon skim milk

3 egg whites or 2 large
  eggs
⅓ cup sugar or 8 packets
  sugar substitute
  (equivalent to 16
  teaspoons sugar)

.... PIE CRUST ....

9-inch Low-Cal Graham
  Cracker Crust (see page
  82), prepared

.... TOPPING ....

Fast Strawberry Sauce or
  other fruit sauce (see
  page 64)

TIPS
....

If you use plain instead of vanilla yogurt, add 1 teaspoon vanilla with the yogurt.

1. Using a food processor, blender, or electric mixer and bowl, combine and process filling ingredients until smooth. Pour into a 1-quart microwave-safe bowl. Microwave for 5 to 6 minutes at HIGH (100%), or until very hot, stirring well every two minutes.

2. Pour into prepared pie crust. Microwave for 5 to 6 minutes at MEDIUM HIGH (70%),† until edges are set. (Cheesecake will still "jiggle" but will become firm as it chills.) Cool slightly, refrigerate at least 4 hours.

3. Serve topped with Fast Strawberry (or Raspberry or Blueberry) Sauce.

Yield: one 9-inch cheesecake

—————————— · ❄ · ——————————

Variations: For Lemon Cheesecake, add 1½ teaspoons grated lemon peel (zest only) and 2 teaspoons fresh lemon juice with filling ingredients in step #1. Proceed as directed.

For Chocolate Cheesecake, add 2 tablespoons carob powder or unsweetened cocoa with filling ingredients in step #1. Proceed as directed.

For Mock Sour Cream Topping, process ½ cup (4 ounces) low-fat cottage cheese, ½ cup (4 ounces) plain or vanilla nonfat yogurt, and 2 packets sugar substitute (equivalent to 4 teaspoons sugar) in a food processor or blender until smooth. Pour over slightly cooled filling (after microwaving) in step #2. Refrigerate 4 hours as directed. Fast Strawberry Sauce is optional.

Nutritional Analysis per Serving (1/10 Cheesecake)

Calories: 148	Sodium: 241 mg
Carbohydrate: 17 g	Diabetic exchanges:
Fat: 2 g	Bread: 0.75
Protein: 8 g	Lean meat: 0.25
Fiber: N/A	Skim milk: 0.5
Cholesterol: 5 mg	

† Rotate dish twice, if necessary, for even cooking.

FAST STRAWBERRY SAUCE

· · · · ·

The perfect low-calorie topping for ice milk, yogurt, or angel food cake.

10-ounce package frozen, unsweetened strawberries, thawed and drained, juice reserved

1½ teaspoons cornstarch
2 packets sugar substitute (equivalent to 4 teaspoons sugar) or 1 tablespoon fructose

In a 1-quart microwave-safe bowl, mix strawberry juice and cornstarch until blended. Microwave 1 to 1½ minutes at HIGH (100%), or until mixture boils for 30 seconds. Stir in strawberries and sugar substitute; cool completely.

Yield: 1¼ cups

—————— · ❄ · ——————

Variation: For Fast Blueberry or Raspberry Sauce, substitute 10 ounces frozen unsweetened blueberries or raspberries for the strawberries. Thaw, drain, and reserve juice. Proceed as directed in step #1.

Nutritional Analysis per 2-Tablespoon Serving	
Calories: 12	Fiber: N/A
Carbohydrate: 3 g	Cholesterol: 0 g
Fat: 0 g	Sodium: 1 mg
Protein: 1 g	Diabetic exchanges: Fruit: 0.25

TIPS
· · · · · · · ·

To thaw 10 ounces frozen fruit, remove any metal packaging (or metal end pieces). Place package on a paper plate or in a microwave-safe bowl. Microwave for 1 to 3 minutes at HIGH (100%), or until slightly icy. Let stand 10 to 15 minutes at room temperature to finish thawing and drain juices.

Gelatin Cookies are the gelatin squares developed by General Foods that get firm enough to eat with your fingers. They are fun to eat and almost calorie-free.

GELATIN COOKIES

——————— · · · · · ———————

Use your microwave to heat the water for this familiar recipe.

2½ cups hot tap water
4 packages (.3 ounces
   each) sugar-free gelatin
   (wild strawberry,
   orange, or any other
   flavor), dry

1. Microwave water in a 1-quart measure for 2½ to 4 minutes at HIGH (100%), or until boiling. Slowly add gelatin to the water, stirring constantly. Blend until gelatin is dissolved.
2. Pour into a 9-inch or 10-inch square pan. Refrigerate at least 4 hours. Using small cookie cutters, cut into pumpkin shapes, stars, and so on.

Yield: 20 to 25 shapes

——————— · ❄ · ———————

Nutritional Analysis per 2-Inch Shape

Calories: 4	Fiber: N/A
Carbohydrate: Trace	Cholesterol: 0 mg
Fat: 0	Sodium: 35 mg
Protein: 1 g	Diabetic exchanges: Free

APPLESAUCE

— · · · · · —

4 cups apples, peeled,
    cored, and sliced
3 tablespoons water
1 teaspoon lemon juice

3 packets sugar substitute
    or 2 tablespoons sugar,
    optional
Dash ground cinnamon

1. Combine apples, water, and lemon juice in a 2-quart microwave-safe bowl. Cover with vented plastic wrap.
2. Microwave for 7 to 8 minutes at HIGH (100%), or until apples are tender. Mash, if desired. Stir in sugar substitute and cinnamon. Serve warm or chilled.

Yield: 4 servings (¾ cup each)

————— · ❄ · —————

Nutritional Analysis per ¾-Cup Serving

Calories: 76 g
Carbohydrate: 20 g
Fat: 2 g
Protein: 1 g

Fiber: 12 g
Cholesterol: 0 g
Sodium: 12 mg
Diabetic exchanges:
    Fruit: 1.0

TIPS

For sweetest applesauce, use Red Delicious, Golden Delicious, Gravenstein, McIntosh, or Jonathan apples.

As unpeeled apples are high in dietary fiber (providing up to half of the recommended daily intake), leave the peel on the apples (wash the apples well). Instead of mashing in step #2, cool slightly and spoon the microwaved apples and juices into a food processor, blender, or food mill. Process until smooth.

To thaw 10 ounces frozen strawberries, microwave in a 1-quart microwave-safe casserole for 1 to 3 minutes at HIGH (100%). Let stand 2 minutes.

8-ounce can juice-packed
    crushed pineapple
1 envelope (7 grams)
    unflavored gelatin, dry
1 cup (8 ounces) nonfat,
    artificially sweetened
    strawberry yogurt

10-ounce package frozen
    unsweetened
    strawberries, thawed
Bed of lettuce, optional

1. Drain pineapple, reserving juice. Mix gelatin and drained juice in a 1-quart microwave-safe bowl. Let stand 1 minute. Stir. Microwave 40 to 60 seconds at HIGH (100%), until gelatin is dissolved. Cool slightly.
2. Mix yogurt into gelatin mixture. Add thawed strawberries (including juice) and drained pineapple. Mix well. Pour into a 1-quart mold. Chill until set. Unmold and serve on a bed of lettuce, if desired.

Yield: 4 servings

Nutritional Analysis per Serving (¼ Mold)

Calories: 93
Carbohydrate: 19
Fat: 1 g
Protein: 5 g
Fiber: N/A

Cholesterol: 1 mg
Sodium: 34 mg
Diabetic exchanges:
    Fruit: 1.25
    Skim milk: 0.25

DELICIOUS BAKED APPLES

2 to 4 small apples, rinsed and cored

1 teaspoon raisins per apple

½ teaspoon ground cinnamon per apple

½ packet sugar substitute (equivalent to 1 teaspoon sugar) or 1 teaspoon brown sugar per apple

2 tablespoons diet cream soda, apple juice, or orange juice per apple

2 tablespoons vanilla nonfat yogurt (artifically sweetened) per apple to garnish, optional

1. Peel top ¼ of the skin from apples and place apples in an 8- × 8-inch microwave-safe casserole.
2. Fill center of each apple with one teaspoon raisins.
3. Combine cinnamon and sugar substitute in a small bowl. Sprinkle over raisins and top of apples. Add apple juice or soda.
4. Cover apples with waxed paper or a loose-fitting lid.
5. Microwave at HIGH (100%) for 5 to 12 minutes. (Calculate total cooking time by allowing 2 to 3 minutes per apple.) Let stand covered 3 minutes before serving. Garnish each apple with a dollop of nonfat yogurt, if desired.

Yield: 2 to 4 servings

Nutritional Analysis per Serving (1 Apple)

Calories: 72
Carbohydrate: 14 g
Fat: 0 g
Protein: 1 g
Fiber: 3 g

Cholesterol: Trace
Sodium: 27 mg
Diabetic exchanges:
  Fruit: 1
  Skim milk: 0.25

Unpeeled apples are especially nutritious due to their fiber content as well as vitamin A and potassium.

To make your apples especially attractive, use the tip of a vegetable peeler and cut a spiral pattern into the peel of the apple. Brush apples with orange juice before microwaving.

Almost any variety of apples can be used here. I especially like to use Jonathan, Golden Delicious, or Gravenstein.

TIPS

For best results, select sweet apples. Try Red Delicious, Yellow Delicious, Gravenstein, or Jonathan.

Try serving each Apple Crisp topped with a tablespoon of vanilla nonfat yogurt.

Do not substitute reduced-calorie margarine in this recipe, as it will make the crisps soggy.

2 large apples or 3 pears, peeled, cored, and chopped
1 teaspoon lemon juice
2 packets sugar substitute or 4 teaspoons sugar
2 tablespoons flour
½ teaspoon ground cinnamon
1½ tablespoons dark-brown sugar, packed
1 tablespoon regular polyunsaturated margarine, softened*
2 tablespoons quick or regular oats, uncooked

1. Combine apples, lemon juice, and sugar substitute in a mixing bowl until mixed. Divide mixture among 4 microwave-safe custard cups. Set aside.
2. Combine flour, cinnamon, and brown sugar. Using a food processor or pastry blender or two knives, cut in margarine until mixture resembles coarse meal. Blend in oats. Divide mixture among the 4 custard cups of apples.
3. Microwave for 5 to 7 minutes at HIGH (100%), or until apples are tender, rearranging cups halfway through cooking time. Let stand 10 minutes.

Yield: 4 crisps

Variation: For Blueberry-Apple Crisps, add 1 cup frozen blueberries and 1 tablespoon additional flour to the apples in step #1. Pour mixture into 5 custard cups. Proceed as directed in step #2. Increase microwaving time to 7 to 9 minutes at HIGH (100%) in step #3.

Nutritional Analysis per Serving (1 Crisp)	
Calories: 120	Cholesterol: 0 mg
Carbohydrate: 24 g	Sodium: 27 mg
Fat: 6 g	Diabetic exchanges:
Protein: 1 g	Fruit: 1.5
Fiber: N/A	Fat: 1

*Use unsalted variety for lowest sodium values, if desired.

FRUIT PIZZA PIE

—————— • • • • • ——————

A delicious idea for summer fruit!

.... PIE ....

1 envelope (7 grams)
   unflavored gelatin, dry
⅔ cup cold water, divided
2 cups (16 ounces) cherry-
   vanilla, vanilla, or
   pineapple artificially
   sweetened, nonfat
   yogurt

4 packets sugar substitute
   or 8 teaspoons sugar

9-inch Low-Cal Graham
   Cracker Crust (see page
   82) or Reduced-Calorie
   Pie Crust (see page 83),
   baked

.... TOPPING ....

1 cup sliced strawberries
½ 11-ounce can mandarin
   orange sections (juice
   packed) or 1 nectarine,
   sliced

1 kiwi fruit, peeled,
   sliced, and each slice cut
   into fourths
1 packet sugar substitute
   (equivalent to 2 tea-
   spoons sugar), optional

1. Pie: Sprinkle gelatin over ⅓ cup cold water in a 2-cup glass measure. Let stand 1 minute. Stir until blended. Microwave for 40 to 60 seconds at HIGH (100%), or until boiling. Stir in remaining ⅓ cup cold water and 4 packets sugar substitute.

2. Using a wire whisk or food processor or blender, combine yogurt with gelatin-water mixture until thoroughly blended. Refrigerate 15 minutes.

3. Pour into cooled pie crust. Chill at least 2 hours.

4. Topping: Arrange fruit attractively over filling. Sprinkle with sugar substitute to help the cut fruit maintain its texture, if desired. Serve immediately or refrigerate until serving time.

Yield: one 9-inch pie

TIPS

For an attractive arrangement of fruit, place strawberry slices on the outside, forming a ring. Form an inner ring with kiwi pieces, form another ring with orange sections, and place one round slice of kiwi in the center. Or form a cross with the strawberry and orange slices and place the kiwi pieces in each section.

❄ ·

Variation: Substitute fruit of your choice for the topping. Try bananas, blueberries, pineapple, peaches, and so on.

Nutritional Analysis per Serving (⅛ Pie)

Calories: 146
Carbohydrate: 19 g
Fat: 2 g
Protein: 5 g
Fiber: N/A
Cholesterol: 3 mg

Sodium: 122 mg
Diabetic exchanges:
  Bread: 0.75
  Fruit: 1.0
  Skim milk: 0.25

TIPS

Cantaloupes, or muskmelons, are rich in vitamins A and C as well as potassium. They even have small amounts of iron and niacin, and only 164 calories per whole melon.

Honeydews are the off-white melons with the light-green interiors. They have some vitamin A but are not as rich in nutrients as cantaloupes.

HONEYDEW OR CANTALOUPE BOATS

· · · · ·

1 large honeydew melon
  (about 3 pounds) or 1
  large cantaloupe
¾ cup strawberries,
  prepared and sliced

1 cup hot water
1 package (.3 ounce)
  sugar-free strawberry
  gelatin, dry
¾ cup cold water

1. Halve and seed the melon. Fill each half with sliced strawberries. Set aside.
2. Microwave hot water for 1 to 2 minutes at HIGH (100%), or until boiling. Stir in gelatin until dissolved. Stir in cold water.
3. Pour strawberry-gelatin mixture over strawberries in melon. (Pour extra gelatin into a custard cup for another use.) Refrigerate at least 4 hours. Cut each melon half into 3 wedges. Serve immediately.

Yield: 6 servings

· ❄ ·

Variation: For Strawberry Chiffon Boats, decrease hot water to ¾ cup. Substitute 1 cup (8 ounces) strawberry nonfat yogurt for the ¾ cup cold water. Proceed as directed in step #1.

Nutritional Analysis per Serving (1 Wedge)

Calories: 81
Carbohydrate: 13 g
Fat: Trace
Protein: 1 g

Fiber: N/A
Cholesterol: 0 mg
Sodium: 12 mg
Diabetic exchanges:
Fruit: 1

MANDARIN MOUSSE
· · · · ·

1 envelope (7 grams) unflavored gelatin, dry
⅓ cup cold water or unsweetened orange juice
⅓ cup cold water
2 cups orange or vanilla artificially sweetened nonfat yogurt

½ cup canned juice-packed mandarin orange sections, drained and chopped
1 packet sugar substitute or 2 teaspoons sugar, optional

1. Sprinkle gelatin over ⅓ cup water, or, if using vanilla yogurt, over orange juice in a 2-cup glass measure. Let stand for 1 minute. Stir until blended. Microwave for 40 to 60 seconds at HIGH (100%), or until steaming hot and gelatin is dissolved, stirring once. Blend in ⅓ cup cold water.

2. Using a wire whisk or food processor or blender, thoroughly combine yogurt with gelatin mixture. Blend in mandarin orange sections and sugar substitute. Divide

evenly among 4 sherbet or champagne glasses. Refrigerate at least 1 hour before serving.

Yield: 4 servings

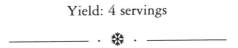

Variation: For Peach, Strawberry, Pineapple, Raspberry, or Blueberry Mousse, substitute 2 cups of appropriate fruit-flavored artificially sweetened nonfat yogurt for the 2 cups orange yogurt, and substitute ½ cup chopped appropriate fruit for the mandarin orange sections. Use water instead of orange juice.

Nutritional Analysis per Serving (1 Sherbet Dish)

Calories: 85	Cholesterol: 3 mg
Carbohydrate: 17 g	Sodium: 64 mg
Fat: Trace	Diabetic exchanges:
Protein: 6 g	Fruit: 0.75
Fiber: N/A	Skim milk: 0.5

LITE CHOCOLATE PUDDING

1 tablespoon carob
  powder†
1½ tablespoons sugar or 2
  packets sugar substitute
1 tablespoon plus 1
  teaspoon cornstarch

1 cup skim milk
½ teaspoon chocolate
  flavoring
½ teaspoon vanilla

1. Combine carob powder, sugar, and cornstarch in a 1-quart microwave-safe bowl. Add milk and mix well. Microwave uncovered for 2 minutes at HIGH (100%). Stir well. Microwave uncovered for 1 to 2 minutes at HIGH (100%), until mixture thickens.
2. Stir in chocolate flavoring and vanilla. Cool slightly. Spoon into dessert dishes. Refrigerate, covered with plastic wrap, until serving time.

Yield: 2 servings

❄

Variation: For 4 servings, double the ingredients. Stir well after microwaving 2½ minutes in step #1. Microwave again for 1½ to 2½ minutes at HIGH (100%), or until mixture thickens.

Nutritional Analysis per ½-Cup Serving

Calories: 93
Carbohydrate: 20 g
Fat: Trace
Protein: 4 g
Fiber: N/A

Cholesterol: 0 mg
Sodium: 65 mg
Diabetic exchanges:
  Bread: 0.75
  Skim milk: 0.5

†Cocoa powder can be substituted for the carob powder, but be sure to consider the extra fat content in your diet. Omit chocolate flavoring if cocoa is used.

For information on carob powder, see tip for Carob and Oat Bran Cake Brownies (page 57).

Sugar or sugar substitute can be adjusted to taste.

TIPS

Those on low-cho- lesterol, egg yolk—free diets, can enjoy custard too! This custard turns out very smooth as long as you are careful to slowly and thor- oughly blend the Egg Substitute and sugar into the hot milk mix- ture.

2 teaspoons cornstarch
    dissolved in 1½ cups
    skim milk
½ cup Egg Substitute (see
    page 91) or Egg Beaters
    or 2 large eggs, beaten

4 tablespoons sugar or 6
    packets sugar substitute
1 teaspoon vanilla
Dash ground nutmeg

1. Microwave cornstarch-milk in a 2-cup glass measure for 1½ to 2 minutes at HIGH (100%), or until very hot. Gradually blend Egg Substitute and sugar into milk, stir- ring constantly. Stir in vanilla and nutmeg. Pour into four 6-ounce microwave-safe custard cups.
2. Arrange in a circle in the microwave oven. Microwave for 4½ to 5½ minutes at MEDIUM (50%), or until custards look set but still jiggle. (Rearrange cups halfway through microwaving time if necessary for even cooking.) Refrig- erate until serving time (custard will set up as it cools).

Yield: 4 servings

Nutritional Analysis per Serving (1 Custard Cup)

Calories: 127
Carbohydrate: 15 g
Fat: 4 g
Protein: 7 g
Fiber: N/A

Cholesterol: 2 mg
Sodium: 102 mg
Diabetic exchanges:
    Bread: 0.5
    Medium meat: 0.5
    Skim milk: 0.5

SLIM APPLE PIE

¾ cup (6-ounce can) frozen apple juice concentrate, thawed
3 tablespoons cornstarch
6 medium Jonathan or Golden Delicious apples (about 6 cups), peeled, cored, and thinly sliced
1 teaspoon ground apple pie spice
2 teaspoons reduced-calorie margarine*
9-inch Low-Cal Graham Cracker Crust, cooled, or Reduced-Calorie Pie Crust, prepared (see pages 82–83)

1. Combine apple juice concentrate and cornstarch in a 2-quart microwave-safe bowl until smooth. Microwave for 2½ to 3½ minutes at HIGH (100%), or until thickened, stirring twice.
2. Add apples, spice, and margarine. Blend well. Cover loosely with waxed paper. Microwave for 9 to 11 minutes at HIGH (100%), or until apples are tender, stirring twice.
3. Immediately pour into cooked pie crust. Let cool ½ hour. Serve warm or refrigerate until serving time.

Yield: one 9-inch pie

❄

Nutritional Analysis per Serving (⅛ Pie)

Calories: 200
Carbohydrate: 38 g
Fat: 2 g
Protein: 1 g
Fiber: N/A
Cholesterol: 1 mg
Sodium: 90 mg
Diabetic exchanges:
  Bread: 0.5
  Fruit: 2.0
  Fat: 0.5

*Use unsalted variety for lowest sodium values, if desired.

TIPS

If necessary, you can substitute 1 teaspoon ground cinnamon and ½ teaspoon ground nutmeg for the apple pie spice.

Serve Slim Apple Pie garnished with a sprinkle of graham cracker crumbs or crunchy cereal (such as Grape Nuts) or a scoop of vanilla ice milk, if desired.

Although this pie will keep in the refrigerator for two days, it is best if eaten on the day of preparation.

BANANA "CREAM" PIE

1 envelope (7 grams) unflavored gelatin, dry
⅔ cup cold water, divided
1½ cups (12 ounces) banana, strawberry-banana, or vanilla artificially sweetened, nonfat yogurt

9-inch Low-Cal Graham Cracker Crust (see page 82), cooled
2 medium bananas, thinly sliced
4 packets sugar substitute or 8 teaspoons sugar, divided
Dash ground cinnamon

1. Sprinkle gelatin over ⅓ cup cold water in a 2-cup glass measure. Let stand 1 minute. Stir until blended. Microwave for 40 to 60 seconds at HIGH (100%), or until steaming hot and gelatin is dissolved. Stir. Blend in remaining ⅓ cup cold water.
2. Using a wire whisk or food processor or blender, combine yogurt with gelatin-water until thoroughly blended. Refrigerate 15 minutes in a covered container. Stir in 3 packets sugar substitute.
3. Spread ⅓ of chilled yogurt mixture into prepared graham cracker crust and cover with sliced bananas. Sprinkle bananas with remaining sugar substitute. Spread remaining yogurt mixture over bananas. Sprinkle with cinnamon to garnish. Refrigerate at least 2 hours or until serving time.

Yield: one 9-inch pie

Nutritional Analysis per Serving (⅛ Pie)

Calories: 140
Carbohydrate: 22 g
Fat: 3 g
Protein: 3 g
Fiber: N/A
Cholesterol: Trace

Sodium : 110 mg
Diabetic exchanges:
Bread: 0.5
Fruit: 0.5
Low-fat milk: 0.5

BLENDER CHOCOLATE "CREAM" PIE

TIPS

For information on using carob in a recipe, see tip on page 57.

½ cup cold water
2 envelopes (7 grams each) unflavored gelatin, dry
1½ cups skim milk
6 packets sugar substitute or 4 tablespoons sugar
2 tablespoons carob or cocoa powder
2 cups low-fat chocolate frozen yogurt or ice milk
1½ teaspoons vanilla flavoring
½ teaspoon chocolate flavoring (omit if using cocoa)
9-inch Low-Cal Graham Cracker Crust (see page 82), prepared

1. Sprinkle gelatin over the cold water in a 1-quart glass measure. Let stand 1 minute; stir until blended. Microwave for 40 to 60 seconds at HIGH (100%), or until very hot and gelatin is dissolved, stirring once. Stir in skim milk until blended.

2. Pour milk mixture into blender or food processor. Add sugar substitute, carob powder, frozen yogurt, and flavorings; process until smooth. Refrigerate 15 minutes until mixture thickens. Pour into prepared graham cracker crust. Refrigerate at least 1 hour to set.

Yield: one 9-inch pie

Variation: For Chocolate-Cream Dessert Cups, omit graham cracker crust. Spoon chocolate-cream mixture into 6 sherbet dishes or champagne glasses. Chill until set.

TIPS

Try using 1 cup vanilla and 1 cup strawberry reduced-calorie nonfat yogurt for a tasty blend of flavors.

Try to buy strawberries in bulk so you can pick the ones that are bright red and firm with hulls attached.

If you buy berries in plastic-web boxes, be sure to look under the box and through the holes to make sure the berries underneath are ripe too.

To keep berries from losing their firmness and texture, rinse and hull just before using them.

STRAWBERRY SUPREME PIE

½ cup cold water, divided
1 package (.3 ounce) sugar-free strawberry gelatin, dry
2 cups (16 ounces) vanilla or strawberry artificially sweetened nonfat yogurt

4 packets sugar substitute or 8 teaspoons sugar, optional
2 cups sliced fresh strawberries, divided
9-inch Low-Cal Graham Cracker Crust (see page 82), cooled

1. Microwave ¼ cup water in a 1-quart microwave-safe bowl for 40 to 60 seconds at HIGH (100%), or until boiling. Stir in strawberry gelatin until dissolved. Stir in remaining ¼ cup cold water.
2. Using a wire whisk or food processor or blender, combine yogurt with gelatin mixture until thoroughly blended. Refrigerate 15 minutes.
3. Combine sugar substitute with sliced strawberries. Fold 1 cup of strawberries into yogurt mixture. Pour into the cooled pie crust. Chill at least 4 hours or overnight. Refrigerate remaining berries. At serving time arrange strawberries attractively on pie.

Yield: one 9-inch pie

· ❄ ·

Variation: Save calories. Try a crustless pie. Omit the pie crust and save 103 calories and 3 grams fat per slice.

Nutritional Analysis per Serving (1/8 Pie)

Calories: 139
Carbohydrate: 18 g
Fat: 3 g
Protein: 4 g
Fiber: N/A
Cholesterol: 1 mg

Sodium: 150 mg
Diabetic exchanges:
  Bread: 0.5
  Fruit: 0.5
  Low-fat milk: 0.25

ENGLISH PUMPKIN PUDDING WEDGES

1 cup evaporated skim milk
1 cup canned pumpkin (1/2 16-ounce can)
3 large egg whites
1 1/2 teaspoons vegetable oil

1/2 cup all-fruit apple butter
1 teaspoon vanilla
1/4 teaspoon ground cinnamon
1 packet sugar substitute or 2 teaspoons sugar

1. Microwave milk in a 2-cup glass measure for 1 to 1 1/2 minutes at HIGH (100%), or until hot but not boiling.
2. Meanwhile, using an electric mixer or wire whisk, beat remaining ingredients until thoroughly blended. Slowly add the hot milk and continue to mix. Pour mixture into a 2-quart microwave-safe ring pan that has been sprayed with vegetable coating. Set on an inverted saucer in the microwave oven.
3. Microwave for 11 to 13 minutes at MEDIUM HIGH (70%), or until almost set. Let stand until cool. Refrigerate until serving time. Cut into wedges.

Yield: 6 servings

TIPS

If a microwave ring is not available, make your own. Place a custard cup, open end up, in the center of an 8- or 9-inch round baking dish.

TIPS

You can substitute 1 teaspoon cinnamon, ½ teaspoon nutmeg, ¼ teaspoon ginger, and ⅛ teaspoon allspice for the pumpkin pie spice.

Adjust the sugar substitute to your liking.

REDUCED-CALORIE PUMPKIN PIE

16 ounces (2 cups) canned pumpkin
½ cup evaporated skim milk
⅓ cup fructose or ½ cup sugar
3 large egg whites
2 teaspoons ground pumpkin pie spice

2 packets sugar substitute (equivalent to 4 teaspoons sugar), optional
1 tablespoon flour
9-inch Reduced-Calorie Pie Crust, baked (see page 83)

1. Combine all ingredients except crust in a 2-quart microwave-safe bowl. Using an electric mixer, beat until smooth. Microwave uncovered for 5 minutes at HIGH (100%), stirring often.
2. Pour into the baked pie crust. Microwave for 12 to 15 minutes at MEDIUM (50%), or until center is almost set but looks slightly moist. (Rotate pan once if necessary for even cooking.) Let stand 10 minutes. Serve warm or cool.

Yield: one 9-inch pie

Variation: To save on calories, try a crustless pie. Omit the pie crust and save 120 calories and 6 grams of fat. Crustless pumpkin pie = only one fruit exchange.

LOW-CAL GRAHAM CRACKER CRUST

3 tablespoons regular   1 cup graham cracker
   polyunsaturated   crumbs (about 7 graham
   margarine*   crackers)
                               4 teaspoons sugar or 2
                                  packets sugar substitute

1. Place margarine in a 9- or 10-inch glass microwave-safe pie plate. Microwave for 40 to 60 seconds at HIGH (100%), or until melted. Stir in graham cracker crumbs and sugar substitute. Press firmly against bottom and sides of pie plate.
2. Microwave for 1 to 1½ minutes at MEDIUM HIGH (70%),† or until pie crust is heated through. Press gently with the back of a spoon to shape further, if necessary. Cool. Fill with desired filling.

Yield: one 9- or 10-inch graham cracker crust

T I P S

Do not substitute re-duced-calorie mar-garine in this recipe; if you do, the crust will become soggy.

Also, to prevent a soggy crust, cool crust completely before fill-ing.

* Use unsalted variety for lowest sodium values, if desired.
† Compacts: Microwave for 1 to 1½ minutes at HIGH (100%) instead of MEDIUM HIGH (70%) in step #2.

Variations: For cheesecakes, press graham cracker mixture into an 8- or 9-inch baking dish in step #1. Proceed as directed.

For food processor graham cracker crust: Do not melt margarine. Process graham cracker crumbs, sliced margarine, and sugar substitute until blended in step #1. Press into pie plate.

Nutritional Analysis per Serving (⅛ Pie)

Calories: 103	Cholesterol: 1 mg
Carbohydrate: 12 g	Sodium: 90 mg
Fat: 3 g	Diabetic exchanges:
Protein: 1 g	Bread: 0.75
Fiber: N/A	Fat: 1.0

TIPS
....

Use your conventional oven for this recipe. The texture and taste just do not turn out in the microwave.

Use this crust in any recipe that calls for a baked pie crust.

REDUCED-CALORIE PIE CRUST

——— · · · · · ———

Use your conventional or convection oven for this one.

1¼ cups all-purpose flour
½ cup reduced-calorie
   margarine*
4 teaspoons ice water

1. Preheat conventional oven to 400° F. Using a food processor or pastry blender or two knives and bowl, blend flour and margarine until mixture is very crumbly.
2. Add ice water to crumbly mixture; using a food processor or fork, mix until dough forms a ball.
3. Roll out pie crust between 2 pieces of waxed paper to fit a 9-inch glass or microwave-safe and oven-safe pie plate.

....
*Use unsalted variety for lowest sodium values, if desired.

Fill plate; flute edges and prick bottom and sides with a fork to prevent bubbling when baking.

4. Bake at 400° F. for 15 to 18 minutes or until lightly browned.

Yield: one 9-inch pie crust

──────── · ❄ · ────────

Nutritional Analysis per Serving (⅛ Pie)	
Calories: 120	Cholesterol: 0
Carbohydrate: 14 g	Sodium: Trace
Fat: 6 g	Diabetic exchanges:
Protein: 2 g	Bread: 1
Fiber: N/A	Fat: 1

FROZEN BLUEBERRY YOGURT

──────── · · · · · ────────

1 envelope (7 grams)
　unflavored gelatin, dry
¼ cup sugar
⅓ cup water
1 tablespoon lemon juice

4 cups fresh or frozen
　(slightly thawed)
　blueberries
1 cup (8 ounces) artificially
　sweetened vanilla non-
　fat yogurt

1. Mix gelatin with sugar in a 2-quart microwave-safe bowl. Add water. Let stand 1 minute. Stir until blended. Microwave for 40 to 60 seconds at HIGH (100%), or until gelatin is completely dissolved, stirring once. Set aside.
2. Using a food processor or blender, process lemon juice and fruit until puréed. Blend in gelatin mixture and yogurt.
3. Freeze in an ice cream maker according to manufacturer's

TIPS

To make frozen yogurt without an ice cream maker, omit step #3. Freeze mixture in a 9-inch pan for 1½ hours or until almost firm. Transfer to a mixing bowl and beat at high speed with an electric mixer until fluffy. Spoon back into pan. Freeze until desired texture (at least 1½ to 2 hours).

instructions. (See tip at left if ice cream maker is not available.) Serve in sherbet glasses.

Yield: 8 servings

——————— · ✳ · ———————

Nutritional Analysis per ½-Cup Serving	
Calories: 55	Cholesterol: Trace
Carbohydrate: 13 g	Sodium: 18 mg
Fat: Trace	Diabetic exchanges:
Protein: 3 g	Fruit: 0.5
Fiber: N/A	Milk: 0.25

Variation: Raspberries, strawberries, or diced cantaloupe may substitute the blueberries.

TIPS
· · · · · · · ·

A few years ago electric yogurt makers were a fad—who needs them now if you have a microwave oven?

If you can program your microwave oven and probe setting to "hold" at a specified temperature, use this feature to hold the mixture at 110° F. for 2 hours in step #2.

HOMEMADE YOGURT
——————— · · · · · ———————

Use your microwave probe or microwave candy thermometer for this recipe.

½ cup instant nonfat dry milk powder
3 cups 1% or 2% low-fat milk
½ cup (4 ounces) plain low-fat cultured yogurt (no additives)

1 teaspoon vanilla
6 packets sugar substitute or 4 tablespoons sugar, optional

1. Combine dry milk powder and milk in a 2-quart microwave-safe bowl until thoroughly blended. Microwave for 8 to 9 minutes at HIGH (100%), or until a microwave probe (or microwave candy thermometer) registers 190° F.

or until mixture just starts to bubble, stirring halfway through cooking time. Cool about ½ hour, or to 110° F.

2. Blend yogurt into milk mixture. Cover with plastic wrap. Let stand in your microwave oven for 2 to 2½ hours, maintaining temperature at 110° F. Check thermometer every 30 minutes. (If temperature falls below 110° F., microwave for 1 minute at DEFROST (30%), or until temperature probe registers 110° F. again.) Stir in vanilla and sugar substitutes and refrigerate when mixture looks set.

Yield: 3 cups

————————— · ❄ · —————————

Variation: For Fruit-Flavored Yogurt, stir in 1 cup of your favorite sliced fruit after yogurt is chilled in step #2.

Nutritional Analysis per 1-Cup Serving

Calories: 100   Cholesterol: 8 mg
Carbohydrate: 12 g   Sodium: 145 mg
Fat: 2 g   Diabetic exchanges:
Protein: 8 g   Low-fat milk: 1
Fiber: N/A

BLENDER STRAWBERRY SORBET

————————— · · · · · —————————

1 envelope (7 grams)
  unflavored gelatin, dry
⅓ cup sugar
2½ cups cold water,
  divided

20 ounces frozen
  unsweetened
  strawberries, slightly
  thawed (see *Note*)

TIPS
·······

To make sorbet without an ice cream maker, omit step #3. Freeze mixture in a 9-inch pan for 1½ hours, or until almost firm. Using a blender or food processor, process one-half of mixture at a time until smooth. Freeze again for 1½ to 2 hours.

You can substitute one quart fresh fruit, cleaned and prepared, or 3 cups sliced juice-packed canned fruit for the 20 ounces frozen fruit. You can also substitute juice from the canned fruit for part of the water.

1. Mix gelatin with sugar in a 1-quart microwave-safe bowl. Add 1 cup water. Let stand 1 minute. Stir until blended. Microwave for 2 to 2½ minutes at HIGH (100%), or until gelatin is completely dissolved, stirring twice. Stir in 1½ cups ice-cold water.
2. Using a food processor or blender, process berries until puréed. Add gelatin liquid and process until fully blended. Freeze 20 minutes in a freezerproof bowl.
3. Transfer to an ice cream maker and freeze according to manufacturer's instructions. (See tip at left if ice cream maker is not available.) Serve in sherbet or champagne glasses.

Yield: 10 servings

——————— · ❄ · ———————

Note: To slightly thaw frozen strawberries, microwave for 2 to 2½ minutes at HIGH (100%). Let stand 1 minute.

Variations: For Sugarless Strawberry Sorbet, omit sugar in step #1. Process 6 packets sugar substitute (equal to 12 teaspoons sugar) with the strawberries or other fruit in step #2. Proceed as directed.

For Strawberry à l'Orange Sorbet, add ⅓ cup (3 ounces) frozen orange juice concentrate and 1 tablespoon orange liqueur (optional) with the strawberries in step #2.

For Peach, Raspberry, Blueberry, or Melon Sorbet, substitute 16 to 20 ounces frozen fruit, slightly thawed, for the strawberries.

Nutritional Analysis per ½-Cup Serving

Calories: 39	Cholesterol: 0 g
Carbohydrate: 7 g	Sodium: 12 mg
Fat: Trace	Diabetic exchange:
Protein: 1 g	Fruit: 0.5
Fiber: N/A	

CHAMPAGNE SORBET

1 envelope (7 grams)
  unflavored gelatin, dry
½ cup sugar
¾ cup orange juice

½ cup cold water
2 cups pink champagne

1. Mix gelatin with sugar in a 1-quart microwave-safe bowl. Add water. Let stand 1 minute. Stir until blended. Microwave for 2 to 2½ minutes at HIGH (100%), stirring twice, or until gelatin is completely dissolved. Stir in orange juice and the champagne. Freeze 20 minutes in a freezerproof bowl.
2. Transfer to an ice cream maker and freeze according to manufacturer's instructions. (See tip at left if an ice cream maker is not available.) Serve in sherbet or champagne glasses.

Yield: 10 servings

— · ❄ · —

Variations: For Nonalcoholic Champagne Sorbet, substitute pink sparkling catawba for the champagne.

For Cranberry-Grape Sorbet, reduce sugar to 1 tablespoon. Reduce champagne to 1 cup. Substitute 2 cups cran-grape juice cocktail for the cold water and orange juice in step #1. Proceed as directed.

Nutritional Analysis per ½-Cup Serving

Calories: 85	Cholesterol: 0 mg
Carbohydrate: 13 g	Sodium: 1 mg
Fat: 0 g	Diabetic exchanges:
Protein: 1 g	No exchange for alcohol
Fiber: N/A	

I first tasted Champagne Sorbet in the gourmet restaurant at a hotel in Tralee, Ireland. It was served as an appetizer before our meal. Everyone in our tour group loved the light, delicious flavor. Upon returning home, I immediately tried to replicate the recipe. The lightness of the sorbet makes it a perfect dessert too.

To make sorbet without an ice cream maker, omit step #2. Freeze mixture in a 9-inch pan for 2 hours, or until almost firm. Using a food processor, process one-half of the mixture at a time until smooth. Freeze again for 1½ to 2½ hours, or until ice cream consistency.

EGGS AND BREAKFAST FOODS

GENERAL TIPS FOR MICROWAVING EGGS

- *Do not microwave eggs in the shell*—they will explode (the yolk cooks quickly and causes pressure against the shell).

- Always cover whole eggs to seal in the moisture and keep the yolk from becoming tough.

- *Always gently prick the yolk and white* with a toothpick or tines of a fork when cooking hard-cooked or poached eggs to allow the steam to escape.

- If your egg "pops" or explodes in the oven (when cooking hard-cooked or poached eggs), you forgot to prick the yolk and white or you used HIGH (100%) power instead of MEDIUM (50%) or MEDIUM HIGH (70%) as recommended (see following chart).

- Microwaved eggs are done even when they still look very moist. They will continue to cook for 1 minute after microwaving (standing time). (See following chart.)

EGG MICROWAVING TIME CHART

TYPE/AMOUNT	PREPARATION/INSTRUCTIONS	TIME*/POWER LEVEL
Scrambled eggs 1–8 medium or large eggs or equivalent Egg Substitute	Beat eggs with 1 tablespoon milk per egg and place in a Styrofoam cup (for easy cleanup) or a custard cup (for 1 or 2 eggs) or casserole (for 3 to 8 eggs). Cover with waxed paper. Stir halfway through microwaving time or every 2 minutes. Let stand, covered, for 1 to 2 minutes after microwaving to complete cooking.	*Microwave 1 egg* for 40 to 60 seconds at HIGH (100%). *Microwave 2 eggs* for 1¼ to 1½ minutes at HIGH (100%). *Microwave 4 eggs* for 1 minute at HIGH (100%). Stir, then microwave for 1½ to 3 minutes at MEDIUM HIGH (70%). *Microwave 6 eggs* for 2 minutes at HIGH (100%). Stir, then microwave for 2 to 4 minutes at MEDIUM HIGH (70%). *Microwave 8 eggs* for 2 minutes at HIGH (100%). Stir, then microwave for 3 to 5 minutes at MEDIUM HIGH (70%).
Poached eggs 1–4 medium or large eggs	Microwave 2 tablespoons water and ¼ teaspoon white vinegar in a custard cup (for each egg) for 30 seconds at HIGH (100%), or until boiling. Break egg into boiling water. Prick yolk and white with toothpick or fork. Cover with waxed paper. Let stand 1 minute after cooking; remove from water to prevent overcooking.	*Microwave 1 egg* for 35 to 40 seconds at MEDIUM HIGH (70%). *Microwave 2 eggs* for 45 to 60 seconds at MEDIUM HIGH (70%). *Microwave 3 eggs* for 1 to 1½ minutes at MEDIUM HIGH (70%). *Microwave 4 eggs* for 1½ to 2½ minutes at MEDIUM HIGH (70%).
Hard-cooked eggs 1–4 medium or large eggs	Break each egg into an individual custard cup that has been sprayed with vegetable coating. Prick yolk and white with toothpick or fork. Cover with waxed paper. Let stand 5 minutes after cooking to complete cooking.	*Microwave 1 egg* for 1½ to 2 minutes at MEDIUM (50%). *Microwave 2 eggs* for 2½ to 3 minutes at MEDIUM (50%). *Microwave 4 eggs* for 4 to 5 minutes at MEDIUM (50%).

*Amount of time per egg is approximate and will vary depending on egg size.

GENERAL TIPS FOR MICROWAVING CEREALS

- Use a 2-quart microwave-safe bowl (or a bowl at least double the size of the amount of cereal to be cooked), as cereal "boils up" during microwaving.

- Microwave cereal uncovered at HIGH (100%) power.

- Stir cereal halfway through microwaving to avoid lumps.

- Start with warm or hot tap water to speed microwaving time.

- For oatmeal or Cream of Wheat, there's no need to use instant cereal or even heat the water first. Simply mix 1 cup hot tap water for every ½ cup cereal in a 2-quart microwave-safe bowl. Microwave for 3 to 4 minutes at HIGH (100%), stirring once. (See recipe, page 106.)

TIPS
....

Anytime a recipe calls for 2 eggs or ½ cup Egg Substitute, this recipe through step #1 may be used.

For added flavoring, add ¼ teaspoon garlic powder to the egg mixture in step #1.

Some people tell me they would rather buy store-bought egg substitute than have to throw the yolks away. Why pay twice as

EGG SUBSTITUTE
OR NO-CHOLESTEROL SCRAMBLED EGGS

——————— · · · · · ———————

A perfect substitute for 2 eggs or ½ cup Egg Beaters!

4 medium or large egg whites
2 tablespoons skim milk

1 tablespoon safflower, canola, or vegetable oil
2 drops yellow food coloring

1. Using a fork or electric mixer, beat all the ingredients in a bowl until foamy. (Yield: ½ cup liquid egg substitute.)

2. For No-Cholesterol Scrambled Eggs: Turn mixture into a 1-quart microwave-safe casserole that has been sprayed with vegetable coating. Cover with lid or vented plastic wrap.

3. Microwave for 1 minute at HIGH (100%).† Stir. Recover and microwave for 30 to 60 seconds at MEDIUM HIGH (70%), or until almost set. Let stand 1 minute.

Yield: 1 serving

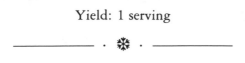

Variation: For 2 servings, double ingredients. Microwave for 2 minutes at HIGH (100%); stir and microwave for 1 to 1½ minutes at MEDIUM HIGH (70%), or until almost set.

Nutritional Analysis per Serving	
Calories: 190	Cholesterol: 1 mg
Carbohydrate: 1 g	Sodium: 215 mg
Fat: 14 g	Diabetic exchanges:
Protein: 13 g	Lean meat: 2
Fiber: N/A	Fat: 2

much money for someone else to get rid of the yolks? I recommend mixing each leftover yolk with ¼ teaspoon sugar (to preserve texture) and placing in a freezer container that has a visible measure. Freeze and keep adding to the same container. Use ½ cup yolks for every 2 eggs called for in a recipe for baked goods (the goods you will take to the next bazaar!).

----

†Compacts: Microwave at HIGH (100%) instead of MEDIUM HIGH (70%) for the same amount of time listed in step #3.

Dieters may find the Low-Calorie Cheesy Omelet quite appealing and filling.

SCRAMBLED EGGS
OR EGG OMELET IN A STYROFOAM CUP

· · · · ·

1–2 large eggs
1 tablespoon water or milk
  per egg

1. Break each egg into an 8- to 10-ounce Styrofoam cup. Add water or milk.
2. Whip with a fork.
3. Microwave 1 egg for 25 seconds at HIGH (100%). Stir. Microwave again for 15 to 20 seconds at HIGH (100%). Let stand 1 minute to set (while you make the toast!). For two eggs: Microwave for 30 seconds at HIGH (100%), stir. Microwave again for 25 to 35 seconds at HIGH (100%). Let stand 1 minute to set.
4. Eat, enjoy, and throw away the cup for easy cleanup.

Yield: 1 egg per serving

—————— · ❄ · ——————

Variation: Try a Low-Calorie Cheesy Omelet. For every egg, stir in 1 tablespoon cottage cheese with the milk. Microwave 10 seconds longer than recommended after stirring. Top with 2 tablespoons grated reduced-fat cheddar cheese. Let stand 1 minute.

Nutritional Analysis per Serving (1 Egg)

Calories: 80	Fiber: N/A
Carbohydrate: 1 g	Cholesterol: 273 mg
Fat: 6 g	Sodium: 146 mg
Protein: 6 g	Diabetic exchanges:
	Medium-fat meat: 1

"NO CHOLESTEROL" OMELET FOR TWO

TIPS

What to do with the leftover yolks is always a dilemma. See the tip on page 91.

5 teaspoons vegetable oil
2 tablespoons diced onion
2 tablespoons chopped
  mushrooms and/or
  green pepper, optional
6 extra-large egg whites or
  8 medium egg whites

2 tablespoons nonfat dry
  milk solids
3 drops yellow food
  coloring
2 tablespoons chopped
  tomato to garnish
  (optional)

Using 4 egg whites instead of 2 whole eggs will supply you with twice the protein but none of the "bad" (saturated) cholesterol.

1. Mix 1 teaspoon vegetable oil, onion, mushrooms, and/or pepper in a small microwave-safe bowl. Cover loosely with plastic wrap. Microwave for 1 to 2 minutes at HIGH (100%), or until onion is translucent. Set aside.
2. Beat egg whites, nonfat dry milk solids, 4 teaspoons vegetable oil, and food coloring in a bowl until foamy using a fork or an electric mixer. Turn into a 1-quart microwave-safe casserole or 9-inch pie plate sprayed with vegetable coating. Cover with lid or vented plastic wrap.
3. Microwave for 1 minute at HIGH (100%). Stir. Cover and microwave again for 2 to 3 minutes at MEDIUM HIGH (70%), or until almost set, lifting edge to allow uncooked portion to spread to bottom at least once. Let stand 2 minutes. Place cooked vegetables and tomatoes (optional) on half of omelet; fold over and serve.

Yield: 2 servings

Nutritional Analysis per Serving (½ Recipe)

Calories: 172
Carbohydrate: 3 g
Fat: 12 g
Protein: 12 g
Fiber: N/A
Cholesterol: Trace

Sodium: 197 mg
Diabetic exchanges:
  Medium-fat meat: 1.5
  Skim milk: 0.25
  Fat: 1.5

You can make your own Egg Substitute for this one, if you're on a cholesterol-restricted diet (see page 91).

ITALIAN OMELET

· · · · ·

Delicious when served at breakfast or for a light dinner.

1 cup Egg Substitute (see page 91) or 1 cup Egg Beaters or 3 large eggs

1 cup (8 ounces) low-fat cottage cheese, lightly drained

1 tablespoon grated Parmesan cheese

¼ teaspoon Italian seasoning or oregano

Chopped parsley to garnish

8-ounce can tomato sauce,* optional

1. In a medium bowl, mix Egg Substitute, cheeses, and Italian seasoning until blended well. Pour into a 9-inch microwave-safe pie plate that has been sprayed with vegetable coating.

2. Microwave for 3 to 4 minutes at MEDIUM (50%), or until edges start to set. Lift edge to allow uncooked portion to spread to the bottom. Continue to microwave for 2 to 3 minutes longer at MEDIUM (50%), or until almost set. Let stand 1 minute. Garnish with chopped parsley.

3. For optional topping, microwave tomato sauce in a small glass bowl or pitcher for 1 minute at HIGH (100%), or until heated. To serve, cut omelet into thirds and pour heated sauce over each slice.

Yield: 3 servings

· ❋ ·

Nutritional Analysis per Serving (⅓ Omelet)

Calories: 228	Cholesterol: 8 mg
Carbohydrate: 9 g	Sodium: 502 mg
Fat: 12 g	Diabetic exchanges:
Protein: 21 g	Medium-fat meat: 2.5
Fiber: N/A	Vegetable: 1.75

*Use no-salt-added variety for lowest sodium value, if desired.

POACHED EGGS

Use a Styrofoam or custard cup for easy cleanup.

2 tablespoons water per
  medium or large egg
¼ teaspoon white vinegar
  per egg
1 to 4 eggs

1. Place 2 tablespoons water and ¼ teaspoon vinegar in a Styrofoam, custard, or muffin cup for each egg. Microwave for ½ to 1½ minutes at HIGH (100%), until boiling.
2. Break 1 egg into each cup. Gently prick yolk and white with a toothpick. Cover with waxed paper. Microwave as directed, until whites are opaque and yolks are soft set. Let stand 1 minute, then remove from water to prevent overcooking.

    For 1 egg: Microwave for 35–45 seconds at MEDIUM HIGH (70%). For two eggs: Microwave for 45–60 seconds at MEDIUM HIGH (70%). For 3 eggs: Microwave for 1 to 1½ minutes at MEDIUM HIGH (70%). For 4 eggs: Microwave for 1½ to 2½ minutes at MEDIUM HIGH (70%).

Yield: 1 egg per serving

You will not taste the vinegar. It helps the whites coagulate, or set.

You can microwave 4 eggs in a 1-quart microwave-safe casserole with 1 cup boiling water and ½ teaspoon vinegar instead of using the individual cups, if desired. Follow the same cooking time as listed in step 2.

Nutritional Analysis per Serving (1 Egg)

Calories: 80
Carbohydrate: 1 g
Fat: 6 g
Protein: 6 g

Fiber: N/A
Cholesterol: 273 mg
Sodium: 146 mg
Diabetic exchanges:
  Medium-fat meat: 1

TIPS

Cool eggs in the refrigerator at least 15 minutes if the salad will be eaten later. If the salad will be eaten immediately, proceed as directed.

Add 1 to 2 teaspoons dill pickle juice with the mayonnaise for a moister salad, if desired.

If eggs pop or explode in your oven, you did not prick the whites and yolks enough to allow built-up steam to escape, or you microwaved the eggs at HIGH (100%) instead of MEDIUM (50%) as recommended.

Delicious served on toast, rye crackers, reduced-calorie bread, or on a bed of lettuce.

2 large eggs or 1 extra-large egg
1 tablespoon reduced-calorie mayonnaise or plain nonfat yogurt
1 tablespoon finely chopped dill pickle or celery

¼ packet sugar substitute (equivalent to ½ teaspoon sugar)
Dill pickle slices to garnish, optional

1. Spray 2 small custard cups with vegetable coating. Break each egg into one of the cups, being careful not to break the yolk. Gently prick each yolk and white with a fork twice. Cover each dish with a small piece of waxed paper. Microwave for 2½ to 3 minutes at MEDIUM (50%), or until white is set and yolk is almost cooked. Let stand 2 to 5 minutes to complete cooking. (See tip at left if salad will be eaten at a later time.)

2. Turn eggs out of custard cups into a small mixing bowl or luncheon plate. Using a table fork and knife or two knives, slice and chop eggs until completely chopped. Stir in mayonnaise until well mixed. Blend in chopped pickle and sugar substitute. Serve garnished with additional dill pickle slices, if desired.

Yield: 1 serving

Nutritional Analysis per Serving

Calories: 206	Cholesterol: 551 mg
Carbohydrate: 4 g	Sodium: 478 mg
Fat: 17 g	Diabetic exchanges:
Protein: 12 g	Medium-fat meat: 2
Fiber: N/A	Fat: 1

LEAN SAUSAGE BREAKFAST FRITTATA

—————————— · · · · · ——————————

Easy breakfast or brunch idea!

8 ounces uncooked Lean Breakfast Sausage (see page 176), crumbled
Dash salt-free browning powder for meat
¾ cup shredded reduced-fat cheddar cheese*
2 tablespoons green onion, finely sliced

1 cup Egg Substitute (see page 91) or Egg Beaters or 4 large eggs, beaten
1 cup evaporated skim milk
Dash Seasoned Salt Substitute #2 (see page 24⁵), or store-bought alternative
1 tablespoon chopped parsley

A frittata is a quiche without a crust (and without the crust's calories).

You may use any lean ground sausage in this recipe, but Lean Breakfast Sausage yields the lowest number of calories and fat per serving.

1. Place crumbled sausage in a 9-inch glass pie plate. Sprinkle with browning powder. Cover with waxed paper. Microwave for 3 to 4 minutes on HIGH (100%), or until no longer pink, stirring twice. Drain well.
2. Sprinkle cheese over sausage and add green onion.
3. Beat Egg Substitute with milk, Seasoned Salt Substitute, and parsley in a medium bowl.
4. Pour into the pie plate. Cover with vented plastic wrap. Microwave for 4 minutes at HIGH (100%). Stir. Cover again. Microwave again for 7 to 8 minutes at MEDIUM (50%), or until center is set but not dry, rotating and stirring once during cooking. Let stand 5 minutes.

Yield: one 9-inch frittata

—————————— · ❄ · ——————————

· ·
*Use reduced-salt variety for lowest sodium values, if desired.

Nutritional Analysis per Serving ($\frac{1}{6}$ Frittata)

Calories: 186
Carbohydrate: 7 g
Fat: 10 g
Protein: 16 g
Fiber: N/A
Cholesterol: 16 mg

Sodium: 184 mg
Diabetic exchanges:
Fat: 0.5
Lean meat: 2
Skim milk: 0.5

TIPS
....

Try serving frittata slices garnished with fresh parsley sprigs and a tomato slice, if desired.

If you substitute imitation crabmeat, keep in mind you will at least double the milligrams of sodium per serving.

CRABMEAT FRITTATA

· · · · ·

A tasty crustless luncheon quiche.

3 medium tomatoes, seeded and cubed
1 medium zucchini, peeled and shredded to equal 1 cup
½ medium onion (½ cup), finely chopped
1 cup Egg Substitute (see page 91) or Egg Beaters or 4 large eggs
½ cup grated Parmesan cheese, divided

1 teaspoon Italian seasoning
1 teaspoon dried parsley
Dash salt substitute or salt*
4 ounces frozen chopped crabmeat, flaked
½ cup grated reduced-fat Swiss cheese
½ cup grated reduced-fat cheddar cheese*

1. Combine tomatoes, zucchini, and onion in a 1-quart flat microwave-safe casserole. Cover with lid or vented plastic wrap. Microwave for 8 to 9 minutes at HIGH (100%), or until crisp-tender. Let stand to cool.
2. Beat Egg Substitute, ¼ cup Parmesan cheese, and remaining seasonings in a medium bowl until blended. Add crabmeat and cooled vegetables. Pour into a 10-inch glass pie plate that has been sprayed with vegetable coating.

....
*Use reduced-salt variety for lowest-sodium values, if desired.

Top with remaining Parmesan cheese, Swiss cheese, and cheddar cheese, distributing evenly.

3. Cover with vented plastic wrap. Microwave for 18½ to 22½ minutes at MEDIUM (50%), or until center is almost set, lifting edge to allow uncooked portion to spread to bottom at least once. Let stand 5 to 10 minutes to complete cooking.

Yield: one 10-inch frittata

──────── · ❄ · ────────

┌───┐
│ *Nutritional Analysis per Serving (⅙ Frittata)*   │
│   │
│ Calories: 197   Sodium: 440 mg   │
│ Carbohydrate: 6 g   Diabetic exchanges: │
│ Fat: 11 g   Lean meat: 2   │
│ Protein: 17 g   Vegetable: 1.5   │
│ Fiber: N/A   Fat: 1   │
│ Cholesterol: 22 mg   │
└───┘

FAST EGG AND POTATO FRITTATA

──── · · · · · ────

1 large potato (8 ounces), peeled and shredded
1 small onion, chopped (about ⅔ cup)
1½ cups Egg Substitute (see page 91) or Egg Beaters, or 6 medium eggs
⅓ cup skim milk
½ teaspoon Seasoned Salt Substitute #2 (see page 245) or store-bought alternative

1. Combine potato and onion in a 9-inch glass pie plate or microwave-safe casserole. Cover loosely with waxed paper or vented plastic wrap. Microwave for 6 to 8 minutes at HIGH (100%), or until vegetables are tender.

TIPS
....
Serve this crustless quiche for any meal— breakfast, brunch, lunch, or dinner.

2. Mix Egg Substitute, skim milk, and Seasoned Salt Substitute in a small bowl. Pour over vegetables. Cover
again. Microwave for 2 to 3 minutes at HIGH (100%), or
until edges start to set. Lift edges to allow uncooked portion to spread to bottom. Microwave for 3 to 4 minutes at
MEDIUM HIGH (70%), or until almost set. Let stand 2
minutes.

Yield: one 9-inch frittata

———————— · ❄ · ————————

Variation: For Calico Frittata, add ¼ cup grated carrot, ¼
cup chopped red pepper, and/or ¼ cup chopped celery with
the onion in step #1. Proceed as directed.

Nutritional Analysis per Serving (¼ Frittata)

Calories: 217   Sodium: 176 mg
Carbohydrate: 18 g   Diabetic exchanges:
Fat: 10 g   Bread: 1.0
Protein: 12 g   Medium-fat meat: 1.25
Fiber: N/A   Milk (skim): 0.25
Cholesterol: 1 mg

TOFU-MUSHROOM QUICHE

· · · · ·

To add color to this delicious high-protein quiche, serve each wedge garnished with a tomato slice and chopped fresh parsley.

To ensure that the bottom of the quiche is done, place quiche on an inverted saucer before microwaving in step #5.

Be sure to use regular margarine in the crust, as reduced-calorie margarine will cause the crust to become soggy.

·········· CRUST ··········

4 slices high-fiber reduced-calorie white or whole wheat bread (crusts removed)

1 tablespoon regular polyunsaturated margarine
2 tablespoons ice water

·········· FILLING ··········

3 cups (12 ounces) sliced fresh mushrooms
2 green onions, chopped
1 cup (4 ounces) shredded Swiss cheese
½ cup Egg Substitute (see page 91) or Egg Beaters or 2 large eggs
6 ounces tofu, drained and wrapped in paper towel to remove excess liquid

⅔ cup evaporated skim milk
⅓ cup plain nonfat yogurt
2 teaspoons snipped fresh parsley, or 1 teaspoon dried
¼ teaspoon each Seasoned Salt Substitute #2 (see page 245) or store-bought alternative and pepper

1. For crust: Using a food processor or blender, process bread into fine crumbs. Blend in margarine until thoroughly mixed. Stir in water with a fork until a dough forms.
2. Press dough into a 9-inch microwave-safe pie plate that has been sprayed with vegetable coating. Microwave crust for 2 to 3 minutes at MEDIUM HIGH (70%), or until sides look dry. Set crust aside.
3. For filling: Microwave mushrooms and onion in a 1-quart microwave-safe casserole covered with lid or vented plastic wrap for 5 to 6 minutes at HIGH (100%), until tender. Drain well and spread into pie crust. Sprinkle with shredded cheese. Set aside.
4. Blend remaining filling ingredients in a food processor or blender until smooth.
5. Pour blended egg mixture into a 1-quart casserole and

microwave for 3 to 4 minutes at HIGH (100%), or until hot, stirring twice. Pour egg mixture over mushrooms and cheese. Microwave quiche for 10 to 14 minutes at MEDIUM (50%) until soft set (rotating pan twice if necessary for even cooking). Let stand 5 minutes before serving.

Yield: one 9-inch quiche

———————— · ❄ · ————————

Nutritional Analysis per Serving (1/6 Quiche)

Calories: 204

Carbohydrate: 12 g

Fat: 11 g

Protein: 15 g

Fiber: N/A

Cholesterol: 19 mg

Sodium: 209 mg

Diabetic exchanges:

  Skim milk: 1

  Lean meat: 1

  Fat: 1

CHEDDAR, BROCCOLI, AND TORTILLA
BRUNCH PIE

10-ounce package frozen chopped broccoli

1 cup (3 to 4 ounces) sliced fresh mushrooms

½ medium onion (½ cup), chopped

1 clove garlic, minced

1 teaspoon olive oil

½ cup Egg Substitute (see page 91) or Egg Beaters or 2 large eggs, beaten

1 cup (8 ounces) low-fat cottage cheese

½ cup (2 ounces) shredded reduced-fat cheddar cheese*

Dash ground nutmeg

½ teaspoon Seasoned Salt Substitute #1 (see page 244) or store-bought alternative

3 (6-inch) flour or corn tortillas

Tomato slices to garnish, optional

1. Place package of broccoli on a paper plate or paper towel–lined plate in the microwave (remove any foil wrapping). Microwave for 5 minutes at HIGH (100%), or until hot. Drain in a colander. Set aside.

2. Combine mushrooms, onion, garlic, and olive oil in a 1½-quart microwave-safe casserole. Microwave for 3 to 4 minutes at HIGH (100%), or until tender. Stir in broccoli and remaining ingredients except tortillas and tomato.

3. Line a 9-inch glass pie plate with the tortillas, overlapping at bottom and extending over sides. Pour egg-broccoli mixture over tortillas. Cover with waxed paper.

4. Microwave for 5 minutes at HIGH (100%), or until edges begin to set. Rotate pan and, using a spoon, lift up edges of egg mixture to allow uncooked portion to spread to the outside. Cover again. Microwave again for 9 to 10 minutes at MEDIUM (50%), or until center is almost set. Let

TIPS
....

Leftovers can be served either cold or hot. To heat, Microwave 1 wedge for 1½ to 2 minutes at MEDIUM HIGH (70%).

* Use reduced-salt variety for lowest sodium values, if desired.

stand 5 minutes, cut into wedges, and serve garnished with tomato slices, if desired.

Yield: one 9-inch pie

——————— · ❋ · ———————

Nutritional Analysis per Wedge (⅙ Pie)

Calories: 178

Carbohydrate: 17 g

Fat: 7 g

Protein: 14 g

Fiber: N/A

Cholesterol: 3 mg

Sodium: 229 mg

Diabetic exchanges:

Bread: .5

Lean meat: 1

Vegetable: 2

Fat: 0.5

OATMEAL OR CREAM OF WHEAT
(REGULAR AND QUICK)

— · · · · · —

Oatmeal or Cream of
Wheat (⅓ cup per
serving)

Water (use 2 times the
quantity of cereal, or ⅔
cup per serving)
½ apple, grated, optional

1. Place cereal, apple, and water in a 2-quart microwave-safe bowl. (You can cook up to 3 to 4 servings at once.)
2. Microwave for 3 to 4 minutes at HIGH (100%) for 1 to 3 servings. Microwave for 4 to 5 minutes at HIGH (100%) for more than 4 servings. Let stand 2 minutes.

Yields: ⅔ cup per serving

——— · ❄ · ———

Nutritional Analysis per Serving (⅔ Cup)

Calories: 125
Carbohydrate: 25 g
Fat: 2 g
Protein: 3 g
Fiber: N/A

Cholesterol: 0 mg
Sodium: 253 mg
Diabetic exchanges:
    Bread: 1.25
    Fruit: 0.5

TIPS
· · · · · · · ·

Be sure to use a deep bowl, as the cereal boils up while cooking.

You can use either regular or quick-cooking cereal. Do *not* use instant. For quick cereals, reduce microwaving time by 1 minute.

Serve oatmeal with ¼ cup skim milk, a drop of butter flavoring, and a packet of sugar substitute or 1 teaspoon fructose per serving, if desired.

FISH

· ❄ ·

GENERAL TIPS FOR MICROWAVING FISH

- A microwave steams, poaches, and bakes fish perfectly in 75 percent less time than a conventional oven.

- Use your favorite recipe but use one-quarter *less* liquid and butter. Microwaving most fish with as little as 2 teaspoons to 2 tablespoons lemon juice works just fine.

- Always defrost frozen fish before cooking. To defrost fish, microwave for 6 to 8 minutes per pound at DEFROST (30%), turning over once. Let stand 3 minutes. Rinse under cold water.

- To prevent the corners of boxed blocks of fillets from over-cooking during defrosting time, shield corners with small strips of foil (see shielding tips, pages 15–16).

- Fish fillets microwave best when they are of equal and uni-form size. For a one-pound block of fish, simply cut the icy block into 4 or 6 chunks halfway through defrosting time. Finish defrosting and rinse. Then microwave the fish in chunks for even cooking.

- If the ends of fillets are especially thin, fold them under each fillet and toward the center.

- For fish with skin, place in a casserole with skin side down.

- Arrange fish fillets like spokes on a wagon wheel in the casserole.

- To cook fish, place in a flat 9- to 10-inch microwave-safe casserole, cover with waxed paper, and microwave for 4 to 6 minutes per pound at HIGH (100%).

- If sensitive foods such as cheese, eggs, mushrooms, or mayonnaise are included in a fish recipe, microwave for 9 to 10 minutes per pound at MEDIUM HIGH (70%) or MEDIUM (50%).

- Microwave clams or mussels only until shells pop open. (See following chart.) Discard any that don't pop open.

- Cook shrimp in shells for added flavor.

- Cook fish until it flakes when lifted gently with a fork. *Do not overcook,* as overcooked fish is firm, dry, and crumbly. When fish is opaque, losing its translucence, it is done.

- Does your microwave smell fishy? Microwave 1 slice lemon or 2 tablespoons lemon juice in ½ cup water for 2½ minutes at HIGH (100%). The odor will disappear. Wipe oven interior clean with a damp cloth.

FISH MICROWAVING TIME CHART

TYPE/AMOUNT	PREPARATION*/INSTRUCTIONS	TIME/POWER LEVEL†
Fish fillet 1 fillet (4 ounces)	Tuck under thin ends, sprinkle each fillet with 2 teaspoons lemon juice and seasonings. Cover with waxed paper.	Microwave for 1 to 2½ minutes at HIGH (100%). Let stand 2 minutes.
2 fillets (4 ounces each)	Same as above.	Microwave for 2 to 3 minutes at HIGH (100%). Let stand 2 minutes.

TYPE/AMOUNT	PREPARATION*/INSTRUCTIONS	TIME/POWER LEVEL

Fish fillet
  1 pound thin
  fillets (1/2- to 3/4-
  inch thick)
	Same as above.	Microwave for 4 to 6 minutes at HIGH (100%).

1 pound very
  thick fillets or
  steaks (1-inch
  thick)
	Same as above.	Microwave for 7 to 10 minutes at MEDIUM HIGH (70%) or MEDIUM (50%), turning over halfway through cooking time.

Whole fish
  2 pounds (trout,
  pike, and so on)
	Remove head or place a strip of foil around eyes and head (see shielding tips, page 15). Place skin side down in a microwave-safe casserole. Sprinkle with seasonings and 2 tablespoons lemon juice. Cover with vented plastic wrap.	Microwave for 12 to 15 minutes at MEDIUM (50%), turning over halfway through cooking time. Let stand 5 minutes.

3 pounds	Same as above.	Microwave for 20 to 24 minutes at MEDIUM (50%), turning over halfway through cooking time. Let stand 5 minutes.

Shrimp or prawns
  (1 pound shelled
  or unshelled)
	Sprinkle with 2 tablespoons lemon juice. Cover with vented plastic wrap.	Microwave for 3 to 5 minutes at HIGH (100%), or until pink and opaque, stirring once.

Scallops (1 pound)	Use a ring mold or place a glass tumbler open side up in the center of a 9- or 10-inch microwave-safe casserole. Place scallops in ring or around tumbler. Sprinkle with 2 tablespoons lemon juice. Cover with vented plastic wrap.	Microwave for 4 to 6 minutes at MEDIUM (50%), stirring once. Let stand 2 minutes.
Lobster (one 6- ounce tail)	Using scissors, cut through bottom side of tail. Place cut side up in casserole. Sprinkle with 1 tablespoon lemon juice. Cover with vented plastic wrap.	Microwave for 3 to 4 minutes at MEDIUM (50%). Let stand 3 minutes.
4 lobster tails (6 ounces each)	Same as above. Arrange tails like spokes on a wagon wheel with thin ends toward the center of microwave-safe casserole.	Microwave for 12 to 14 minutes at MEDIUM (50%). Let stand 5 minutes.

12 clams or
  mussels (about
  1 pound)
	Same as for scallops.	Microwave for 3 to 5 minutes at HIGH (100%), or until clams pop open.

. . . .

*See General Tips for Microwaving Fish, page 107.

COD ITALIANO

TIPS

Cod is naturally high in protein as well as calcium, phosphorus, and potassium.

························ SAUCE ························

½ medium onion (½ cup), chopped
½ medium green bell pepper (½ cup), seeded and chopped, optional
1 clove garlic, minced
1 medium tomato, seeded and chopped (½ cup)

1 cup (about 4 ounces) sliced fresh mushrooms
1 tablespoon vegetable oil or olive oil
2 teaspoons lemon juice
1 tablespoon chopped fresh parsley
1 teaspoon Italian seasoning

························ FISH ························

4 cod or other white fish fillets (4 ounces each)

························ TOPPING ························

3 tablespoons grated Parmesan cheese

1. Combine sauce ingredients in a 2-quart flat microwave-safe casserole, until well blended. Cover with lid or vented plastic wrap.
2. Microwave for 4 to 5 minutes at HIGH (100%), or until vegetables are tender, stirring twice.
3. Slip fish under vegetables, spooning vegetables over fish and arranging thickest portions of fish to the outside. Cover again.
4. Microwave for 6 to 7 minutes at HIGH (100%), or until fish flakes easily with a fork. Sprinkle with Parmesan cheese topping. Let stand 3 minutes. Serve immediately.

Yield: 4 servings

Nutritional Analysis per Serving (3-ounce Cooked Fillet and ¼ Sauce)

Calories: 165

Carbohydrate: 6 g

Fat: 6 g

Protein: 23 g

Fiber: N/A

Cholesterol: 60 mg

Sodium: 147 mg

Diabetic exchanges:

Lean meat: 3

Vegetable: 1

CAJUN CATFISH OR REDFISH

·········· FISH ··········

4 farm-raised catfish fillets or redfish fillets (4 ounces each)

1 lime, sliced, for garnish
2 tablespoons skim milk

·········· CAJUN SEASONING MIX ··········

1½ teaspoons paprika
½ teaspoon onion powder
½ teaspoon garlic powder
¼ teaspoon dried oregano
¼ teaspoon dried thyme

¼ teaspoon red pepper flakes
¼ teaspoon ground white pepper
¼ teaspoon ground black pepper

1. Rinse fillets in water and dry with paper toweling. Place in a 2-quart or 10-inch flat microwave-safe casserole. Brush fillets with skim milk.
2. Combine Cajun Seasoning Mix ingredients; pat mixture onto fish. Cover with waxed paper.
3. Microwave for 3 minutes at HIGH (100%). Rearrange fillets and top each with a slice of lime. Cover again. Microwave for 1½ to 3 minutes at HIGH (100%), or until fish flakes easily with a fork.

Yield: 4 servings

* · ❄ · *

Nutritional Analysis per Serving (3-Ounce Cooked Fillet)

Calories: 147
Carbohydrate: 3 g
Fat: 5 g
Protein: 21 g

Fiber: N/A
Cholesterol: 65 mg
Sodium: 77 mg
Diabetic exchanges:
    Lean meat: 3

If you like "hot stuff," you'll love Cajun Catfish.

Farm-raised catfish have advantages over those in the rivers: They grow in unpolluted waters and are fed a fixed diet.

YOGURT-BAKED FLOUNDER

— · · · · · —

4 flounder fillets (4 ounces each)
1 teaspoon cornstarch
3 tablespoons plain nonfat yogurt
1 tablespoon reduced-calorie mayonnaise

½ teaspoon prepared mustard
¼ teaspoon dried tarragon
2 tablespoons Seasoned Bread Crumbs or Cornflakes (see page 243)

1. Arrange fillets in a 10-inch flat microwave-safe casserole with thickest portions to the outside.
2. Combine cornstarch and yogurt in a small bowl until blended. Stir in mayonnaise, mustard, and tarragon. Spread mixture on fish fillets. Sprinkle with bread crumbs.
3. Cover with waxed paper. Microwave for 4 to 6 minutes at HIGH (100%), or until fish flakes easily with a fork, rearranging fillets halfway through cooking time. Let stand 3 minutes.

Yield: 4 servings

——— · ❄ · ———

Variation: For 2 servings, cut ingredients in half. Proceed as directed. Microwave for 2½ to 4 minutes at HIGH (100%), or until fish flakes with a fork.

Nutritional Analysis per Serving (4-Ounce Fillet)

Calories: 117	Cholesterol: 59 mg
Carbohydrate: 3 g	Sodium: 195 mg
Fat: 3 g	Diabetic exchanges:
Protein: 19 g	Bread: 0.25
Fiber: N/A	Lean Meat: 2.5

STUFFED FLOUNDER

.... STUFFING ....

1 teaspoon corn oil or
   reduced-calorie
   margarine*
½ medium onion,
   chopped (½ cup)
¼ cup chopped celery (½
   stalk)

2 tablespoons chopped
   fresh parsley or 1½
   teaspoons dried parsley
1½ cups apple, peeled,
   cored, and chopped
1 tablespoon fresh lemon
   juice
Dash dried tarragon leaves

.... FISH ....

4 flounder fillets (4 ounces
   each)

.... TOPPING ....

2 tablespoons grated
   Parmesan cheese

1. Combine corn oil, onion, and celery in an 8-inch or 9-inch flat microwave-safe casserole. Cover with lid or vented plastic wrap. Microwave for 3 minutes at HIGH (100%). Stir in parsley, apple, lemon juice, and tarragon. Microwave for 2 to 3 minutes at HIGH (100%), until vegetables and apple are tender. Spread evenly over bottom of the casserole.
2. Place fish on top of apple mixture. Cover with waxed paper. Microwave for 4 minutes at HIGH (100%). Sprinkle with Parmesan cheese. Cover again. Microwave for 3 to 5

*Use unsalted variety for lowest sodium value, if desired.

Choose a Jonathan or Gravenstein apple for best results in this recipe.

minutes at HIGH (100%), or until fish flakes easily. Serve garnished with additional parsley, if desired.

Yield: 4 servings

❄

Nutritional Analysis per Serving (3-Ounce Cooked Fillet)

Calories: 149
Carbohydrate: 12 g
Fat: 3 g
Protein: 20 g
Fiber: N/A
Cholesterol: 59 mg

Sodium: 201 mg
Diabetic exchanges:
  Lean meat: 2.5
  Vegetable: Free
  Fruit: 0.5

LEMON FLOUNDER OR SOLE

· · · · ·

2 teaspoons reduced-
  calorie margarine*
1 cup (3 to 4 ounces) sliced
  mushrooms
¼ medium onion (¼ cup),
  chopped
2 tablespoons fresh
  chopped parsley

4 (4 ounces each) flounder
  or sole fillets
2 tablespoons lemon or
  lime juice
½ teaspoon dried oregano
⅛ teaspoon ground pepper

TIPS
· · · · · · · ·

For a low-calorie yet
vitamin-rich accom-
paniment to Lemon
Flounder or Sole, try
spooning hot Rata-
touille (see page 316)
over the fish before
standing time in step
#2.

1. Microwave margarine, mushrooms, and onions in a 10-inch flat microwave-safe casserole, covered with waxed paper, for 3 to 4 minutes at HIGH (100%).
2. Place fish fillets on top of vegetables, sprinkle with lemon juice and then parsley, oregano, and pepper. Cover with waxed paper. Microwave for 5 to 7 minutes at HIGH (100%), until fish flakes with a fork. Let stand 5 minutes.

Yield: 4 servings

· ❄ ·

Nutritional Analysis per Serving (3-ounce Cooked Fillet)

Calories: 115
Carbohydrate: 5 g
Fat: 2 g
Protein: 19 g
Fiber: N/A

Cholesterol: 57 mg
Sodium: 148 mg
Diabetic exchanges:
  Lean meat: 2.0
  Vegetable: 1

· ·
*Use unsalted variety for lowest sodium value, if desired.

Halibut is a lean fish, mild in flavor. It should be done in about 2 minutes of microwaving time and about 1 minute of standing time. Halibut dries out easily, so be careful not to overmicrowave it.

HALIBUT IN LEMON SAUCE
(OR PARMESAN CHEESE SAUCE)

· · · · ·

············· FISH ·············

2 halibut fillets (3 to 4 ounces each)

············· LEMON SAUCE ·············

1 tablespoon reduced-calorie margarine*
2 tablespoons chopped onion
2 teaspoons dried parsley

1 teaspoon lemon juice
¼ teaspoon prepared mustard
¼ teaspoon garlic powder

1. Place halibut in a 9-inch microwave-safe casserole. Set aside.
2. Combine ingredients for Lemon Sauce in a 1-cup glass measure. Microwave for 1 minute at HIGH (100%). Pour sauce over halibut.
3. Cover with vented plastic wrap and microwave for 2 to 3 minutes at HIGH (100%), until fish is fork-tender. Let stand 1 minute.

Yield: 2 servings

· ❄ ·

Nutritional Analysis per Serving (3-Ounce Cooked Fillet and ¼ Sauce)

Calories: 124
Carbohydrate: 1 g
Fat: 3 g
Protein: 21 g

Fiber: N/A
Cholesterol: 50 mg
Sodium: 61 mg
Diabetic exchanges:
    Lean meat: 3

*Use unsalted variety for lowest sodium value, if desired.

LOBSTER TAILS AND LEMON OR ORANGE SAUCE

· · · · ·

·· LOBSTER ····················

4 frozen lobster tails (6
    ounces each), thawed
1 tablespoon lemon juice

···················· ORANGE SAUCE ····················

½ cup orange juice
1 teaspoon cornstarch
1 tablespoon reduced-
    calorie margarine*

Dash ground ginger,
    optional

···················· LEMON SAUCE ····················

½ cup cold water
1 teaspoon cornstarch
½ teaspoon chicken
    bouillon granules*

2 tablespoons reduced-
    calorie margarine*
2 tablespoons lemon juice

1. Using kitchen scissors or a sharp knife, cut through bottom of each lobster tail. Arrange tails, cut side up, like wagon spokes on a wheel (with thin tail ends toward the center) in a 9- or 10-inch glass pie plate. Sprinkle with lemon juice. Cover with a glass lid or vented plastic wrap.
2. Microwave for 12 to 14 minutes at MEDIUM (50%), or until shells look bright pink and flesh is opaque. (Rotate plate halfway through cooking time, if necessary, for even cooking.) Let stand 5 minutes.
3. Meanwhile make Orange (or Lemon) Sauce. Combine orange juice and cornstarch (or cold water, cornstarch, and bouillon granules). Stir until smooth. Microwave for

* Use unsalted variety for lowest sodium values, if desired.

········

Live lobster does not microwave well, but frozen lobster tails will turn out tender and delicious after microwaving.

40 to 60 seconds at HIGH (100%), or until thickened and bubbly, stirring once. Blend in margarine and ginger (or lemon juice), stirring until melted. If necessary, microwave 1 minute at HIGH (100%) to heat. Serve lobster tails with Orange or Lemon Sauce for dipping.

Yield: 4 servings

———————— · ❄ · ————————

Nutritional Analysis per Tail with Sauce

Calories: 107
Carbohydrate: 5 g
Fat: 2 g
Protein: 16 g
Fiber: N/A

Cholesterol: 81 mg
Sodium: 323 mg
Diabetic exchanges:
　Lean meat: 2.5
　Fruit: 0.25

FISH FILLETS IN CUCUMBER SAUCE

· · · · ·

························ FISH ························

4 halibut, flounder, cod,
   perch, or any white fish
   fillets (4 ounces each)
1 tablespoon lemon juice

···················· CUCUMBER SAUCE ····················

1 small cucumber, peeled
   and sliced
3 green onions, chopped
⅔ cup plain nonfat yogurt
½ teaspoon dill weed
2 teaspoons lemon juice

½ teaspoon Seasoned Salt
   Substitute #2 (see page
   245) or store-bought
   alternative
Parsley sprigs and lemon
   slice to garnish, optional

1. Arrange fish in a flat 1½-quart microwave-safe casserole.
   Sprinkle with lemon juice. Cover with waxed paper. Microwave for 4 to 5 minutes at HIGH (100%), until fish
   flakes easily with a fork. Let stand during step #3.
2. Meanwhile, purée Cucumber Sauce ingredients using a
   blender or food processor.
3. Microwave sauce in a 2-cup glass measure for 2 to 3 minutes at MEDIUM (50%), or until hot. Pour over cooked
   fish. Serve garnished with parsley and lemon, if desired.

Yield: 3 to 4 servings

· ❄ ·

Nutritional Analysis per Serving (3-Ounce Cooked Fillet)

Calories: 110
Carbohydrate: 3 g
Fat: 1 g
Protein: 22 g
Fiber: N/A

Cholesterol: 58 mg
Sodium: 99 mg
Diabetic exchanges:
   Lean meat: 2.75
   Skim milk: 0.25

I prefer using halibut or flounder in this recipe, but any lean white fish fillets will work.

As it is always best to use the freshest fish possible, you may have to purchase whatever type is available at your market or grocery store on shopping day.

Always smell fish be-fore purchasing it. If it smells fishy, don't buy it.

Mackerel is one of the kinds of fish that contain the omega-3 (long chain) fatty acid fish oils. When consumed regularly, these fish oils have been associated with reduced risk of heart disease because they help lower the level of cholesterol in the blood and reduce the formation of blood clots. Combined with the cholesterol-lowering benefits of the oat bran, this mackerel and mushroom loaf may be of special help to those on low-cholesterol diets.

MACKEREL AND MUSHROOM LOAF WITH CREAM SAUCE

· · · · ·

½ small onion (⅓ cup), finely chopped
1 cup (3 to 4 ounces) sliced fresh mushrooms
15 ounces canned mackerel, packed in water, drained
10½ ounces Cream Soup Substitute, prepared (see page 259)

⅓ cup rolled oats
¼ cup dry oat bran
2 large egg whites
1 teaspoon prepared mustard
¼ teaspoon each dried marjoram, dried basil, and black pepper

1. Combine onion and mushrooms in a 1-quart microwave-safe casserole. Cover with lid or vented plastic wrap. Microwave for 2 to 2½ minutes at HIGH (100%), or until crisp-tender. Let stand 2 minutes. Set aside 2 tablespoons cooked vegetables for step #4.

2. Flake mackerel and stir into remaining cooked vegetables. Add ½ cream soup mixture and all remaining ingredients. Blend well using a fork. Spread mixture into a 5-cup microwave ring mold or 8 × 4-inch loaf pan that has been sprayed with vegetable coating. Cover with waxed paper.

3. Microwave for 15 to 20 minutes at MEDIUM (50%), or until the center is firm. (Rotate casserole halfway through cooking, if necessary, for even cooking.) Let stand 5 minutes. Invert onto a serving dish.

4. Meanwhile, mix remaining cream soup mixture with reserved cooked mushrooms and onions and a dash each marjoram and basil in a 1-cup measure. Microwave for 1½ to 2½ minutes at HIGH (100%), or until hot. Drizzle over mackerel loaf.

Yield: 6 servings

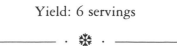

ORANGE ROUGHY ALMONDINE

······· FISH ·······

4 orange roughy fillets (4 ounces each)

1 teaspoon plain gelatin, dry

½ teaspoon Seasoned Salt Substitute #2 (see page 245) or store-bought alternative

2 tablespoons snipped fresh parsley

1½ tablespoons lime juice

······· TOASTED ALMONDS ·······

¼ cup sliced almonds *

1 tablespoon regular polyunsaturated margarine *

1. Fish: Place fish fillets in a flat 1½-quart microwave-safe casserole. Sprinkle with gelatin, Seasoned Salt Substitute, parsley, and lime juice. Cover with a lid or vented plastic wrap.

2. Microwave for 4 to 5 minutes at HIGH (100%), or until fish flakes easily with a fork. Let stand 5 minutes.

* Use unsalted variety for lowest sodium values, if desired.

TIPS

You can substitute lemon juice for the lime juice, if desired.

3. Topping: Mix almonds and margarine in a 9-inch round or square glass dish. Microwave uncovered for 1½ to 3 minutes at HIGH (100%), until almonds are toasted, stirring often.
4. Serve fish topped with almonds.

Yield: 4 servings

———————— · ❄ · ————————

Nutritional Analysis per Serving (3-Ounce Cooked Fillet)

Calories: 162
Carbohydrate: 2 g
Fat: 10 g
Protein: 14 g
Fiber: N/A

Cholesterol: 17 mg
Sodium: 54 mg
Diabetic exchanges:
   Lean meat: 2.25
   Fat: 1.0

TIPS
....

Swordfish is higher in fat than halibut, flounder, or cod, but its fat content is made up of the omega-3 fatty acids, which have been found to lower blood cholesterol and reduce the risk of heart disease. Swordfish has more than four times the amount of omega-3 fatty acids as halibut, but only half as much as salmon.

ORANGE-BAKED SWORDFISH FILLETS

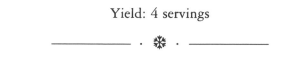

4 swordfish or other white fish fillets (4 ounces each, thawed if frozen)
2 tablespoons orange juice concentrate, slightly thawed
1 large egg white, beaten until foamy

1 teaspoon Worcestershire sauce, optional
8 whole wheat cracker squares (1½-inch), * made into crumbs
4 teaspoons reduced-calorie margarine*

1. Pat thawed fish dry with a paper towel.
2. Mix orange juice concentrate, egg white, and Worcestershire sauce in a small flat dish. Dip fish into this mixture, then into the cracker crumbs.

....
*Use unsalted variety for lowest sodium values, if desired.

3. Place prepared fish in a 10-inch microwave-safe casserole dish. Dot with margarine. Cover with waxed paper.
4. Microwave for 4 to 5 minutes at HIGH (100%), or until fish flakes with a fork. Let stand 2 minutes.

Yield: 4 servings

· ❄ ·

Nutritional Analysis per Serving (3-Ounce Cooked Fillet)

Calories: 185
Carbohydrate: 7 g
Fat: 8 g
Protein: 24 g
Fiber: N/A

Cholesterol: 43 mg
Sodium: 165 mg
Diabetic exchanges:
  Bread: 0.5
  Lean Meat: 3

SHRIMP PRIMAVERA

2 cups (6 ounces) rotini (thin macaroni twists), uncooked
1 teaspoon vegetable oil
4 cups very hot water
2 packages (10 ounces each) frozen mixed vegetables (broccoli, carrots, and water chestnuts)
1 clove garlic, minced
1 small onion, chopped (⅔ cup)
2 teaspoons reduced-calorie margarine*

2 teaspoons cornstarch
1 teaspoon chicken bouillon granules*
¾ cup evaporated skim milk
Dash each ground basil, ground nutmeg, and dried parsley
6 ounces frozen, deveined, cooked medium-sized shrimp, thawed and rinsed
2 tablespoons grated Parmesan cheese
Dried parsley

*Use unsalted variety for lowest sodium values, if desired.

TIPS
·········
For frozen mixed vegetables I also like to use a combination of broccoli, carrots, mushrooms, green beans, water chestnuts, and pea pods, but any 16- to 20-ounce combination works well.

When microwaving packaged frozen vegetables, lay packages side by side. Do not stack.

To microwave a 16- or 20-ounce bag of frozen vegetables, make a large "X" slit in the bag. Place in a microwave-safe casserole, slit side down. Microwave as directed in step #2. Pull bag off vegetables, using tongs.

1. Combine rotini, oil, and water in a 2-quart microwave-safe bowl. Microwave uncovered for 10 to 11 minutes at HIGH (100%), or until pasta is tender. Drain, rinse, and set aside.

2. Microwave frozen mixed vegetables in boxes (remove foil if foil-wrapped) on a paper plate or on three layers of paper towels for 8 to 9 minutes at HIGH (100%), or until tender-crisp. Unwrap, drain, and set aside.

3. Microwave garlic, onion, and margarine in a 2-quart bowl for 2 to 3 minutes at HIGH (100%), or until almost tender. Set aside. Stir cornstarch and bouillon granules into milk in a 1-quart glass measure until smooth; add basil, nutmeg, and parsley. Microwave uncovered for 3 to 4 minutes at HIGH (100%), or until sauce comes to a boil and thickens. Stir in shrimp, garlic, onion, and margarine. Toss rotini and mixed vegetables with cooked sauce. Microwave for 2 to 3 minutes at HIGH (100%), or until heated through. Transfer to a serving bowl and serve garnished with Parmesan cheese and a dash of parsley.

Yield: 6 servings

———————— · ❄ · ————————

Variation: Substitute 2 cups broken vermicelli for the rotini.

Nutritional Analysis per Serving (⅙ Recipe)

Calories: 220	Sodium: 134 mg
Carbohydrate: 33 g	Diabetic exchanges:
Fat: 4 g	Bread: 2.0
Protein: 15 g	Lean meat: 1.5
Fiber: N/A	Vegetable: Free
Cholesterol: 46 mg	

MICRO-STEAMED SHRIMP

· · · · ·

1 pound medium shrimp,
  unpeeled
1 clove garlic, minced
2 tablespoons lemon juice
1 tablespoon dry white
  wine, optional

½ teaspoon Seasoned Salt
  Substitute #1 (see page
  244) or store-bought
  alternative

1. Combine all ingredients in a 9- or 10-inch microwave-safe
   pie plate. Place a small glass custard cup or tumbler in
   the center of the plate so shrimp are arranged in a circular
   fashion around it. Cover with vented plastic wrap.
2. Microwave for 3 to 5 minutes at HIGH (100%), or until
   shrimp shells look bright pink and flesh is opaque, stirring twice to redistribute shrimp. Let stand 2 minutes.
   Peel before serving (see tip).

Yield: 4 servings

—————— · ❄ · ——————

Variations: Shrimp can be served with a low-calorie cocktail
sauce by mixing ⅓ cup reduced-calorie catsup, 1 tablespoon
horseradish, 1 tablespoon lemon juice, and a dash hot sauce.

Substitute peeled and deveined shrimp for the unpeeled
shrimp before microwaving.

Nutritional Analysis per Serving (3 Ounces Cooked Shrimp)

Calories: 124
Carbohydrate: 2 g
Fat: 2 g
Protein: 23 g

Fiber: N/A
Cholesterol: 172 mg
Sodium: 168 mg
Diabetic exchanges:
  Lean meat: 3.25

Shrimp is tasty when served with either the Low-Calorie Cocktail Sauce (see variation) or store-bought salsa. Shrimp can be chilled (after microwaving) and served as an appetizer, if desired.

If you like stove-top steamed shrimp, you will like Micro-Steamed Shrimp. You will probably want to devein large shrimp after cooking because the intestinal vein will contain grit. However, medium shrimp often do not contain grit, so the vein does not need to be removed.

To peel shrimp, remove shell from the head with one hand while pulling on the tail with the other. The shell should slide off.

Instead of using a pie plate and custard cup, you can use an 8-cup microwave-safe ring pan.

To cover with "vented plastic wrap" means to cover a bowl or casserole with plastic wrap, but leave a small edge turned back so steam can escape.

SHRIMP CREOLE
· · · · ·

1 tablespoon vegetable oil or reduced-calorie margarine*

½ medium onion (½ cup), chopped

½ cup celery (1 stalk), chopped

¼ medium green bell pepper (¼ cup), chopped

1½ tablespoons cornstarch

16-ounce can stewed tomatoes*

8-ounce can tomato sauce*

½ teaspoon chili powder

½ teaspoon garlic powder

1 pound raw shrimp, shelled and deveined

½ packet sugar substitute (equivalent to 1 teaspoon sugar)

1. In a 1-quart microwave-safe casserole, combine oil, onion, celery, and green pepper. Cover with lid or vented plastic wrap, and microwave for 3 to 4 minutes at HIGH (100%), until vegetables are tender.
2. Stir cornstarch into stewed tomatoes until blended. Add to vegetables.
3. Add all remaining ingredients except for shrimp. Cover. Microwave for 5 to 6 minutes at HIGH (100%), or until bubbly. Stir in shrimp. Cover again. Microwave for 3 to 5 minutes at HIGH (100%), or until shrimp are opaque and tender, stirring once. Let stand 2 minutes.

Yield: 4 servings

· ❄ ·

Nutritional Analysis per Serving (¼ Recipe)

Calories: 209
Carbohydrate: 19 g
Fat: 4 g
Protein: 25 g
Fiber: N/A

Cholesterol: 172 mg
Sodium: 242 mg
Diabetic exchanges:
   Lean meat: 3
   Vegetable: 3

* Use no-salt-added variety for lowest sodium values, if desired.

SHRIMP SALSA

2 teaspoons vegetable or
olive oil
1 medium jalapeño pepper
or 2 fresh green chilies,
seeds removed and
minced
½ medium tomato, seeds
removed and minced
½ medium onion (½ cup),
chopped

½ medium green bell
pepper (½ cup),
chopped
1 clove garlic, minced
8-ounce can tomato
sauce*
1 teaspoon dried cilantro
or parsley
1 pound raw shrimp,
shelled and deveined

1. Combine oil, jalapeño pepper, tomato, onion, green pepper, and garlic in a 1-quart microwave-safe casserole or bowl. Cover with lid or vented plastic wrap. Microwave for 3 to 4 minutes at HIGH (100%), or until vegetables are tender.
2. Stir in tomato sauce and cilantro. Cover. Microwave for 4 to 5 minutes at HIGH (100%), or until mixture boils well. Stir in shrimp. Cover again. Microwave for 3 to 5 minutes at HIGH (100%), or until shrimp are opaque and tender. Serve immediately.

Yield: 4 servings

* ❄ *

Nutritional Analysis per Serving (¼ Recipe)	
Calories: 170	Cholesterol: 172 mg
Carbohydrate: 8 g	Sodium: 277 mg
Fat: 5 g	Diabetic exchanges:
Protein: 24 g	Lean meat: 3
Fiber: N/A	Vegetable: 1.5

*Use no-salt-added variety for lowest sodium values, if desired.

TIPS

"Salsa" means "sauce" in Spanish and is most often used as a dip for tortilla chips or fresh vegetables. This Shrimp Salsa tastes delicious over cooked vegetables as well as pasta.

Select scallops that smell sweet, not fishy. Refrigerate and use within two days, or freeze for up to three months.

"SAUTÉED" GARLIC SCALLOPS

· · · · ·

2 tablespoons reduced-
    calorie margarine*
1 clove garlic, minced
12 ounces scallops, rinsed
    and drained

3 tablespoons Seasoned
    Bread Crumbs (see page
    243) or Dry Bread
    Crumbs (see page 54)
    and a dash of Seasoned
    Salt Substitute #2 (see
    page 245), optional
Lemon wedges to garnish,
    optional

1. Microwave margarine and garlic in a 9- or 10-inch glass pie plate for 40 to 50 seconds at HIGH (100%). Stir in scallops. Sprinkle with bread crumbs. Cover with a paper towel.
2. Microwave for 4 to 5 minutes at MEDIUM (50%), or until scallops are opaque in appearance. Let stand 2 minutes. Serve garnished with lemon wedges, if desired.

Yield: 4 servings

· ❄ · ─────

Nutritional Analysis per Serving (3 Ounces Cooked Scallops)

Calories: 121
Carbohydrate: 4 g
Fat: 5 g
Protein: 15 g
Fiber: N/A
Cholesterol: 29 mg

Sodium: 176 mg
Diabetic exchanges:
    Bread: 0.25
    Lean meat: 2.25
    Fat: 0.5

* Use unsalted variety for lowest sodium values, if desired.

SCALLOPS IN WINE SAUCE

· · · · ·

Tasty individual casseroles.

1 pound fresh scallops, rinsed and drained
¼ cup Colombard or other dry white wine
1 tablespoon lemon juice
1 clove garlic, minced
2 green onions, thinly sliced
1 cup (3 to 4 ounces) fresh mushrooms, sliced

1 cup skim milk
2 tablespoons cornstarch
Dash nutmeg
½ teaspoon Seasoned Salt Substitute #2 (see page 245) or store-bought alternative
4 whole wheat cracker squares (1½-inch), made into crumbs

1. Combine scallops, wine, lemon juice, garlic, onion, and mushrooms in a 2-quart microwave-safe casserole. Cover with lid or vented plastic wrap. Microwave for 6 to 7½ minutes at MEDIUM (50%), or until scallops are tender, stirring twice. Drain, reserving ½ cup liquid. Leave scallops in colander or strainer.

2. Mix milk and cornstarch in measuring cup until smooth. Stir into reserved liquid in casserole. Microwave uncovered for 2 to 3 minutes at HIGH (100%), or until thickened, stirring twice. Add nutmeg and Seasoned Salt Substitute and stir.

3. Place scallops in 4 individual microwave-safe casseroles or custard cups. Pour milk mixture over scallops. Sprinkle with crushed crackers. Microwave for 1 to 2 minutes at MEDIUM HIGH (70%), or until heated through.

Yield: 4 servings

———— · ❄ · ————

To thaw frozen scallops, microwave for 6 to 8 minutes at DEFROST (30%), separating with a fork after 3 minutes. Let stand 10 minutes before proceeding with step #1.

Variation: Substitute 16 ounces of frozen scallops thawed for the fresh ones (see tip at left).

For 2 casseroles, use ½ the ingredients. Proceed as directed, cutting microwaving time by one-half in each step.

Nutritional Analysis per Serving (¼ Recipe)

Calories: 175

Carbohydrate: 15 g

Fat: 2 g

Protein: 21 g

Fiber: N/A

Cholesterol: 38 mg

Sodium: 216 mg

Diabetic exchanges:

    Bread: 0.5

    Lean meat: 2.5

    Vegetable: Free

    Skim milk: 0.25

POACHED SALMON COLOMBARD AND VEGETABLES

—————— · · · · · ——————

4 salmon steaks (4 ounces each)
1 small zucchini, cut into julienne strips
1½ cups (6 ounces) sliced fresh mushrooms
3 tablespoons Colombard wine or skim milk

½ teaspoon Seasoned Salt Substitute #2 (see page 245) or store-bought alternative
¼ teaspoon dried dill weed
4 lemon slices
Dried parsley flakes to garnish, optional

1. Place salmon steaks in a 9- or 10-inch flat microwave-safe casserole. Arrange equal amounts of zucchini and mushrooms over each. Sprinkle salmon and vegetables with wine, Seasoned Salt Substitute, and dill weed. Top each with a lemon slice. Cover with lid or vented plastic wrap.

2. Microwave for 7 to 9 minutes at medium HIGH (70%), or until fish flakes easily with a fork, rearranging salmon halfway through cooking time. Let stand 2 to 3 minutes. Serve garnished with parsley flakes, if desired.

Yield: 4 servings

—————— · ❈ · ——————

Variation: Substitute ½ cup finely chopped onion for the zucchini and/or mushrooms. Proceed as directed.

Nutritional Analysis per Serving (¼ Recipe)

Calories: 150
Carbohydrate: 3 g
Fat: 4 g
Protein: 23 g

Fiber: N/A
Cholesterol: 59 mg
Sodium: 81 mg
Diabetic exchanges:
    Lean meat: 3

TIPS
....

Salmon is high in calcium, protein, and omega-3 (long chain) fatty acids. These fatty acids have been found to help lower the level of blood cholesterol.

Any 1-inch-thick frozen fish fillets can be used successfully in this recipe.

Salmon is high in fat—however, the fat is the type that is composed of omega-3 (long chain) fatty acids, which can help lower blood cholesterol.

LEMON SALMON WITH CUCUMBER SAUCE

——————— · · · · · ———————

···························· FISH ····························

4 salmon steaks (4 ounces each, fresh or frozen, thawed)

2 green onions, thinly sliced
1 lemon, sliced

···················· CUCUMBER SAUCE ····················

½ cup low-fat cottage cheese
3 tablespoons nonfat plain yogurt
½ teaspoon lemon juice
¼ teaspoon dill weed
½ teaspoon Seasoned Salt Substitute #2 (see page 245) or store-bought alternative

½ medium cucumber, peeled and sliced
Lemon and cucumber slices to garnish, optional

1. Fish: Arrange salmon in a 10-inch flat microwave-safe casserole with thickest portions toward outside. Top with onion and lemon slices. Cover loosely with plastic wrap or waxed paper. Microwave for 7 to 9 minutes at MEDIUM HIGH (70%), or until fish flakes easily with a fork. Let stand 3 minutes.
2. Cucumber Sauce: Meanwhile, purée all sauce ingredients using a blender or food processor. Refrigerate or heat. (Sauce can be served chilled or heated.) To heat, microwave for 2 to 3 minutes at MEDIUM (50%).
3. Serve chilled or heated sauce over salmon. Garnish with additional lemon slices and cucumber slices, if desired.

Yield: 4 servings

——————— · ❄ · ———————

Variations: Omit cottage cheese and use ⅔ cup yogurt total. Proceed as directed.

For White Fish Fillets with Cucumber Sauce, substitute 1 pound of any white fish fillets for the salmon steaks.

Nutritional Analysis per Serving (¼ Recipe)

Calories: 175

Carbohydrate: 4 g

Fat: 5 g

Protein: 24 g

Fiber: N/A

Cholesterol: 62 mg

Sodium: 198 mg

Diabetic exchanges:

Lean meat: 3

Vegetable: 0.5

TIPS
....

Any lean white fish can be used in this recipe. However, for best results, choose fillets that have the least fishy flavor.

3 tablespoons Seasoned Bread Crumbs (see page 243)
3 tablespoons grated Parmesan cheese
4 (4-ounce) thin red snapper fillets or other white fish

2 tablespoons grated onion
4 teaspoons frozen reduced-calorie margarine*
Parsley sprigs and lemon slices to garnish, optional

1. In a small bowl, combine bread crumbs and Parmesan cheese. Set aside.
2. Sprinkle each fillet with grated onion. Place 1 teaspoon frozen margarine on each fillet. Tuck in sides and roll up. Fasten with toothpicks. Coat each roll in bread crumb mixture. Place seam side down in a 1½-quart microwave-safe casserole. Refrigerate at least 15 minutes to set coating.
3. Cover with waxed paper. Microwave for 4 to 6 minutes at HIGH (100%), or until fish flakes easily with a fork, spooning juices over fish halfway through the cooking time. Remove toothpicks. Serve garnished with parsley and lemon slices, if desired.

Yield: 4 servings

❄

Nutritional Analysis per Serving (3-Ounce Cooked Fillet)

Calories: 155
Carbohydrate: 2 g
Fat: 9 g
Protein: 21 g
Fiber: N/A

Cholesterol: 44 mg
Sodium: 147 mg
Diabetic exchanges:
  Lean meat: 3
  Fat: 0.25

*Use unsalted variety for lowest sodium values, if desired.

SAUCY VEGETABLE FISH FILLETS

TIPS

½ cup celery (1 stalk), chopped

½ small onion (⅓ cup), chopped

⅔ cup (2½ ounces) fresh mushrooms, sliced

¼ cup water

4 fish fillets (torsk, cod, or other white fish; 4 ounces each; thawed if frozen)

1 tablespoon cornstarch dissolved in 1 tablespoon water

1 teaspoon dried parsley to garnish, optional

If you need a lean low-calorie entree, this is the one. This recipe works well with just about any white fish fillets.

1. Combine celery, onion, mushrooms, and water in a flat 2-quart microwave-safe casserole. Cover with waxed paper. Microwave for 3 to 4 minutes at HIGH (100%).

2. Slip fish under vegetables. Cover again. Microwave for 4 to 5 minutes at HIGH (100%), until fish flakes easily with a fork.

3. Drain fish juices into a custard cup. Stir cornstarch and water into the juices until thoroughly blended. Microwave for 1 to 2 minutes at HIGH (100%), until thickened, stirring once.

4. Pour mixture over fish. Microwave again for 1 to 2 minutes. Sprinkle with parsley, if desired.

Yield: 4 servings

Nutritional Analysis per Serving (¼ Recipe)

Calories: 107

Carbohydrate: 44

Fat: 1 g

Protein: 20 g

Fiber: N/A

Cholesterol: 57 mg

Sodium: 79 mg

Diabetic exchanges:

Lean meat: 1.5

Vegetable: 1

TIPS
....

Serve Quick Fish Creole over traditional rice, if desired (see page 230).

QUICK FISH CREOLE

——————— · · · · · ———————

Delicious served over brown rice.

2 white fish fillets (such as cod or sole; 4 ounces each)
½ cup chopped medium onion
½ cup (2 ounces) sliced fresh mushrooms

½ cup chopped green bell pepper
½ cup diagonally sliced celery
8-ounce can tomato sauce*

1. Place fish fillets in a 1-quart microwave-safe baking dish or casserole. Combine remaining ingredients and spoon over fish. Cover.
2. Microwave for 6 to 7 minutes at HIGH (100%). Let stand 5 minutes.

Yield: 2 servings

——————— · ❄ · ———————

Nutritional Analysis per Serving (½ Recipe)

Calories: 159
Carbohydrate: 13 g
Fat: 2 g
Protein: 25 g
Fiber: N/A

Cholesterol: 64 mg
Sodium: 132 mg
Diabetic exchanges:
   Lean meat: 3
   Vegetable: 2.5

....
*Use unsalted for lowest sodium values, if desired.

EASY CRUMB-COATED SNAPPER OR PIKE

2 tablespoons reduced-
  calorie margarine*
8 whole wheat cracker
  squares (1½-inch), made
  into crumbs
4 red snapper or walleye
  pike fillets (4 ounces
  each), thawed

3 tablespoons skim milk
½ teaspoon Seasoned Salt
  Substitute #1 (see page
  244) or store-bought
  alternative

1. Microwave margarine in a flat 2-quart microwave-safe casserole for 1 minute at HIGH (100%), or until melted.
2. Stir in cracker crumbs. Remove half of the crumb mixture.
3. Arrange fish over crumb mixture in casserole. Sprinkle
   fish with Seasoned Salt Substitute and remaining cracker-
   crumb mixture. Pour milk over fish. Cover with waxed
   paper.
4. Microwave for 5 to 7 minutes at HIGH (100%), or until
   fish flakes with a fork.

Yield: 4 servings

Nutritional Analysis per Serving (3-Ounce Cooked Fillet)

Calories: 156
Carbohydrate: 4 g
Fat: 4 g
Protein: 23 g
Fiber: N/A

Cholesterol: 40 mg
Sodium: 13 mg
Diabetic exchanges:
  Bread: 0.25
  Lean meat: 3

You can substitute any cracker crumbs or bread crumbs (see page 54) for the wheat cracker crumbs.

Pour the milk gently over and around the fish so the coating does not slide off.

The milk in this recipe helps reduce the "fishy taste" of some fish.

*Use unsalted variety for lowest sodium values, if desired.

MEATS AND MAIN DISHES

·❄·

GENERAL TIPS FOR DEFROSTING MEATS

- Always defrost frozen meats before cooking.

- Always remove the clear plastic butcher packaging and Styrofoam tray before defrosting. The clear plastic (polyvinyl chloride) can give off a poisonous gas, and the Styrofoam can slow down defrosting.

- For large roasts, shield bony tips or thin ends of meat with foil strips to prevent overcooking while defrosting (see shielding tips, page 15).

- Freeze ground meats in a doughnut shape whenever possible to speed defrosting and to help with even defrosting.

- Always defrost meats at DEFROST (30%) or MEDIUM (50%). (See the following defrosting time chart.)

- Standing time is very important for defrosting meats. If the defrosting instructions say to microwave for 5 minutes at

DEFROST (30%) and let stand 5 minutes, the total defrosting time is 10 minutes. (The meat will not be defrosted until after the standing time.)

GENERAL TIPS FOR MICROWAVING MEATS

- Tender meats such as hamburger, steaks, or chops can be microwaved quickly at HIGH (100%). Use waxed paper, a paper towel, or a napkin to cover tender meats to prevent splattering during microwaving.

- Less tender meats such as roasts, fresh hams, stew meat, and round steaks should be microwaved slowly with liquid added and covered tightly with a lid or vented plastic wrap. Microwave at HIGH (100%) to heat through and then at MEDIUM (50%) or DEFROST (30%) to cook and tenderize.

- Microwave tough meats such as chuck roast in a plastic cooking bag for 20 to 30 minutes per pound at DEFROST (30%) to tenderize.

- Do not expect pot roasts to flake off the fork like those braised for three to four hours in a conventional oven. They will, however, turn out tender, firm, and flavorful.

- Cooked or cured ham, pork, Canadian bacon, and so on should be microwaved at MEDIUM HIGH (70%) or MEDIUM (50%) to prevent the outer edges from drying out.

- DO NOT use a conventional meat thermometer in the microwave oven. If you don't have a microwave meat thermometer, insert a conventional one when you remove the meat from the oven to quickly check the temperature. You can use a microwave temperature probe, if desired. (See tips on pages 16–17.)

- Roasts will cook more evenly if microwaved in a plastic cooking bag and turned over twice during microwaving.

- Arrange meat with the thickest pieces to the outside.

- Meat tastes better when microwaved above juices on a rack (or on onion slices or celery ribs to improvise a rack).

- Do not salt meat until after microwaving. (Salt will toughen meat.)

- To cook ground meats for casseroles and eliminate much of the fat, crumble meat into a plastic strainer and place it over a casserole, to cook and drain the grease at once.

- Standing time is very important to help complete the cooking. Small cuts of meat require about 5 minutes of standing time, covered.

- Large cuts of meat require 10 to 15 minutes of standing time, covered tightly. Internal temperature may rise as much as 15° F. during standing time.

MEAT DEFROSTING TIME CHART

TYPE/AMOUNT	PREPARATION/INSTRUCTIONS*	TIME/POWER LEVEL
Hamburger, ground pork, ground veal, or ground turkey (1–3 pounds)	Break apart ground meat halfway through cooking time.	Microwave for 5 to 8 minutes per pound at DEFROST (30%). Let stand 5 minutes.
Steaks, chops, stew meat, cutlets, and other small packages of meat (1–2 pounds)	Separate pieces halfway through microwaving time, and if any end pieces feel warm, shield with foil strips (see Shielding Tips, page 15).	Microwave 5 to 8 minutes per pound at DEFROST (30%). Let stand 10 minutes.
Roasts, corned beef, ribs, and other large pieces of meat over 2 inches thick	Turn over twice during defrosting. If end pieces feel warm, shield with foil strips (see Shielding Tips, page 15).	Microwave 5 to 6 minutes per pound at MEDIUM (50%). Let stand 15 to 30 minutes.
Bacon, hot dogs, or sausage links	Turn over halfway through microwaving time.	Microwave for 3 to 4 minutes at DEFROST (30%). Let stand 2 to 3 minutes.

*For all meats, use a microwave-safe casserole and cover with waxed paper.

MEAT MICROWAVING TIME CHART

TYPE/AMOUNT	PREPARATION/INSTRUCTIONS	TIME/POWER LEVEL
Hamburger patties 1 patty (4–5 ounces each)	Shape like a doughnut. Sprinkle with browning powder. Place on roasting rack above juices. Cover with waxed paper.	Microwave 2 to 2½ minutes at HIGH (100%). Let stand 1 minute.
2 patties	Same as above.	Microwave 3 to 4½ minutes at HIGH (100%). Let stand 2 minutes.
4 patties	Same as above.	Microwave for 6 to 8 minutes at HIGH (100%). Let stand 2 minutes.
Tender-cut steaks (1 pound or more): rib eye, sirloin, T-bone (beef, pork, venison, or veal)	Sprinkle with browning powder. Place on roasting rack above juices. Cover with waxed paper.	Microwave for 5 minutes per pound at HIGH (100%).
Pork or lamb chops (per 5-ounce chop)	Same as for steaks.	Microwave for 1 minute per chop at HIGH (100%) and then for 5 minutes per chop at MEDIUM (50%). Let stand 3 minutes.
Pot or chuck roast (1–4 pounds)	Sprinkle with browning powder. Place in a plastic cooking bag. Tie with a string or plastic tie, leaving a ½-inch opening. (Do not pierce bag.) Place in a casserole. Turn over twice during microwaving.	Microwave for 20 to 30 minutes per pound at DEFROST (30%). Let stand 10 minutes.
Rib roast (Standing rib, rolled or sirloin, 3–8 pounds)	Place roast on rack fat side up. Cover or tent with waxed paper. Turn over halfway through microwaving time.	Microwave for 5 minutes at HIGH (100%) and then for 12 to 15 minutes per pound at MEDIUM (50%), or until desired doneness. Let stand 10 minutes tented with foil.

TYPE/AMOUNT	PREPARATION/INSTRUCTIONS	TIME/POWER LEVEL
Cooked ham (2–4 pounds)	See recipe on page 167. Turn over halfway through microwaving time.	Microwave for 10 minutes at HIGH (100%) and then for 10 to 12 minutes per pound at MEDIUM (50%). Let stand 5 minutes.
Stew meat (1 pound or more)	Place in a cassrole. Sprinkle with browning powder.	Microwave for 5 minutes at HIGH (100%), add liquid and vegetables, and microwave again for 15 minutes per pound at DEFROST (30%) or MEDIUM (50%). Let stand 5 minutes.
Bacon slices	Place on a roasting (or bacon) rack. Cover with two layers of paper towels.	Microwave for 30 to 60 seconds per slice at HIGH (100%).
Hot dogs, without bun (1–4)	Place on a roasting rack or glass plate.	Microwave for 25 to 35 seconds at MEDIUM HIGH (70%) per hot dog.
Hot dogs in the bun (1–4)	Place hot dogs in bun. Wrap up in two layers of paper towels to prevent sogginess. (Do not spread with condiments before microwaving).	Microwave for 40 seconds at MEDIUM HIGH (70%) per hot dog in bun.

CHINESE BEEF AND VEGETABLE STIR FRY

——————— · · · · · ———————

14–16 ounces boneless top
  round or sirloin steak,
  cut into thin 2 × 4-inch
  strips
⅓ cup water
3 tablespoons reduced-
  sodium soy sauce
3 tablespoons red wine
  vinegar or dry red wine
1 clove garlic, minced

2 teaspoons vegetable oil
16-ounce package frozen
  mixed vegetables
  (broccoli, carrots, and
  water chestnuts),
  slightly thawed
2 teaspoons cornstarch
  dissolved in 2
  tablespoons cold water

1. Combine meat, water, soy sauce, vinegar, and garlic in a 2-quart microwave-safe casserole. Cover; refrigerate at least 2 hours or overnight to marinate.
2. Preheat 10-inch microwave browning skillet by microwaving for 5 to 6 minutes at HIGH (100%). Add vegetable oil and tilt to coat surface. Using tongs, place meat in preheated browning skillet, reserving liquid. Microwave uncovered for 3 to 4 minutes at HIGH (100%), or until no longer pink, stirring halfway through cooking time. Set aside.
3. Place vegetables in the 2-quart microwave-safe casserole with reserved liquid from meat. Cover with lid or vented plastic wrap. Microwave for 6 to 7 minutes at HIGH (100%), or until tender-crisp. Add dissolved cornstarch-water to vegetables; stir. Microwave uncovered for 5 to 6 minutes at HIGH (100%), or until thickened, stirring once.
4. Add meat to vegetables. Microwave uncovered for 2 to 3 minutes at HIGH (100%), or until heated through.

Yield: 4 servings

——————— · ❄ · ———————

TIPS
· · · · · · · ·

For slicing ease, partially freeze steak (about 2 hours) before slicing. Then a sharp knife will almost glide through meat.

Try serving Chinese Beef and Vegetable Stir Fry over heated bean sprouts (see Tip, page 152) or Parsleyed Rice (see page 239).

For the appetizer, serve Egg Drop Soup (see page 273).

A microwave browning skillet can be purchased from department stores or kitchen accessory stores for about $12 to $18. It works similarly to a frying pan in that it heats up to about 500° F. to quickly sear and brown the food while cooking it. Follow the manufacturer's instructions for use and for preheating your skillet.

If you do not have a browning skillet, instead of Step #2, place oil and drained meat in a 10-inch or 2-quart microwave-safe casserole. Microwave for 6 to 8 minutes at MEDIUM HIGH (70%), or until no longer pink, stirring twice.

Nutritional Analysis per Serving (¹⁄₄ Recipe)	
Calories: 202	Cholesterol: 60 mg
Carbohydrate: 12 g	Sodium: 376 mg
Fat: 6 g	Diabetic exchanges:
Protein: 26 g	Lean meat: 2.75
Fiber: 4 g	Vegetable: 2

TIPS

Marinating the meat overnight gives the steaks time to absorb the flavors and at the same time helps tenderize them.

MARINATED TERIYAKI STEAK

· · · · ·

·················· MARINADE ·····················

3 tablespoons reduced-sodium soy sauce

3 tablespoons unsweetened pineapple juice

2 tablespoons garlic-wine or cider vinegar

1 green onion, thinly sliced

1 clove garlic, minced

½ teaspoon ground ginger

1 packet sugar substitute (equivalent to 2 teaspoons sugar) or 1½ teaspoons fructose

1 tablespoon vegetable oil or dry red wine

························· MEAT ·····················

1½ pounds beef flank steak or top round steak, scored

1. Combine marinade ingredients in a small bowl. Place steak in a microwave-safe 10-inch flat casserole or 10 × 7-inch baking dish. Pour marinade over steak, coating top and bottom. Cover with plastic wrap. Refrigerate at least 4 hours or overnight.
2. Lightly drain marinade from meat. Cover meat with lid or vented plastic wrap. Microwave for 6 minutes at HIGH

(100%). Turn meat over. Cover again. Microwave for 40 to 50 minutes at DEFROST (30%), or until meat is tender. Cut meat into thin slices and serve with cooking juices.

Yield: 6 servings

————————— · ❄ · —————————

Nutritional Analysis per Serving (⅙ Recipe)

Calories: 195

Carbohydrate: 1 g

Fat: 7 g

Protein: 26 g

Fiber: N/A

Cholesterol: 70 mg

Sodium: 250 mg

Diabetic exchanges:

Lean meat: 3.5

Vegetable: 0.25

BEEF BURGUNDY

————————— · · · · · —————————

14–16 ounces boneless beef sirloin steak, sliced into ¼-inch-wide strips

½ teaspoon browning powder for meat*

½ medium onion (½ cup), chopped

1 clove garlic, minced

½ small carrot (½ cup), grated

1 teaspoon beef bouillon granules,* dissolved in ½ cup hot water

¼ cup burgundy or other dry red wine

2 teaspoons cornstarch dissolved in 2 tablespoons water

4-ounce can sliced mushrooms, drained, optional

1. Place beef in a 2-quart microwave-safe casserole. Sprinkle with browning powder. Add onion, garlic, and carrot.

. . . .

*Use unsalted variety for lowest sodium values, if desired.

Red cooking wine works well in this recipe, but be sure to use a brand that is salt-free. Salted wine will not only add sodium but will cause the meat to dry out.

Cover. Microwave for 5 to 6 minutes at HIGH (100%), stirring once.

2. Stir in bouillon-water, burgundy, cornstarch-water, and mushrooms (optional). Microwave for 16 to 20 minutes at MEDIUM (50%), or until fork-tender. Let stand 5 minutes. Serve warm over cooked vegetables (broccoli, carrots, and water chestnuts) or Parsleyed Rice (see page 239).

Yield: 4 servings

———————— · ❄ · ————————

Variation: Add 6 ounces sliced fresh mushrooms with the onion in step #1, if desired. Omit canned mushrooms.

Nutritional Analysis per Serving (¼ Recipe)

Calories: 218   Cholesterol: 65 mg
Carbohydrate: 5 g   Sodium: 79 mg
Fat: 9 g   Diabetic exchanges:
Protein: 24 g   Lean meat: 3
Fiber: N/A   Vegetable: 1

BEEF STROGANOFF

· · · · ·

14–16 ounces boneless
  beef top round or sirloin
  steak, cut into cubes or
  2-inch-long strips
Dash browning powder
  for meat,* optional
1 small onion, thinly sliced
  and cut into rings
½ teaspoon garlic powder
  or 1 clove garlic, minced
1 cup (3 to 4 ounces) sliced
  fresh mushrooms

1 teaspoon beef bouillon
  granules* dissolved in
  ¾ cup hot water
¼ cup dry sherry or water
2 teaspoons cornstarch
1 cup (8 ounces) plain
  nonfat yogurt mixed
  with 1 teaspoon
  cornstarch
Snipped parsley to
  garnish, optional

TIPS
·········
Serve Beef Stroganoff over the traditional noodles or brown rice, or for low calories and high nutrition, serve over cooked slivered vegetables.

1. Sprinkle meat with browning powder, if desired. Combine meat and onion in a flat 10-inch microwave-safe casserole. Cover with lid or waxed paper. Microwave for 4 to 5 minutes at HIGH (100%).
2. Stir in garlic powder and mushrooms. Cover and microwave again for 2 to 3 minutes at HIGH (100%).
3. Mix bouillon-water, sherry, and cornstarch until smooth. Stir liquids into meat and vegetables. Cover.
4. Microwave for 15 to 20 minutes at MEDIUM (50%), or until fork-tender.
5. Stir in yogurt-cornstarch and microwave again, covered, for 3 to 4 minutes at MEDIUM (50%) to heat. Let stand 1 minute. Sprinkle with parsley to garnish, if desired.

Yield: 4 servings

——————— · ❊ · ———————

Variation: Substitute 1 cup cottage cheese blended smooth in a food processor with 1 tablespoon lemon juice for the yogurt-cornstarch.

···
*Use unsalted variety for lowest sodium values, if desired.

Nutritional Analysis per Serving (¹/₄ Recipe)

Calories: 249   Cholesterol: 65 mg

Carbohydrate: 10 g   Sodium: 123 mg

Fat: 5 g   Diabetic exchanges:

Protein: 27 g   Lean meat: 3.5

Fiber: N/A   Vegetable: 2

TIPS
....

This entree actually improves in flavor when reheated the next day.

LOW-CALORIE ROUND STEAK ROYAL

——————— · · · · · ———————

An easy one-dish microwave oven meal.

1 cup tomato juice*
1 tablespoon cornstarch
1½ packets sugar
    substitute (equivalent to
    3 teaspoons sugar) or 2
    teaspoons fructose
1 teaspoon beef bouillon
    granules*
Seasoned Salt Substitute
    #2 (see page 245) or
    store-bought alternative
14–16 ounces boneless
    round steak, thinly
    sliced into strips and
    sprinkled with 1
    teaspoon browning
    powder for meat*

4 carrots, thinly sliced
2 ribs celery, thinly sliced
1 onion, thinly sliced and
    separated into rings
2 medium white potatoes
    (10 ounces), peeled and
    thinly sliced
1 tomato, chopped,
    optional

1. In a 3-quart microwave-safe casserole, blend tomato juice, cornstarch, sugar substitute, beef bouillon granules, and

....
*Use unsalted variety for lowest sodium values, if desired.

Seasoned Salt Substitute. Add steak strips, stirring to coat. Stir in remaining vegetables, except for the tomato. Cover with lid or vented plastic wrap.

2. Microwave for 5 minutes at HIGH (100%). Stir. Cover again.

3. Microwave for 30 to 40 minutes at MEDIUM (50%) or DEFROST (30%), or until meat and vegetables are fork-tender. (Stir in tomato for the last 5 minutes of cooking time.) Let stand covered 5 minutes before serving.

Yield: 6 servings

———————— · ❄ · ————————

┌───┐

Nutritional Analysis per Serving (¼ Recipe)

Calories: 209
Carbohydrate: 22 g
Fat: 4 g
Protein: 20 g
Fiber: N/A
Cholesterol: 46 mg

Sodium: 74 mg
Diabetic exchanges:
  Bread: 0.5
  Lean meat: 2.5
  Vegetable: 2

└───┘

Be sure to use top round steak or sirloin steak for this recipe.

If you must use bottom round steak, reduce power level from ME-DIUM (50%) to DE-FROST (30%) in step #3 and microwave for 40 to 50 minutes at DEFROST (30%).

COMPANY ROUND STEAK

──────── • • • • • ────────

1½ pounds top round steak, cut into serving pieces

Dash browning powder for meat*

1 onion, sliced and separated into rings

1 tablespoon Worcestershire sauce

1 teaspoon dried parsley or 1 tablespoon chopped fresh parsley

10-ounce can Cream Soup Substitute (see page 259)

1 teaspoon beef bouillon granules*

Sprigs of parsley to garnish, optional

1. Pound or score steak pieces. Sprinkle with browning powder.
2. Combine remaining ingredients except parsley in a 1-quart microwave-safe casserole. Place steak pieces in the casserole and blend. Cover tightly with lid or vented plastic wrap.
3. Microwave for 8 minutes at HIGH (100%). Stir. Cover and microwave again for 30 to 40 minutes at MEDIUM (50%). Let stand 5 minutes. Serve garnished with sprigs of parsley, if desired.

Yield: 6 servings

──────── • ❄ • ────────

Nutritional Analysis per Serving (⅙ Recipe)

Calories: 200

Carbohydrate: 6 g

Fat: 7 g

Protein: 27 g

Fiber: N/A

Cholesterol: 70 mg

Sodium: 111 mg

Diabetic exchanges:

Bread: 0.25

Lean meat: 3

Fat: 0.25

*Use unsalted variety for lowest sodium values, if desired.

MARINATED BEEF KABOBS

· · · · ·

···················· MARINADE ····················

1 tablespoon garlic-wine
   vinegar
3 tablespoons pineapple
   juice
2 tablespoons reduced-
   sodium soy sauce
1 packet sugar substitute
   (equivalent to 2
   teaspoons sugar) or 1½
   teaspoons fructose

1 tablespoon green onion,
   finely chopped
½ clove garlic, minced, or
   ¼ teaspoon garlic
   powder
¼ teaspoon ground ginger
2 teaspoons vegetable oil

···················· KABOBS ····················

8- or 9-ounce sirloin tip
   roast or beef flank steak,
   cut into 1-inch pieces
1 medium onion, cut into
   16 pieces

1 small zucchini, cut into
   16 pieces
Dash browning powder
   for meat*
4 cherry tomatoes,
   optional

1. Combine marinade ingredients. Place meat in a 12 × 8-
   inch microwave-safe casserole. Pour marinade over meat
   and marinate 3 or 4 hours.
2. Drain and reserve marinade. Alternately thread meat,
   onion, and zucchini on 4 10-inch wooden skewers.
3. Place the kabobs in the baking dish. Brush with half of
   marinade. Sprinkle meat with browning powder. Cover
   with waxed paper. Microwave for 3 minutes at HIGH
   (100%). Turn kabobs over, brush with marinade, and
   sprinkle with browning powder. Add tomatoes to

·······································
*Use salt-free variety for lowest sodium values, if desired.

Try serving kabobs
over Parsleyed Rice
(see page 239) or over
heated bean sprouts.
To heat bean sprouts,
microwave 2 cups for
1½ to 2 minutes at
HIGH (100%).

Do not marinate the
meat for longer than
four hours. Although
marinating adds flavor
and helps tenderize
meat, longer soaking
of small meat cubes ex-
tracts too many of the
juices.

skewers, if desired. Cover again. Microwave for 3 minutes at HIGH (100%), or until meat reaches desired doneness.

Yield: 4 kabobs

——————— · ❄ · ———————

Nutritional Analysis per Serving (1 Kabob)

Calories: 143

Carbohydrate: 6 g

Fat: 4 g

Protein: 12 g

Fiber: N/A

Cholesterol: 32 mg

Sodium: 205 mg

Diabetic exchanges:

   Lean meat: 1.75

   Vegetable: 1.5

SLOPPY JOES

· · · · ·

1¼ pounds ground turkey
½ medium onion (½ cup),
    chopped
1 clove garlic, minced
8-ounce can tomato
    sauce*
6 tablespoons tomato
    paste* or ⅓ cup
    reduced-caloric catsup*
2 teaspoons garlic-wine
    vinegar
1 packet sugar substitute
    or 2 teaspoons sugar

½ teaspoon Seasoned Salt
    Substitute #2 (see page
    245) or store-bought
    alternative
3 whole wheat hamburger
    buns, split and lightly
    toasted, or 3 whole
    wheat English muffins,
    split and toasted

1. Combine ground turkey, onion, and garlic in a 2-quart microwave-safe casserole. Cover with lid or vented plastic wrap. Microwave for 5 to 6 minutes at HIGH (100%), or until no longer pink, stirring twice. Drain well.
2. Stir remaining ingredients except for buns into cooked turkey. Cover again. Microwave for 3½ to 4½ minutes at HIGH (100%), until heated through and bubbly, stirring once. Serve ½ cup Sloppy Joe mixture over each toasted half bun.

Yield: 6 servings

———— · ❋ · ————

Nutritional Analysis per Serving (⅙ Recipe)

Calories: 218
Carbohydrate: 17 g
Fat: 8 g
Protein: 18 g
Fiber: N/A
Cholesterol: 50 mg

Sodium: 202 mg
Diabetic exchanges:
    Bread: 1
    Lean meat: 2
    Vegetable: 1

*Use no-salt-added variety for lowest sodium values, if desired.

Sloppy Joes are an all-American favorite in many households. Using turkey in this recipe instead of ground beef can cut cholesterol as well as calories—and your family will probably never notice the difference.

To cook the meat and drain the grease at the same time, crumble ground meat into a plastic strainer and place over a casserole. Add onion and garlic and proceed with step #1.

Meat loaf is another way to sneak cholesterol-lowering and vitamin B–rich oats into your diet. Either regular or quick oats will work in meat-loaf recipes.

For a special topping, combine in a small bowl 1 tablespoon tomato paste with ½ packet sugar substitute (equivalent to 1 teaspoon sugar) and a dash of ground nutmeg. Spread over meat loaf after microwaving in step #2; let stand 3 minutes as directed.

MEAT LOAF FOR ONE OR TWO
(IN A MUG)

—————— · · · · · ——————

4–5 ounces ground turkey
  or lean ground beef
1 tablespoon dry oatmeal
  or bread crumbs,
  optional
1 tablespoon dried parsley
  flakes

1 teaspoon dried onion
  flakes
1 teaspoon beef bouillon
  granules* dissolved in 1
  tablespoon skim milk
Dash browning powder
  for meat,* optional

1. Combine all ingredients except browning powder in a small bowl. Pat into a microwave-safe mug or custard cup. Make a small hole in the center. Sprinkle with browning powder, if desired.
2. Microwave for 2 to 3 minutes at HIGH (100%), or until no longer pink. Drain fat. Let stand 3 minutes.

Yield: 1 serving

—————— · ❄ · ——————

Variation: For Meat Loaf for Two, double the ingredients. Place in 2 mugs. Microwave for 5 to 6 minutes at HIGH (100%).

<hr>

Nutritional Analysis per Serving (1 Mug)

Calories: 183	Cholesterol: 73 mg
Carbohydrate: 6 g	Sodium: 151 mg
Fat: 12 g	Diabetic exchanges:
Protein: 23 g	For bread: 1
Fiber: N/A	For lean meat: 3.0

· ·
*Use unsalted variety for lowest sodium values, if desired.

TRIM MICROWAVE MEAT LOAF OR TURKEY LOAF

..... • • • • • .....

.... **MEAT LOAF** ....

1¼ pounds ground turkey, ground veal, or lean ground beef
1 large egg white, slightly beaten
¼ cup dried parsley flakes
1 small onion (⅔ cup), finely chopped
1 clove garlic, minced, optional

1 teaspoon beef bouillon granules* dissolved in 3 tablespoons water
½ cup dry whole wheat bread crumbs (see page 54), optional
Dash browning powder* for meat, optional

.... **TOPPING** ....

2 tablespoons tomato paste*
Dash each ground nutmeg and dry mustard

1 packet sugar substitute (equivalent to 2 teaspoons sugar)

1. Combine all meat-loaf ingredients, except browning powder. Place in a glass pie plate or 1-quart microwave-safe casserole, shaping into a ring and leaving a 2-inch hole in the center. Sprinkle with browning powder, if desired. Cover with waxed paper. Microwave for 12 minutes at MEDIUM HIGH (70%), rotating dish halfway through cooking.
2. Combine tomato paste, nutmeg, mustard, and sugar substitute in a small bowl. Spread topping evenly over cooked meat loaf. Microwave again for 2 to 3 minutes at

Choose veal over beef if you're counting calories. Lean veal has only about 120 calories per 3-ounce serving compared to lean beef, which has about 190 calories per serving. However, veal is slightly higher in cholesterol than beef.

Choose ground turkey (an excellent source of protein) for the least amount of cholesterol and fat. Be sure to read the label on pre-packaged ground turkey, to make sure it doesn't contain the skin. If it does, the fat content will be about the same as that of ground beef.

If your diet must be low in cholesterol and fat, ask your butcher to grind a turkey breast like hamburger.

*Use unsalted variety for lowest sodium values, if desired.

MEDIUM HIGH (70%), or until meat is no longer pink. Let stand 3 minutes.

Yield: 5 servings

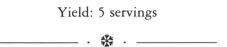

Variations: For Cajun Meat Loaf, add ¼ teaspoon each ground black pepper, ground white pepper, and crushed red pepper to the meat-loaf ingredients in step #1. Proceed as directed.

Nutritional Analysis per Serving (⅕ Ring)

Calories: 193
Carbohydrate: 5 g
Fat: 9 g
Protein: 20 g
Fiber: N/A

Cholesterol: 62 mg
Sodium: 140 mg
Diabetic exchanges:
    For bread: 0.5
    For lean meat: 3

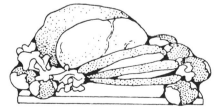

CHEESY MEAT LOAF FLORENTINE

——————— • • • • • ———————

Delicious spinach- and cheese-stuffed meat loaf.

························· STUFFING ·························

2 packages (10 ounces
    each) frozen chopped
    spinach
¾ cup (6 ounces) cottage
    cheese, drained, *or*
    grated mozzarella cheese
    (3 ounces)

¼ teaspoon ground
    nutmeg

························· MEAT LOAF ·························

1¼ pounds ground turkey,
    ground veal, or lean
    ground beef
1 large egg white, slightly
    beaten
¼ cup dried parsley flakes
½ medium onion (½ cup),
    finely chopped

½ teaspoon garlic powder,
    optional
1 teaspoon beef bouillon
    granules* dissolved in 2
    tablespoons hot water
Dash browning powder
    for meat,* optional

1. Place spinach packages on a paper plate or paper
   towel–lined glass pie plate (remove any foil wrapping).
   Microwave for 5 to 6 minutes at HIGH (100%), or until
   thawed and warmed. Drain spinach in a colander or
   strainer and pat dry with a paper towel to absorb excess
   liquid. Mix spinach, drained cottage cheese, and nutmeg
   in a small bowl. Set aside.
2. Combine meat-loaf ingredients except browning powder
   in a bowl. Pat ⅔ mixture in a microwave ring pan, making a small indentation or tunnel in the middle of the

···
*Use unsalted variety for lowest sodium values, if desired.

If a microwave ring pan is not available, create your own: Place a custard cup or small glass tumbler in the center of a 9-inch glass pie plate or round microwave-safe casserole, open side up.

For a special topping, mix 2 tablespoons tomato paste, a dash each of ground nutmeg and dry mustard, and sugar substitute (equivalent to 1 to 2 teaspoons sugar). Spread over meat loaf for the last 2 minutes of microwaving time.

meat. Spread spinach stuffing into the tunnel. Top with remaining meat loaf, sealing seams. Sprinkle with browning powder, if desired. Microwave for 12 to 16 minutes at MEDIUM HIGH (70%), or until no longer pink. Let stand 3 minutes.

Yield: 6 servings

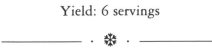

Variation: For Swiss Mushroom Meat Loaf, substitute a 4-ounce can sliced mushrooms, drained, for the cooked spinach. Use ¾ cup (3 ounces) grated Swiss cheese instead of the cottage cheese. Mix mushrooms, Swiss cheese, and nutmeg to make stuffing. Proceed with step #2.

Nutritional Analysis per Serving (⅙ Loaf)

Calories: 203	Cholesterol: 53 mg
Carbohydrate: 10 g	Sodium: 305 mg
Fat: 9 g	Diabetic exchanges:
Protein: 24 g	Lean meat: 3
Fiber: N/A	Vegetable: 2

LITE LASAGNA

————— · · · · · —————

Tastes like traditional lasagna, but zucchini replaces the noodles for fewer calories.

2 medium zucchini (about 9 inches long), peeled
1 pound ground turkey, ground veal, or lean ground beef
½ medium onion (about ½ cup), chopped
1 clove garlic, minced, or ½ teaspoon garlic powder
1 teaspoon Italian seasoning
½ packet sugar substitute (equivalent to 1 teaspoon sugar)

Dash salt substitute* or salt, optional
16-ounce jar sugar-free spaghetti sauce*
1½ cups (12 ounces) low-fat cottage cheese, drained
¾ cup (3 ounces) shredded part-skim mozzarella cheese
¼ cup grated Parmesan cheese, optional

1. Slice peeled zucchini lengthwise into long ¼-inch-thick strips. Arrange zucchini strips in a 9- or 10-inch microwave-safe square casserole or baking dish. Cover with waxed paper. Microwave 7 to 8 minutes at HIGH (100%), or until fork-tender. Drain off liquid. Pat zucchini with paper towel to absorb excess liquid. Set aside to cool.
2. Crumble ground meat and combine with onion and garlic in a 2-quart microwave-safe casserole. Cover with waxed paper. Microwave for 4 to 6 minutes at HIGH (100%), or until no longer pink, stirring twice. Drain off fat. Stir in Italian seasoning, sugar substitute, salt substitute, and spaghetti sauce. Set aside.
3. Arrange half the zucchini slices (about 6) to cover the bottom of the 9- or 10-inch casserole or baking dish.

··
*Use no-salt-added variety for lowest sodium values, if desired.

TIPS
········

To drain cottage cheese, place in a colander and press lightly with a spoon, allowing liquid to drain off.

This is my all-time favorite low-calorie main dish. I used to love traditional lasagna made with pasta, and this tastes just as good. I don't even miss the noodles.

If Italian seasoning is not available, substitute 1 teaspoon dried oregano and ½ teaspoon dried basil.

Next layer half the cottage cheese over zucchini; then half of the mozzarella cheese; then half of the sauce mixture. Repeat layers starting with zucchini and ending with sauce.

4. Cover loosely with waxed paper or plastic wrap. Microwave for 20 to 22 minutes at MEDIUM HIGH (70%), or until lasagna is hot and flavors have blended. Sprinkle with Parmesan cheese, if desired. Let stand 5 minutes.

Yield: 8 servings

———————— · ❄ · ————————

Variation: For Meatless Lite Lasagna, omit ground turkey or meat. Proceed as directed (omit microwaving meat in step #2).

Nutritional Analysis per Serving (¹/₈ Recipe)

Calories: 197   Cholesterol: 41 mg
Carbohydrate: 9 g   Sodium: 330 mg
Fat: 8 g   Diabetic exchanges:
Protein: 21 g   Lean meat: 2.5
Fiber: N/A   Vegetable: 2

HOMEMADE SPAGHETTI MEAT SAUCE

_____ · · · · · _____

Serve this low-fat sauce with spaghetti squash for a low-calorie taste sensation.

1 pound ground turkey,
   ground veal, or lean
   ground beef, crumbled
½ medium onion (about ½
   cup), finely chopped
1 clove garlic, minced
16-ounce can whole or
   stewed tomatoes*

8-ounce can tomato
   sauce*
1 teaspoon Italian
   seasoning
1 teaspoon dried parsley

1. Combine crumbled ground meat, onion, and garlic in a 2-quart microwave-safe casserole. Cover with waxed paper. Microwave for 5 to 6 minutes at HIGH (100%), or until no longer pink, stirring twice.
2. Stir in remaining ingredients. Cover with waxed paper. Microwave for 8 to 10 minutes at HIGH (100%), or until bubbly. Stir.
3. Microwave for 8 to 10 minutes at MEDIUM (50%), or until sauce thickens. Let stand 5 minutes.

Yield: 5 servings

_____ · ❄ · _____

Variation: Try Homemade Spaghetti Sauce with Meatballs. To make meatballs, combine 1 pound ground turkey with ¼ cup chopped onion, 1 large egg white or 1 medium egg, 3 tablespoons dried bread crumbs, and 2 teaspoons dried parsley. Shape into 12 meatballs and place in a 10-inch microwave-safe casserole. Sprinkle with garlic- and onion-flavored browning powder (optional). Cover with waxed paper. Microwave for 6 to 8 minutes at HIGH (100%), or until meatballs

....

* Use no-salt-added variety for lowest sodium values, if desired.

TIPS
....

If Italian seasoning is not available, substitute 1 teaspoon dried oregano and ½ teaspoon dried basil.

are no longer pink, stirring and rearranging halfway through cooking time. Drain. Set aside.

For sauce, omit ground turkey in step #1 above. Microwave onion and garlic with 1 tablespoon water for 1½ to 2 minutes at HIGH (100%) to soften. Gently mix meatballs, cooked onion, garlic, and remaining ingredients in the 2-quart casserole. Proceed as directed in steps #2 and #3.

Nutritional Analysis per Serving (⅕ Recipe)

Calories: 218
Carbohydrate: 13 g
Fat: 9 g
Protein: 21 g
Fiber: N/A

Cholesterol: 62 mg
Sodium: 136 mg
Diabetic exchanges:
    Lean meat: 2.5
    Vegetable: 2.5

T I P S
· · · · · · · ·

Serve Quick Spaghetti Meat Sauce with low-calorie spaghetti squash (see page 318) or with whole wheat spaghetti (cooked according to directions on the box).

QUICK SPAGHETTI MEAT SAUCE

1 pound ground turkey, ground veal, or lean ground beef
½ medium onion (about ½ cup), chopped
2 cloves garlic, minced

2 16-ounce jars sugar-free spaghetti sauce*
¼ cup grated Parmesan cheese, optional
½ cup (2 ounces) grated reduced-fat cheddar cheese,* optional

1. Combine crumbled ground meat, onion, and garlic in a 2-quart microwave-safe casserole. Cover with waxed paper. Microwave for 5 to 6 minutes at HIGH (100%), or until no longer pink, stirring twice.
2. Stir in spaghetti sauce, Parmesan, and cheddar cheese.

....
*Use salt-free or reduced-sodium variety for lowest sodium values, if desired.

Microwave for 8 to 10 minutes at HIGH (100%), or until bubbly. Serve immediately (see tip).

Yield: 8 servings

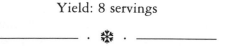

Variation: For Quick Spaghetti Sauce and Meatballs, see Homemade Spaghetti Meat Sauce variation (page 162). Follow directions for making meatballs. Proceed with step #2 in this recipe.

Nutritional Analysis per ½-Cup Serving

Calories: 145

Carbohydrate: 8 g

Fat: 7 g

Protein: 14 g

Fiber: N/A

Cholesterol: 32 mg

Sodium: 131 mg

Diabetic exchanges:

   Lean meat: 1.5

   Vegetable: 2

TIPS

Pork tenderloin is used in this recipe because it is the leanest cut of pork available (always remove any fat).

Try serving Chinese Pork and Vegetables over heated bean sprouts (see Tip, page 152) or Parsleyed Rice (see page 239).

16-ounce package frozen broccoli, carrots, and water chestnuts
⅓ cup cold water
1 tablespoon garlic-wine vinegar
2 tablespoons reduced-sodium soy sauce

2 teaspoons cornstarch
½ teaspoon grated orange peel
1 pound pork tenderloin, thinly sliced into strips and sprinkled with browning powder for meat*

1. Place frozen vegetables in a 2-quart or 10-inch flat microwave-safe casserole. Mix water, vinegar, soy sauce, cornstarch, and orange peel in a small bowl until smooth. Stir into frozen vegetables. Cover with lid or vented plastic wrap. Microwave for 4 to 5 minutes at HIGH (100%), or until vegetables are thawed and hot.
2. Add pork. Cover again. Microwave for 6 to 8 minutes at HIGH (100%), or until pork is no longer pink, stirring twice. Let stand covered for 3 minutes.

Yield: 4 servings

Nutritional Analysis per Serving (¼ Recipe)

Calories: 196
Carbohydrate: 11 g
Fat: 4 g
Protein: 27 g
Fiber: N/A

Cholesterol: 80 mg
Sodium: 286 mg
Diabetic exchanges:
　Lean meat: 3
　Vegetable: 2

*Use unsalted variety for lowest sodium values, if desired.

SWEET-AND-SOUR PORK

3 tablespoons garlic-wine
   vinegar
5 teaspoons cornstarch
2 tablespoons reduced-
   sodium soy sauce
¼ teaspoon ginger
4 packets sugar substitute
   (equivalent to 8
   teaspoons sugar) or 2
   tablespoons fructose

8-ounce can juice-packed
   pineapple chunks, juice
   reserved
1 pound boneless pork
   tenderloin, cut into 1-
   inch cubes
1 small onion, thinly sliced
   and separated
1 green bell pepper,
   cut into strips

1. Combine vinegar, cornstarch, soy sauce, ginger, sugar substitute, and pineapple juice in a 2-quart microwave-safe casserole until cornstarch is dissolved. Stir in pork. Cover with lid or vented plastic wrap.
2. Microwave for 7 to 10 minutes at MEDIUM (50%),† or until pork is no longer pink, stirring halfway through cooking time.
3. Stir in pineapple chunks, onion slices, and pepper strips. Cover again and microwave for 7 to 8 minutes at MEDIUM HIGH (70%),† or until the onion slices are tender and pepper strips are tender-crisp. Let stand 5 minutes.

Yield: 4 servings

Nutritional Analysis per Serving (¼ Recipe)

Calories: 215
Carbohydrate: 17 g
Fat: 5 g
Protein: 24 g
Fiber: N/A
Cholesterol: 93 mg

Sodium: 263 mg
Diabetic exchanges:
   Lean meat: 3
   Vegetable: 1
   Fruit: 0.5

† Compacts: Microwave for recommended time at HIGH (100%) instead of MEDIUM (50%) in step #2 and at HIGH (100%) instead of MEDIUM HIGH (70%) in step #3.

Try serving Sweet-and-Sour Pork over heated bean sprouts (see Tip, page 152) or Parsleyed Rice (see page 239).

The tenderloin is the leanest cut of pork. (Always remove any fat.) Pork tenderloin has only 166 calories per 3-ounce cooked serving but is high in vitamin B (thiamine) and niacin.

LITE CHERRY-GLAZED HAM

————————— · · · · · —————————

2½ pounds "lower-salt" boneless cooked ham
10 ounces can "lite" cherry fruit filling

1½ teaspoons lemon juice
Dash ground cloves

1. Place ham, rounded side down, on a microwave roasting rack. Cover loosely with plastic wrap. Microwave for 10 minutes at HIGH (100%). Turn ham over. Cover again. Microwave for 20 minutes at MEDIUM (50%).
2. Meanwhile, mix remaining ingredients together to make glaze.
3. Spread half of glaze over ham. Microwave 2 minutes at MEDIUM (50%), or until 130° F. Top with remaining glaze. Tent with aluminum foil and let stand 5 minutes on counter.

Yield: 10 servings

————————— · ❄ · —————————

Variation: For a 1-pound ham slice, place ham slice on a microwave-safe roasting rack. Cover loosely with plastic wrap. Microwave for 6 to 8 minutes at MEDIUM HIGH (70%). Cut remaining ingredients in half and mix together to make glaze. Spread glaze on ham slice. Microwave 1 minute longer at MEDIUM HIGH (70%).

Nutritional Analysis per Serving
(3 Ounces Ham, with Glaze)

Calories: 185
Carbohydrate: 7 g
Fat: 6 g
Protein: 21 g
Fiber: N/A

Cholesterol: 1 mg
Sodium: 735 mg
Diabetic exchanges:
  Lean meat: 3.0
  Fruit: 0.5

ITALIAN PIZZA BURGERS

12 ounces ground turkey or lean ground beef

¼ cup oat bran cereal or quick-cooking oats

½ small onion (⅓ cup), chopped

½ teaspoon Italian seasoning or dried oregano

Dash garlic powder and dried parsley

2 tablespoons shredded mozzarella cheese

2 English muffins or whole wheat buns, split

4 tablespoons tomato sauce*

1. Combine ground meat, oat bran, onion, and herbs. Form into 4 thin patties; make a small hole in the center of each. Arrange on a microwave-safe roasting rack; cover with waxed paper. Microwave for 4 to 5 minutes at HIGH (100%), or until meat is no longer pink. Sprinkle each burger with ½ tablespoon cheese; microwave 30 seconds at HIGH (100%).
2. While burgers are microwaving, toast muffins or buns.
3. Spread 1 tablespoon tomato sauce over each muffin or bun half. Top with burgers.

Yield: 4 servings

Nutritional Analysis per Serving (¼ Recipe)

Calories: 248

Carbohydrate: 18 g

Fat: 10 g

Protein: 22 g

Fiber: N/A

Cholesterol: 86 mg

Sodium: 277 mg

Diabetic exchanges:

Bread: 1

Lean meat: 2.5

Vegetable: 0.75

*Use no-salt-added variety for lowest sodium values, if desired.

Serve Italian Pizza Burgers with a fresh vegetable salad and Italian dressing to complete the meal.

If you or your family prefer browned looking burgers, sprinkle each burger with salt-free browning powder for meat (such as Micro Shake) before microwaving in step #1.

Make a hole in the center of each burger to make sure the center is done before the outside is overcooked.

To microwave ½ pound ground meat or turkey for Variation, crumble and place in a small microwave-safe casserole. Cover with a paper towel. Microwave for 2 to 3 minutes at HIGH (100%), or until no longer pink, stirring once. Drain.

To drain cottage cheese, see the tip on page 211.

Mock Lasagna Rolls can also be garnished with 1 tablespoon grated mozzarella cheese.

MOCK LASAGNA ROLLS WITH CHEESE FILLING

————— • • • • • —————

Low-calorie eggplant substitutes for the pasta.

1 large eggplant, peeled and sliced lengthwise into 6-inch by ¼-inch-long thin slices
1 small onion (⅔ cup), finely chopped
2 cloves garlic, minced
1 teaspoon olive oil
2 teaspoons water
¼ cup grated Parmesan cheese
½ cup grated mozzarella cheese, optional

1¼ cups low-fat cottage cheese, drained
1 teaspoon Italian seasoning
1 teaspoon dried chives
1 large egg white
16-ounce jar sugar-free spaghetti sauce with mushrooms*
Parmesan cheese and chives to garnish, optional

1. Place eggplant slices in a 10-inch or 12 × 8-inch flat microwave-safe casserole. Cover with lid or vented plastic wrap. Microwave for 10 to 11 minutes at HIGH (100%), or until tender, rearranging once. Drain and set aside.
2. Combine onion, garlic, olive oil, and water in a small microwave-safe dish. Microwave uncovered for 2 to 3 minutes at HIGH (100%), or until tender-crisp. Stir in cheeses, Italian seasoning, chives, and egg white until mixed.
3. Place 2 spoonfuls of cheese mixture on each slice, distributing more toward one end. Start at that end and roll up. Place rolls seam side down in the flat casserole. Pour spaghetti sauce over rolls. Cover with vented plastic wrap or lid. Microwave for 12 to 13 minutes at HIGH (100%), rearranging rolls halfway through cooking. Sprinkle each

....
*Use no-salt-added variety for lowest sodium values, if desired.

roll with a dash of Parmesan cheese and chives to garnish, if desired. Let stand 2 minutes.

Yield: 6 servings

———————— · ❄ · ————————

Variation: For Lasagna Rolls with Meat Filling, add ½ pound cooked ground turkey, veal, or lean ground beef (see tip) with the cheese in step #2.

Nutritional Analysis per Serving (⅙ Recipe)

Calories: 128
Carbohydrate: 14 g
Fat: 3 g
Protein: 11 g
Fiber: N/A

Cholesterol: 7 mg
Sodium: 286 mg
Diabetic exchanges:
   Lean meat: 1
   Vegetable: 3

STUFFED GREEN PEPPERS

You can add a 2½-ounce jar of mushrooms, drained, with the ingredients in step #2, if desired. Proceed as directed.

Microwaving the peppers before stuffing in step #1 will help prevent them from cracking during later microwaving.

Try garnishing each stuffed pepper with 1 tablespoon grated reduced-fat cheddar cheese during standing time in step #3.

2 large green bell peppers
5 ounces ground turkey, veal, or lean ground beef
½ small onion (⅓ cup), chopped
¼ cup cottage cheese (2 ounces)
½ teaspoon dried sage, optional
2 tablespoons dried chopped parsley or ¼ cup fresh
1 teaspoon Worcestershire sauce
2 tablespoons dry bread crumbs (see page 00) or cracker crumbs
¼ cup tomato sauce,* beef bouillon, tomato juice, or water
Dash browning powder for meat,* optional

1. Prepare peppers by washing and removing tops, core, and seeds. Arrange in a 1½-quart flat microwave-safe casserole. Microwave covered with vented plastic wrap for 2 minutes at HIGH (100%). Let stand 5 minutes.
2. Combine remaining ingredients except browning powder in a small mixing bowl. Spoon meat mixture into peppers. Sprinkle with browning powder, if desired. Cover with waxed paper.
3. Microwave for 9 to 10 minutes at HIGH (100%), until meat is well done. Let stand 5 minutes.

Yield: 2 servings

Variation: For 1 serving, cut recipe in half. Microwave for 6 to 7 minutes at HIGH (100%) in step #3..

For 4 servings, double recipe. Microwave for 15 to 17 minutes at HIGH (100%) in step #3, or until meat is no longer pink.

*Use no-salt-added variety for lowest sodium values, if desired.

LEAN TACO SALAD

· · · · ·

1 pound ground turkey,
  veal, or lean ground
  beef, crumbled
½ medium onion (½ cup),
  finely chopped
1 tablespoon chili powder
1 teaspoon paprika
1 teaspoon ground cumin
½ teaspoon Seasoned Salt
  Substitute #1 (see page
  244) or store-bought
  alternative

¼ cup reduced-calorie
  French or Russian
  salad dressing *
4–5 cups torn lettuce
  and/or romaine leaves
1 large tomato, chopped
1 medium cucumber,
  chopped
4 radishes, sliced
4 wheat cracker squares
  (1½-inch), crumbled

TIPS
....

Try substituting any of
your favorite chopped
garden vegetables for
the tomato, cucumber,
and radishes.

Instead of using store-
bought French dress-
ing, try making your
own (see page 252).

1. Combine ground meat and onion in a 1-quart microwave-
   safe casserole. Cover with waxed paper. Microwave for 3
   minutes at HIGH (100%). Stir in chili powder, paprika,
   cumin, and Seasoned Salt Substitute. Cover again. Microwave for 1 to 2 minutes at HIGH (100%), or until meat
   is no longer pink, stirring once or twice to separate.
   Drain well. Stir in salad dressing. Cover again and let
   stand 2 minutes.
2. Divide lettuce, tomato, cucumber, and radishes among 4

....
* Use less-salt variety for lowest sodium values, if desired.

serving bowls. Put ¼ ground beef mixture on top of each salad; toss lightly. Top each with a crumbled cracker.

Yield: 4 servings

———————— · ❊ · ————————

Variation: Substitute ¼ cup tomato sauce mixed with ½ packet sugar substitute (equivalent to 1 teaspoon sugar) for the salad dressing. Add one 15-ounce can kidney beans, drained and rinsed in hot water, in step #2.

Nutritional Analysis per Serving (¼ Recipe)

Calories: 222

Carbohydrate: 13 g

Fat: 10 g

Protein: 21 g

Fiber: N/A

Cholesterol: 61 mg

Sodium: 116 mg

Diabetic exchanges:

Bread: 0.25

Lean meat: 2.5

Vegetable: 2

LEG OF LAMB WITH SHERRY-MUSHROOM SAUCE

————— · · · · · —————

···················· LEG OF LAMB ·······················

4- to 5-pound leg of lamb
  or shank half, bone in
3 cloves garlic, peeled and
  pressed or processed in
  a food processor to
  make a paste
1 teaspoon dried thyme
1 teaspoon dried rosemary

1 tablespoon vegetable or
  olive oil
Dash Seasoned Salt
  Substitute #1 (see page
  244) or store-bought
  alternative

················ SHERRY-MUSHROOM SAUCE ·················

2 tablespoons reduced-
  calorie margarine*
1 tablespoon all-purpose
  flour
4-ounce can sliced
  mushrooms,* drained
  and liquid reserved
1 tablespoon sherry or
  white wine

1 cup evaporated skim
  milk
½ teaspoon Seasoned Salt
  Substitute #1 (see page
  244) or store-bought
  alternative
¼ teaspoon each dried
  tarragon and rosemary

1. Cut several ½-inch slits in lamb. Rub garlic paste into
   each slit. In a small bowl mix thyme, rosemary, and oil;
   rub mixture over entire surface of lamb.
2. Place lamb fat side down on a microwave-safe roasting
   rack. Cover or tent with waxed paper. Microwave for 6 to
   8 minutes at HIGH (100%).
3. Reduce power to MEDIUM (50%). Microwave for half
   the calculated microwaving time (see chart).
4. Turn lamb fat side up. Cover again. Microwave for remainder of cooking time at MEDIUM (50%), or to de-

··
*Use unsalted variety for lowest sodium values, if desired.

To avoid overcooking,
shield about 2 inches
of the bone end of the
lamb leg with a strip of
foil before microwav-
ing in step #2. (See
shielding tips, page
15.)

sired internal temperature/doneness. Cover with foil and let stand on kitchen counter for 10 minutes.

5. While lamb is standing, prepare the sauce: Microwave margarine in a 1-quart microwave-safe bowl for 30 to 40 seconds at HIGH (100%). Stir flour into liquid from mushrooms until blended; stir into melted margarine. Add sherry and milk. Stir in Seasoned Salt Substitute, tarragon, and rosemary. Microwave for 3 to 3½ minutes at MEDIUM HIGH (70%), or until thickened. Stir in sliced mushrooms. Microwave for 1 minute at MEDIUM HIGH (70%) to heat mushrooms through.

6. Season lamb with salt substitute, if desired. Slice and serve immediately with Sherry-Mushroom Sauce.

Yield: 8 servings

——————— · ❄ · ———————

Variation: You can substitute a rolled lamb roast for the leg of lamb.

Nutritional Analysis per Serving (3-Ounces Boneless)

Calories: 173

Carbohydrate: Trace

Fat: 8 g

Protein: 24 g

Fiber: N/A

Cholesterol: 80 mg

Sodium: 59 mg

Diabetic exchanges:

  Lean meat: 3

Nutritional Analysis per 3-Tablespoon Sauce Serving

Calories: 44

Carbohydrates: 5 g

Fat: 2 g

Protein: 3 g

Fiber: N/A

Cholesterol: 1 mg

Sodium: 38 mg

Diabetic exchanges:

  Vegetable: 0.5;

  Skim milk: 0.25

LEAN BREAKFAST SAUSAGE

TIPS

1 pound ground turkey
½ medium onion, finely
   chopped (½ cup)
1 teaspoon paprika
1 teaspoon ground sage
1 teaspoon Seasoned Salt
   Substitute #2 (see page
   245) or store-bought
   alternative

½ teaspoon black pepper
2 teaspoons vegetable oil
¼ cup Dry Bread Crumbs
   (see page 54)

One average serving (2 ounces) of grilled pork sausage has about 208 calories and 19 grams fat. Using Lean Breakfast Sausage will save you about one-third of the calories (80) and over one-half the fat (11 grams).

1. Combine all ingredients thoroughly in a mixing bowl. Cover. Refrigerate overnight. Use in recipes to replace bulk pork sausage.
2. For microwaved Lean Breakfast Sausage Patties, shape into 6 small doughnut shape patties. Make a pencil-size hole in the center of each. Place on a microwave-safe roasting rack. Sprinkle with salt-free browning powder for meat (such a Micro Shake). Microwave 1 patty for 1 to 2 minutes at HIGH (100%). Let stand 2 minutes. For 2 patties, microwave for 2 to 3 minutes at HIGH (100%). For 4 patties, microwave for 4 to 5 minutes at HIGH (100%). For 6 patties, microwave for 6 to 7 minutes at HIGH (100%).

Yield: 6 servings

Nutritional Analysis per Serving (1 Cooked Patty = 2 Ounces)

Calories: 128
Carbohydrate: 2 g
Fat: 7 g
Protein: 14 g
Fiber: N/A

Cholesterol: 40 mg
Sodium: 70 mg
Diabetic exchanges:
   Bread: 0.25
   Lean meat: 2

POULTRY

· ❄ ·

GENERAL TIPS FOR MICROWAVING
POULTRY

- When possible, choose poultry that is not injected with a butter solution. The bird will microwave better without the fat and you will save calories.

- "Pop-out" temperature doneness indicators do not work in microwave ovens. The turkey will be cooked before the timer pops out. It may pop out during standing time.

- Do not use a conventional meat thermometer in the microwave oven—it could break. You can insert one when you remove the poultry from the oven to quickly check the temperature (175° to 180° F. means the breast of poultry is done). The temperature will rise another 10° F. after 10 to 15 minutes of standing time.

- Always defrost chicken or chicken pieces before microwaving. To defrost, microwave a whole chicken, chicken pieces, or turkey (breast only) for 6 to 8 minutes at DEFROST (30%) per pound. Let stand 10 minutes.

- Always defrost turkey completely before cooking and re-move giblets. To defrost a whole turkey, remove packaging, shield bony parts, and place on a microwave roasting rack. Microwave for 2 minutes per pound at DEFROST (30%). Let stand 15 to 20 minutes (to allow outside to cool off while inside continues to defrost. This is called equalization time). Turn over. Microwave again for 2 minutes per pound at DEFROST (30%). Let stand in cool water 30 minutes for breasts and 1 hour for whole turkey before cooking.

- Use a microwave-safe roasting rack when cooking whole birds *or* place the bird on celery stalks to raise it out of its juices.

- When microwaving a whole bird, shield wings and drumsticks with foil for half the cooking time to prevent them from drying out.

- For outdoor grilling, precook poultry pieces by microwaving 2½ to 3 pounds for 15 minutes at MEDIUM HIGH (70%). Then grill chicken or turkey for 20 to 25 minutes basted with barbeque sauce.

POULTRY MICROWAVING TIME CHART

TYPE/AMOUNT	PREPARATION/INSTRUCTIONS	TIME/POWER LEVEL
Whole chicken (2–6 pounds)	Tie legs together with string. Fasten wings with toothpicks. Season (see recipes this section) and shield any bony parts with foil. Place on a microwave-safe roasting rack. Cover loosely with plastic wrap. (Turn over halfway through cooking time.)	Microwave 3 minutes at HIGH (100%) and then 9 minutes per pound at MEDIUM HIGH (70%). Let stand 5 minutes.
Bone-in chicken split-breast or leg with thigh attached (about 8 ounces each)	Season or coat as recipes in this section suggest. Arrange small bony pieces toward the center. Cover with waxed paper. Let stand 3 minutes after microwaving to complete cooking.	Microwave 1 piece for 1 minute at HIGH (100%) and then 4 to 5 minutes at MEDIUM HIGH (70%).

TYPE/AMOUNT	PREPARATION/INSTRUCTIONS	TIME/POWER LEVEL
		Microwave 2 pieces for 2 minutes at HIGH (100%) and then 9 to 10 minutes at MEDIUM HIGH (70%) Microwave 4 pieces for 4 minutes at HIGH (100%) and then 16 to 20 minutes at MEDIUM HIGH (70%).
Boneless chicken breasts, fillets or pieces (1 pound)	Place in a microwave-safe casserole. Season as recipes in this section suggest. Cover with waxed paper. Rearrange or stir halfway through microwaving time.	Microwave 12 to 14 minutes at MEDIUM (50%). Let stand 5 minutes.
Stewing chicken (3–5 pounds)	Stuff cavity with ½ cup each chopped onion and chopped celery. Tie legs together with string. Shield any bony parts with foil. Place in a prepared plastic cooking bag on a roasting rack. Tie bag closed with a string or plastic leaving a ½-inch opening.	Microwave for 3 minutes at HIGH (100%) and then 10 minutes per pound at MEDIUM (50%). Let stand 10 minutes.
Whole turkey (12–22 pounds)	Tie legs together with string. Season as recipes in this section suggest. Shield any bony parts with foil. Place in a prepared plastic cooking bag on a microwave-safe roasting rack. Tie bag closed with string or plastic tie leaving a ½-inch opening.	Microwave for 10 minutes at HIGH (100%) and then 9 minutes per pound at MEDIUM HIGH (70%). Let stand 15 minutes.
Convection micro-waved turkey (6–22 pounds)	Same as for whole turkey.	Low Mix Bake 350° (or Combination 2 or Code 2) for 10 to 12 minutes per pound. Let stand 15 minutes.
Speed-browned turkey (12–22 pounds)	Same as for whole turkey.	Microwave 10 minutes at HIGH (100%) and then 5 minutes per pound at MEDIUM HIGH (70%). Transfer to conventional oven, preheated at 350°F. Bake 1 hour or until done. Let stand 10 minutes.

(cont'd)

TYPE/AMOUNT	PREPARATION/INSTRUCTIONS	TIME/POWER LEVEL
Turkey breast (3—6 pounds)	Same as for whole turkey.	Microwave for 14 to 16 minutes per pound at MEDIUM (50%). Let stand 10 minutes.
Cornish game hens (2 to 4, 1 pound each)	Remove giblets. Brush with vegetable oil, sprinkle with browning powder. Cover with waxed paper. Turn over halfway through cooking time.	Microwave for 7½ to 9 minutes per pound at MEDIUM HIGH (70%) Let stand 5 minutes, covered with foil.
Duck, goose, pheasant, or capon (4—6 pounds)	Remove extra fat and giblets. Prick skin with a fork. Place on a microwave-safe roasting rack. Brush lightly with vegetable oil, sprinkle with browning powder. Tent with a piece of waxed paper. Turn over halfway through cooking time.	Microwave 8 to 9 minutes per pound at MEDIUM HIGH (70%). Let stand 10 minutes tented with foil.

COOKED (POACHED) CHICKEN

FOR MAIN DISHES OR SALADS

———————— · · · · · ————————

Any recipe that calls for cooked chicken—microwave it!

2 teaspoons chicken
   bouillon granules*
2 cups hot water
1 stalk celery, sliced,
   optional

¼ medium onion,
   chopped (about ⅓ cup),
   optional.
2—2½ pounds chicken
   breasts or other chicken
   pieces, skinned

1. Mix bouillon and water in 1-quart microwave-safe bowl until dissolved. Add celery and onion, if desired. Microwave for 5 to 6 minutes at HIGH (100%), or until boiling. Set aside.
2. Place chicken pieces meaty side up in a 10-inch or 3-quart microwave-safe casserole. Arrange meatiest portions to the

....
*Use unsalted variety for lowest sodium values, if desired.

TIPS
....

To microwave 2 chicken breasts or 1 pound chicken, cut ingredients in half. Proceed as directed except decrease microwaving time to 7 to 8 minutes at HIGH (100%) in step #3.

To microwave 4 pounds chicken, double ingredients. Proceed as directed except increase microwaving time to 30 to 32 minutes at HIGH (100%) in step #3.

In a hurry? Use very hot tap water and omit microwaving for 5 to 6 minutes at HIGH (100%) in step #1. Proceed with step #2.

outside and bony pieces to the center. Pour bouillon and vegetables over chicken. Cover with lid or vented plastic wrap.

3. Microwave for 14 to 16 minutes at HIGH (100%), or until tender. Uncover and cool. Strain broth and refrigerate or freeze it for future use. Remove chicken and discard bones and vegetables. Cut chicken into bite-size pieces.

Yield: 4 servings or 2 cups cooked diced chicken and 1 cup chicken broth

————————— · ❄ · —————————

Variations: Add 2 tablespoons white wine with the water to help tenderize the chicken.

Add 1 bay leaf with the water for additional flavoring.

Substitute 2½ pounds turkey breast or turkey pieces, skinned, for the chicken breasts.

Nutritional Analysis per Serving (½ Cup Diced Chicken)

Calories: 157
Carbohydrate: 2 g
Fat: 3 g
Protein: 26 g
Fiber: N/A

Cholesterol: 74 mg
Sodium: 79 mg
Diabetic exchanges:
Lean meat: 3
Vegetable: Free

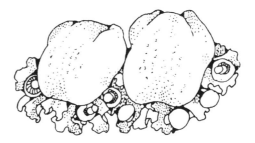

WHOLE ROASTED CHICKEN
STUFFED WITH CELERY AND ONION

——————— · · · · · ———————

3- to 4-pound whole frying
   or roasting chicken
½ medium onion (½ cup),
   chopped
1 clove garlic, minced
2 stalks celery (1 cup),
   chopped

1 tablespoon vegetable oil
Dash poultry seasoning
Dash paprika
Dash browning powder
   for chicken*

TIPS
· · · · · · · ·

Choose a plump chicken. When shopping, allow 8 to 12 ounces uncooked bone-in roasting chicken per person.

1. In a small bowl mix onion, garlic, and celery, and place in chicken cavity. Tie chicken legs together with a string and fasten wings to body with toothpicks.
2. Place chicken on a microwave-safe roasting rack, breast side up. Brush with oil. Sprinkle well with seasonings. Shield wings and bony parts with foil (see tips on shielding, page 15). Cover loosely with waxed paper or plastic wrap.
3. Microwave for 3 minutes at HIGH (100%).
4. Microwave breast side down for 4 minutes per pound at MEDIUM HIGH (70%).† Turn over, sprinkle with seasonings again. Microwave breast side up for 5 minutes per pound at MEDIUM HIGH (70%), or until no longer pink. Let stand 5 minutes.

Yield: 4 to 6 servings

——————— · ❄ · ———————

Variation: For bread stuffing, mix 2–3 pieces of dry bread (cubed) with onions and celery in step #1. Proceed as directed.

· ·
* Use unsalted variety for lowest sodium values, if desired.
† **Compacts:** Microwave at HIGH (100%) instead of MEDIUM HIGH (70%) in step #4.

Nutritional Analysis per Serving (4 Ounces Skinned and
Boned White Meat)

Calories: 162	Cholesterol: 75 mg
Carbohydrate: 2 g	Sodium: 77 mg
Fat: 5 g	Diabetic exchanges:
Protein: 27 g	Lean meat: 3.5
Fiber: N/A	Fat: 0.5

TIPS

For a special dinner, serve Chicken Breasts Parmesan with Wine Sauce (page 248) and a baked potato or Ratatouille (page 316).

CHICKEN BREASTS PARMESAN

1 large egg white or 2
  medium egg whites
1 teaspoon vegetable oil
2 teaspoons skim milk
4 bone-in chicken breast
  halves (about 2 pounds),
  skinned

¾ cup Seasoned Bread
  Crumbs or Cornflakes
  (see page 243) in a
  plastic bag
Fresh parsley to garnish,
  optional

1. Stir together egg white, oil, and milk. Dip chicken breasts in mixture and then shake with Seasoned Bread Crumbs in plastic bag.
2. Arrange chicken in a shallow microwave-safe casserole, so thicker pieces are toward the outside. Microwave for 4 minutes at HIGH (100%).† Rearrange chicken. Microwave for 12 to 16 minutes at MEDIUM HIGH (70%), or until no longer pink. Let stand 5 minutes. Serve garnished with fresh parsley, if desired.

Yield: 4 servings

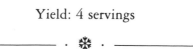

†**Compacts:** Microwave for 15 to 16 minutes at HIGH (100%) in step #2.

Variations: For 1 breast half, omit egg white and oil. Dip in 2 teaspoons milk and 3 tablespoons Seasoned Bread Crumbs. Proceed as directed. Microwave for 1 minute at HIGH (100%) and 4 to 5 minutes at MEDIUM HIGH (70%) in step #2. Let stand 5 minutes.

For 2 breast halves, cut ingredients in half. Proceed as directed. Microwave for 2 minutes at HIGH (100%) and 9 to 10 minutes at MEDIUM HIGH (70%) in step #2. Let stand 5 minutes.

Nutritional Analysis per Serving (1 Breast Half)

Calories: 230
Carbohydrate: 7 g
Fat: 8 g
Protein: 30 g
Fiber: N/A
Cholesterol: 76 mg

Sodium: 240 m
Diabetic exchanges:
  Bread: 0.5
  Lean meat: 3.5
  Fat: 0.25

LEMON CHICKEN IN WINE SAUCE

· · · · ·

4 chicken breast halves or thighs (about 1 pound), deboned
2 tablespoons reduced-calorie margarine*
½ teaspoon Seasoned Salt Substitute #1 (see page 244) or store-bought alternative
2 teaspoons lemon juice

2 tablespoons Colombard wine or white grape juice
¼ cup evaporated skim milk
½ teaspoon chicken bouillon granules*
1½ teaspoons cornstarch
Fresh chopped parsley to garnish, optional

1. Pound chicken breasts flat with a mallet or side of a saucer until ¼-inch thick. Set aside.

....
*Use unsalted variety for lowest sodium values, if desired.

Try serving Lemon Chicken in Wine Sauce over fresh microwaved broccoli (see chart, page 330). Garnish with lemon slices, if desired.

2. Microwave margarine in a microwave-safe 10-inch flat casserole or 12 × 8-inch baking dish for 20 to 30 seconds at HIGH (100°) or until melted. Stir in lemon juice and Seasoned Salt Substitute. Roll chicken breasts in lemon-margarine sauce until coated. Arrange breasts with thickest portions to the outside. Cover with waxed paper. Microwave for 12 to 14 minutes at MEDIUM (50%), or until chicken is tender, rearranging halfway through cooking time.
3. Drain lemon-margarine juices from chicken into a 2-cup glass measure. Discard any juices beyond ¼ cup. Stir wine, milk, bouillon granules, and cornstarch into ¼ cup juices until blended. Microwave for 2 to 2½ minutes at HIGH (100%), or until thickened. Pour over chicken. Sprinkle with parsley, if desired.

Yield: 4 servings

———————— · ❄ · ————————

Nutritional Analysis per Serving (¼ Recipe)

Calories: 183   Cholesterol: 73 mg
Carbohydrate: 2 g   Sodium: 72 mg
Fat: 6 g   Diabetic exchanges:
Protein: 27 g   Lean meat: 3
Fiber: N/A

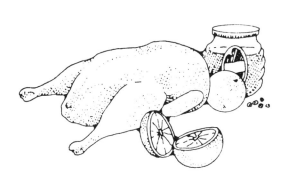

TRIM CHICKEN CORDON BLEU

· · · · ·

1½ pounds boneless,
   skinned chicken breasts
   (6 pieces)
6 thin slices (2 ounces)
   low-sodium 95% lean
   ham
6 thin slices (2 ounces)
   part-skim mozzarella
   cheese
1 tablespoon reduced-
   calorie mayonnaise

1 tablespoon skim milk
¾ cup Seasoned Bread
   Crumbs or Cornflakes
   (see page 243), placed
   on a plate
Dash browning powder
   for chicken*
Chopped fresh parsley to
   garnish, optional

TIPS
· · · · · · · ·

For a complete meal, try
serving Trim Chicken
Cordon Bleu on a bed
of microwaved slivered
or julienned vegetables.

1. Pound chicken breasts flat with a mallet until ¼-inch thick. Place 1 slice ham on flattened breast. Top with 1 slice mozzarella cheese. Roll up chicken breasts, tucking under ends. Set aside.

2. Stir together mayonnaise and milk in a small dish. Roll chicken breasts in mayonnaise mixture and then in bread crumbs. Sprinkle with browning powder. Place in a 10-inch flat microwave-safe casserole. Cover with lid or vented plastic wrap and refrigerate 1 hour.

3. Microwave covered for 16 to 18 minutes at MEDIUM HIGH (70%),† or until meat is no longer pink. (Rotate casserole once and rearrange chicken halfway through microwaving time, if necessary, for even cooking.) Serve garnished with chopped fresh parsley, if desired.

Yield: 6 servings

———— · ❊ · ————

* Use unsalted variety for lowest sodium value, if desired.
† **Compacts:** Microwave 15 to 16 minutes at HIGH (100%) in Step #3.

Nutritional Analysis per Serving (⅙ Recipe)	
Calories: 211	Cholesterol: 83 mg
Carbohydrate: 4 g	Sodium: 261 mg
Fat: 6 g	Diabetic exchanges:
Protein: 32 g	Bread: 0.25
Fiber: N/A	Lean meat: 3.5

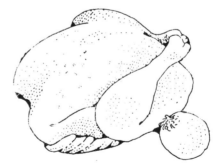

CHICKEN KIEV

・ ・ ・ ・ ・

1½ pounds boneless,
   skinned chicken breasts
   (6 pieces)
6 teaspoons frozen
   reduced-calorie
   margarine*
1 large egg white or 2
   medium egg whites
1 teaspoon safflower or
   vegetable oil

2 teaspoons skim milk
¾ cup Seasoned Bread
   Crumbs or Cornflakes
   (see page 243) placed on
   a plate
Dash browning powder
   for chicken,* optional
Fresh parsley sprigs to
   garnish, optional

1. Pound chicken breasts flat with mallet until ¼-inch thick. Place 1 teaspoon frozen margarine on each piece. Roll up chicken breasts, tucking under ends. Set aside.
2. Beat egg white, oil, and milk until thoroughly mixed. Dip chicken breasts in mixture and then roll in Seasoned Bread Crumbs. Sprinkle with browning powder, if desired. Place in a 10-inch flat microwave-safe casserole. Cover with lid and refrigerate 1 to 24 hours.
3. Microwave, covered, for 15 to 18 minutes at MEDIUM HIGH (70%),† or until meat is no longer pink, rearranging chicken halfway through cooking time. Let stand 3 minutes. Garnish with fresh parsley sprigs, if desired.

Yield: 6 servings

・ ❄ ・

Nutritional Analysis per Serving (⅙ Recipe)

Calories: 221
Carbohydrate: 5 g
Fat: 8 g
Protein: 30 g
Fiber: N/A

Cholesterol: 75 mg
Sodium: 180 mg
Diabetic exchanges:
   Bread: 0.5
   Lean meat: 3.5

* Use unsalted variety for lowest sodium values, if desired.
† Compacts: Microwave 15 to 16 minutes at HIGH (100%) in step #3.

Browning powder enhances the color, especially if bread crumbs are used instead of cornflakes.

For a complete meal, try serving Chicken Kiev with Light Gravy (see page 248) on a bed of cooked slivered vegetables or with a baked potato.

To make a thickened sauce to serve with the chicken or other vegetables, remove chicken to a serving plate. Mix 1 tablespoon cornstarch in 2 tablespoons cold water until smooth; stir into cooking juices and vegetables. Microwave 2½ to 3½ minutes, or until bubbly. Serve over chicken.

Serve Chicken Cacciatore with spaghetti squash (see page 318) as a low-calorie substitute for the traditional side dish of spaghetti.

CHICKEN CACCIATORE

· · · · ·

2 cloves garlic, minced
1 small onion, thinly sliced
16-ounce can stewed
    tomatoes* or whole
    tomatoes,* chopped
3 tablespoons white wine
    or white grape juice
½ teaspoon dried chives
1 teaspoon dried oregano

Dash sugar substitute
1 bay leaf, optional
4 split chicken breasts (2
    pounds), bone in,
    skinned
2 tablespoons grated
    Romano cheese to
    garnish, optional

1. Combine garlic, onion, chopped tomatoes, wine, chives, sugar substitute, bay leaf, and oregano in a 10-inch flat microwave-safe casserole. Cover with lid or vented plastic wrap. Microwave for 7 to 9 minutes at HIGH (100%), or until vegetables are tender, stirring once.

2. Arrange breasts in the sauce so the meatiest portions are to the outside of the casserole. Ladle some of the sauce over the vegetables. Microwave covered for 23 to 25 minutes at MEDIUM HIGH (70%),† rearranging chicken and ladling with sauce halfway through cooking time. Let stand 5 minutes. Remove bay leaf. Serve garnished with grated Romano cheese, if desired.

Yield: 4 servings

──────── · ❄ · ────────

Nutritional Analysis per Serving (¼ Recipe)

Calories: 225
Carbohydrate: 12 g
Fat: 5 g
Protein: 31 g
Fiber: N/A

Cholesterol: 80 mg
Sodium: 194 mg
Diabetic exchanges:
    Lean meat: 3
    Vegetable: 2

....

*Use no-salt-added variety for lowest sodium values, if desired.
†**Compacts:** Microwave at HIGH (100%) instead of MEDIUM HIGH (70%) in step #2 for the same amount of time.

QUICK SAUCY CHICKEN

4 chicken breast halves
    (2–2½ pounds), bone
    in, skinned

½ cup Seasoned Bread
    Crumbs (see page 243)
16-ounce jar sugar-free
    spaghetti sauce*

1. Rinse chicken under running water and dip in Seasoned
   Bread Crumbs. Arrange chicken in a flat 10-inch microwave-safe casserole with bony side up and meatiest portions to the outside. Cover with lid or vented plastic
   wrap.
2. Microwave for 5 minutes at HIGH (100%). Turn chicken
   over. Top with spaghetti sauce. Cover again. Microwave
   for 15 to 18 minutes at MEDIUM HIGH (70%),† or
   until chicken next to bone is no longer pink, rotating
   dish once if necessary for even cooking. Let stand 5 minutes.

Yield: 4 servings

Nutritional Analysis per Serving (¼ Recipe)

Calories: 236
Carbohydrate: 15 g
Fat: 4 g
Protein: 31 g
Fiber: N/A
Cholesterol: 74 mg

Sodium: 168 mg
Diabetic exchanges:
    Bread: 0.25
    Lean meat: 3.5
    Vegetable: 2

---

*Use no-salt-added for lowest sodium values, if desired.
†**Compacts:** Microwave for 18 to 20 minutes at HIGH (100%) after adding
spaghetti sauce in step #2.

TIPS

In the summer, when my garden is flourishing, I also like to add 1 chopped tomato, 2 chopped green onions, and ½ clove garlic, minced, with the spaghetti sauce in step #2. The results are delicious.

Try serving Curried
Chicken and Broccoli
Casserole with Can-
taloupe Boats (see
page 71) or Slim Ap-
ple Pie (see page 76)
to complete the meal.
Curry powder may be
omitted or adjusted to
taste.

CURRIED CHICKEN AND
BROCCOLI CASSEROLE

——————— · · · · · ———————

16-ounce package frozen
   chopped broccoli
2 cups Cooked Chicken
   (see page 180)
1/3 cup dry Cream Soup
   Mix (see page 259)
1 cup water
1/2 cup skim milk

1 teaspoon curry powder,
   optional
1 teaspoon Seasoned Salt
   Substitute #1 (see page
   244) or store-bought
   alternative
Dash paprika to garnish, if
   desired

1. Place broccoli in a 2-quart microwave-safe casserole.
   Cover with lid or vented plastic wrap. Microwave for 7 to
   8 minutes at HIGH (100%), or until heated. Drain. Top
   with chicken. Set aside.
2. Combine soup mix, water, milk, curry powder, and Seasoned Salt Substitute in a 1-quart microwave-safe bowl
   until smooth. Microwave for 2½ to 3½ minutes at HIGH
   (100%), or until thickened, stirring twice. Pour sauce
   over chicken and stir slightly. Cover again.
3. Microwave for 8 to 9 minutes at MEDIUM HIGH (70%),
   or until heated through. Serve garnished with paprika, if
   desired.

Yield: 4 servings

——————— · ❄ · ———————

Nutritional Analysis per Serving (¼ Casserole)

Calories: 225
Carbohydrate: 14 g
Fat: 4 g
Protein: 31 g
Fiber: N/A
Cholesterol: 80 mg

Sodium: 140 mg
Diabetic exchanges:
  Bread: 0.5
  Lean meat: 3.5
  Vegetable: 1

CHICKEN-BROCCOLI DIVAN

· · · · ·

1 pound fresh broccoli
   (about 2 cups), cleaned
   and cut flowerets

⅓ cup hot water

2 tablespoons cornstarch

2 tablespoons cold water

⅔ cup skim milk

⅛ teaspoon ground
   nutmeg

2 tablespoons dry white
   wine, sherry, or water

1½ teaspoons chicken
   bouillon granules*

1 cup Cooked (Poached)
   Chicken, sliced into
   bite-sized pieces (see
   page 180)

⅓ cup grated Parmesan
   cheese

Paprika to garnish,
   optional

No rice or pasta in this casserole, unlike most divans! Although the wine is optional, it does add a nice flavor. You can use unsalted cooking wine or non-alcoholic wine instead of the dry white wine, if you like.

1. Place prepared broccoli and hot water in a 2-quart microwave-safe bowl. Cover with vented plastic wrap. Microwave for 8 to 10 minutes at HIGH (100%), or until tender. Remove broccoli to an 8-inch microwave-safe casserole, reserving ⅓ cup broccoli juice in bowl.

2. Blend cornstarch and cold water until smooth; stir into broccoli juice in bowl. Add milk, nutmeg, wine, and bouillon granules. Stir. Microwave for 1½ to 2½ minutes at HIGH (100%), or until thickened, stirring twice. Pour half the sauce over broccoli; place chicken slices on top, and then pour remaining sauce over chicken.

3. Sprinkle with Parmesan cheese and paprika, if desired. Microwave for 1½ to 3 minutes at HIGH (100%), or until heated through.

Yield: 4 servings

——————— · ❄ · ———————

*Use unsalted variety for lowest sodium values, if desired.

Nutritional Analysis per Serving (⅙ Recipe)

Calories: 180

Carbohydrate: 13 g

Fat: 4 g

Protein: 21 g

Fiber: N/A

Cholesterol: 43 mg

Sodium: 112 mg

Diabetic exchanges:

    Bread: 0.5

    Lean meat: 2

    Vegetable: 1

JUICY BAKED CHICKEN AND MUSHROOMS

· · · · ·

2 tablespoons dried parsley

2 tablespoons dried chives

2 cups fresh mushrooms, sliced (6 to 8 ounces)

2 bone-in chicken breast halves (4½–5 ounces each), skinned

¼ cup lemon juice

½ teaspoon onion powder

½ teaspoon Seasoned Salt Substitute #1 (see page 244) or store-bought alternative

½ teaspoon poultry seasoning

1½ teaspoons unflavored gelatin, dry

1 teaspoon paprika

1. Mix parsley, chives, and mushrooms in a 1-quart microwave-safe casserole dish.
2. Place chicken over mushroom mixture. Pour lemon juice over chicken.
3. Sprinkle remaining ingredients over chicken in order given.
4. Cover with lid or vented plastic wrap. Microwave for 10 to 14 minutes at MEDIUM HIGH (70%), or until tender. Let stand 3 minutes before serving.

Yield: 2 servings

————— · ❄ · —————

Nutritional Analysis per Serving (1 Breast Half)

Calories: 156

Carbohydrate: 6 g

Fat: 3 g

Protein: 26 g

Fiber: N/A

Cholesterol: 64 mg

Sodium: 61 mg

Diabetic exchanges:

Lean meat: 3

Vegetable: 1

This is one of my favorite low-calorie ways to make chicken. The unflavored gelatin gives the chicken a saucy look and texture.

Chicken is the perfect low-calorie red meat substitute. Lean skinless chicken breasts are far lower in calories and fat than red meat.

8-ounce can tomato sauce*
½ teaspoon Italian seasoning
2 teaspoons grated onion
3 tablespoons Seasoned Bread Crumbs (see page 243)

1 tablespoon grated Parmesan cheese
4 pieces chicken breast (about 1 pound), boned and skinned
2 tablespoons skim milk
¼ cup (1 ounce) shredded low-fat mozzarella cheese

1. Combine tomato sauce, Italian seasoning, and onion in a 2-cup glass measure. Microwave for 2 to 3 minutes at HIGH (100%), or until boiling. Set aside.
2. Combine bread crumbs and Parmesan cheese on a small plate. Dip chicken pieces into milk and then in Parmesan-crumbs. Arrange in a 10-inch flat microwave-safe casserole. Cover with waxed paper. Microwave for 12 to 14 minutes at MEDIUM (50%), or until no longer pink.
3. Pour tomato sauce over chicken. Sprinkle with mozzarella cheese. Microwave for 1½ to 2 minutes at HIGH (100%) to heat through.

Yield: 4 servings

Variations: For Turkey Parmigiana, substitute 4 turkey cutlets (4 ounces each) for the chicken breast pieces. Proceed as directed.

For Mexican Chicken, substitute 4 ounces reduced-calorie salsa or picante sauce and ½ teaspoon chili powder for the 8 ounces tomato sauce and ½ teaspoon Italian seasoning. Proceed as directed.

*Use no-salt-added variety for lowest sodium values, if desired.

Nutritional Analysis per Serving (¼ Recipe)

Calories: 192

Carbohydrate: 4 g

Fat: 6 g

Protein: 30 g

Fiber: N/A

Cholesterol: 79 mg

Sodium: 154 mg

Diabetic exchanges:

Lean meat: 3.5

Vegetable: Free

CHICKEN À L'ORANGE

· · · · ·

You'll love this orange curried chicken.

4 chicken breast pieces
(about 1 pound), boned
and skinned

½ teaspoon finely grated
orange peel

½ cup orange juice

Dash each curry powder,
garlic powder, and
paprika

1 tablespoon cold water

1 tablespoon cornstarch

Sprigs of fresh tarragon
and orange slices to
garnish, optional

TIPS
· · · · · · · ·

Try serving this tasty main dish on a bed of Parsleyed White or Wild Rice (see page 239) with a fresh green salad.

If you prefer a browned chicken, substitute a dash of chicken browning powder for the paprika.

1. Place chicken in a 10-inch flat microwave-safe casserole. Arrange thickest portions to the outside of casserole. Combine orange peel, juice, and curry powder; pour over chicken. Sprinkle chicken lightly with garlic powder and paprika. Cover with waxed paper. Microwave for 3 minutes at HIGH (100%).

2. Using a sharp knife, make 5 slashes in each chicken piece, cutting to, but not through, the opposite side. Baste chicken with juices and sprinkle again with paprika. Cover again. Microwave for 6 to 8 minutes at MEDIUM (50%), or until tender.

3. Remove chicken to serving plate, reserving liquid. Strain reserved liquid. Mix water and cornstarch in a small bowl;

stir into reserved liquid. Microwave for 2 to 2½ minutes at HIGH (100%), or until thickened, stirring once. Spoon sauce over chicken. Garnish with tarragon sprigs and orange slices, if desired.

Yield: 4 servings

——————— · ❄ · ———————

Variation: For Oriental Chicken à l'Orange, substitute 2 teaspoons reduced-sodium soy sauce and ¼ teaspoon ground ginger for the curry powder. Proceed as directed.

Nutritional Analysis per Serving (¼ Recipe)

Calories: 170
Carbohydrate: 7 g
Fat: 3 g
Protein: 27 g
Fiber: N/A

Cholesterol: 73 mg
Sodium: 64 mg
Diabetic exchanges:
    Lean meat: 3.5
    Fruit: 0.5

DIET BARBECUE CHICKEN

The barbecue coating tastes great and adds fewen than 5 calories to each breast.

Make up the coating and save the extra for next time.

1 or 2 chicken breast
   halves (6 ounces each),
   bone-in, skinned
2 tablespoons lemon juice

.... BARBECUE COATING ....

2 tablespoons (2 packages)
   unflavored gelatin, dry
2 teaspoons paprika
½ teaspoon garlic powder
½ teaspoon onion powder
½ teaspoon dry mustard

1 packet sugar substitute
   (equivalent to 2
   teaspoons sugar)
1 teaspoon dried parsley
   flakes

1. Coat chicken with lemon juice. Set aside. Mix barbeque coating ingredients. Sprinkle chicken with the barbeque coating.
2. Place chicken on a paper plate or in a 1-quart microwave-safe casserole. Cover with waxed paper.
   For 1 breast half, microwave for 1 minute at HIGH (100%)† and microwave again for 5 minutes at MEDIUM HIGH (70%). For 2 breast halves, microwave for 2 minutes at HIGH (100%)† and microwave again for 9 minutes at MEDIUM HIGH (70%).
   Let stand 3 to 5 minutes.

Yield: 1 to 2 servings

❄

† **Compacts:** For 1 breast half, microwave for 5 to 6 minutes at HIGH (100%) total time in step #2. For 2 breast halves, microwave for 8 to 10 minutes at HIGH (100%) total time.

T I P S
········

This recipe will also make 8 small servings. Use 8 small (6-inch) tortillas. Proceed as directed. Divide ingredients among 8 tortillas in step #3.

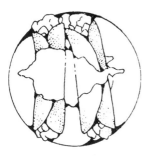

CHICKEN FAJITAS

— · · · · · —

No need to head for the border—you can make this Mexican treat at home in your microwave oven.

1 pound boned and
    skinned chicken breasts,
    cut in thin strips
¼ cup lime juice
1 clove garlic, minced
½ teaspoon Seasoned Salt
    Substitute #2 (see page
    245) or store-bought
    alternative
¼ teaspoon each dried
    oregano, cumin, and
    garlic powder

½ cup (2 ounces) sliced
    fresh mushrooms,
    optional
½ medium onion (½ cup),
    chopped
4 medium flour tortillas
    (7-inch size)
1 small tomato, chopped
1 cup shredded lettuce
¼ cup nonfat plain yogurt

1. Place chicken strips in a 1-quart microwave-safe casserole. Combine lime juice, garlic, seasonings, and herbs in a small bowl. Pour over chicken. Cover with lid. Refrigerate at least 1 hour or overnight.

2. Stir mushrooms and onion into chicken. Cover with waxed paper; microwave for 12 to 14 minutes at MEDIUM (50%), or until chicken is tender, stirring twice.

3. To prepare tortillas, roll up and wrap each individually in a paper towel. Microwave all 4 for 40 to 50 seconds at

HIGH (100%), or until warm. Unroll. Divide chicken mixture among tortillas, placing some in the center of each. Top each with some tomato, lettuce, and yogurt. Roll up and enjoy!

Yield: 4 servings

———————— · ❄ · ————————

Nutritional Analysis per Serving (1 Fajita)

Calories: 246   Sodium: 78 mg
Carbohydrate: 23 g   Diabetic exchange:
Fat: 5 g   Bread: 1
Protein: 29 g   Lean meat: 3
Fiber: N/A   Vegetable: 1
Cholesterol: 73 mg   Skim milk: 0.25

CHICKEN AND VEGETABLES
ROSEMARY FOR TWO

———————— · · · · · ————————

2 tablespoons water
2 stalks celery, thinly
  sliced
1 clove garlic, minced
½ medium onion, thinly
  sliced
2 chicken breast halves
  (about 1 pound), bone
  in, skinned
2 medium carrots, sliced
¼ teaspoon crushed
  rosemary

Dash browning powder
  for chicken*
1 tablespoon water
1 teaspoon cornstarch
½ teaspoon chicken
  bouillon granules*
½ teaspoon Seasoned Salt
  Substitute #2 (see page
  245) or store-bought
  alternative
Dash dried chives or
  parsley to garnish,
  optional

* Use unsalted variety for lowest sodium values, if desired.

If your diet permits, you may want to add 1 medium peeled and quartered potato with the carrots in step #2. If you do, microwave for 15–18 minutes in step #2.

1. Combine 2 tablespoons water, celery, garlic, and onion in a 1-quart microwave-safe casserole. Cover with lid or vented plastic wrap. Microwave for 3 minutes at HIGH (100%), or until vegetables are partially cooked.
2. Add chicken and carrots; sprinkle with rosemary and browning powder. Cover again. Microwave for 13 to 15 minutes at MEDIUM HIGH (70%), rearranging chicken halfway through microwaving time. Let stand covered while making sauce in step #3.
3. Drain juices from chicken and vegetables into a small bowl. Mix 1 tablespoon water, cornstarch, bouillon granules, and Seasoned Salt Substitute in a 1-cup glass measure until smooth. Stir in chicken juices. Microwave for 1 minute at HIGH (100%), or until mixture comes to a boil and thickens, stirring once. Pour sauce over chicken. Serve garnished with chives or parsley, if desired.

Yield: 2 servings

——————— · ❄ · ———————

Nutritional Analysis per Serving (½ Recipe)

Calories: 210
Carbohydrate: 15 g
Fat: 4 g
Protein: 28 g
Fiber: N/A

Cholesterol: 73 mg
Sodium: 125 mg
Diabetic exchanges:
   Lean meat: 3
   Vegetable: 2

CAJUN CHICKEN

_. . . . ._

Try doubling or tripling the seasoning mix so you will have it handy the next time you're in the mood for Cajun Chicken.

If you prefer milder seasoning, omit the crushed red pepper.

.... SEASONING MIX ....

1½ teaspoons paprika
½ teaspoon dried thyme
½ teaspoon onion powder
¼ teaspoon garlic powder
¼ teaspoon black pepper

¼ teaspoon white pepper
¼ teaspoon crushed red pepper and/or ⅛ teaspoon cayenne (ground red pepper)

.... CHICKEN ....

4 boned and skinned chicken breast halves or thighs (about 1 pound)
¼ cup lime juice

Lime slices and fresh parsley sprigs to garnish, optional

1. Mix seasonings together in a small bowl; set aside.
2. Pound chicken breasts flat with a mallet or side of a saucer until ¼-inch thick. Arrange chicken in a microwave-safe 10-inch flat casserole or 12 × 8-inch baking dish, with thickest portions to the outside. Brush chicken thoroughly with lime juice. Sprinkle seasoning mixture evenly over all 4 chicken pieces.
3. Cover with waxed paper. Microwave for 12 to 14 minutes at MEDIUM (50%), or until chicken is tender, rearranging chicken halfway through cooking time. Let stand 5 minutes. Garnish with lime and parsley, if desired.

Yield: 4 servings

_. ❄ ._

Nutritional Analysis per Serving (1 Breast Half)

Calories: 146
Carbohydrate: 4 g
Fat: 3 g
Protein: 27 g
Fiber: N/A

Cholesterol: 72 mg
Sodium: 67 mg
Diabetic exchanges:
    Lean meat: 3.5

Use any 16-ounce package of frozen mixed vegetables in this recipe.

Use a small sharp hand grater to grate only the yellow outer peel of the lemon, called the zest. Avoid using any of the white pith beneath the zest because it has a bitter flavor.

Try serving this hot lemon sauce over the Lemon Chicken Breasts with Vegetables: Drain juices from microwaved chicken and vegetables into a 1-quart microwave-safe bowl. Dissolve 2 tablespoons cornstarch in 1 cup of chicken broth. Add to juices and microwave for 3 to 4 minutes at HIGH (100%), or until sauce thickens.

LEMON CHICKEN BREASTS WITH VEGETABLES

— · · · · · —

4 split chicken breasts (about 2 pounds), bone in and skinned
¼ cup lemon juice
1 teaspoon grated lemon peel (zest only)
½ medium onion, thinly sliced
1 clove garlic, minced, or ½ teaspoon garlic powder

2 teaspoons vegetable oil
½ teaspoon Seasoned Salt Substitute #1 (see page 244) or store-bought alternative
½ teaspoon crushed rosemary
16-ounce package frozen mixed vegetables (broccoli, carrots, and water chestnuts)

1. Place chicken breasts in a 10-inch flat microwave-safe casserole. Combine remaining ingredients except vegetables in a small bowl; pour over chicken. Turn chicken over so bony sides are up and meaty portions remain in marinade. Cover with vented plastic wrap or lid and refrigerate at least 30 minutes.
2. Turn chicken meaty side up with thickest portions to the outside. Cover again. Microwave for 15 minutes at MEDIUM HIGH (70%). Add vegetables. Cover again. Microwave for 9 to 10 minutes at HIGH (100%), or until chicken is tender and vegetables are done. Let stand 5 minutes.

Yield: 4 servings

——— · ❄ · ———

Nutritional Analysis per Serving (¼ Recipe)

Calories: 204
Carbohydrate: 10 g
Fat: 6 g
Protein: 29 g
Fiber: N/A

Cholesterol: 73 mg
Sodium: 82 mg
Diabetic exchanges:
  Lean meat: 3
  Vegetable: 2

CHICKEN KABOBS

· · · · ·

·············· MARINADE ··············

3 tablespoons reduced-
   calorie Italian Salad
   dressing*
2 teaspoons reduced-
   sodium soy sauce

Dash ground ginger
1 teaspoon fructose or
   sugar substitute
   (equivalent to 1½
   teaspoons sugar)

·············· KABOBS ··············

1 pound boned and
   skinned chicken breasts,
   sliced into 24 thin strips
1 green bell pepper and 1
   red bell pepper, cut into
   12 pieces each

2 tablespoons water
12 small fresh mushrooms
1 small zucchini, cleaned
   and unpeeled, cut into
   12 rounds

Chicken Kabobs also make tasty appetizers. Divide ingredients among 24 round wooden toothpicks in step #4 and proceed as directed.

Sometimes I like to substitute pineapple chunks for the mushrooms. (Start with 15-ounce can juice-packed pineapple chunks, drained.)

1. Combine marinade ingredients in a small bowl until thoroughly mixed. Place chicken in an 8 × 12-inch flat microwave-safe casserole; pour marinade over chicken. Cover with plastic wrap and refrigerate at least 1 hour.
2. Microwave green and red pepper and water in a microwave-safe dish for 3 to 4 minutes at HIGH (100%), or until crisp-tender. Drain.
3. Alternately thread chicken pieces, peppers, mushrooms, and zucchini on 12 (6-inch) wooden skewers. Place kabobs in casserole, brushing with marinade. Cover with waxed paper. Microwave for 4 minutes at HIGH (100%). Rearrange kabobs. Microwave again for 4 to 5 minutes at HIGH (100%), or until chicken is tender.

Yield: 12 kabobs or 4 servings

——————— · ❄ · ———————

*Use low-sodium variety for lowest sodium values, if desired.

Variations: For Turkey Kabobs, substitute 1 pound turkey tenderloin, sliced into 24 thin strips, for the chicken. Proceed as directed.

For Chicken, Onion, and Tomato Kabobs: Substitute 1 small onion, cut into 12 pieces, for the red pepper. Proceed as directed in step #2. Add 12 cherry tomatoes, one to each skewer, when threading skewers in step #3.

Nutritional Analysis per 3 Kabobs

Calories: 168

Carbohydrate: 5 g

Fat: 3 g

Protein: 28 g

Fiber: N/A

Cholesterol: 73 mg

Sodium: 99 mg

Diabetic exchanges:

   Lean meat: 3

   Vegetable: 1

ORIENTAL CHICKEN AND VEGETABLES

——————— · · · · · ———————

16-ounce bag frozen
Oriental mixed
vegetables (broccoli,
carrots, and water
chestnuts; or broccoli,
red peppers, bamboo
shoots, and straw
mushrooms)
1 teaspoon chicken
bouillon granules*
dissolved in ½ cup hot
water
3 tablespoons reduced-
sodium soy sauce

2 tablespoons garlic-wine
vinegar
2 teaspoons fructose or 1½
packets sugar substitute
(equivalent to 3
teaspoons sugar)
1 tablespoon cornstarch
1 green onion, thinly
sliced to equal ¼ cup
1 pound boned and
skinned chicken breasts,
sliced into thin strips

TIPS
· · · · · · · · ·

Try serving Oriental
Chicken and Vegeta-
bles over heated fresh
bean sprouts (see Tip,
page 152) or Pars-
leyed White Rice (see
page 239). To heat
bean sprouts, micro-
wave 2 cups for 1½ to
2 minutes at HIGH
(100%).

1. Cut a large "X" in the plastic bag of frozen vegetables to
   allow steam to escape. Place bag "X" side down in a glass
   pie plate or microwave-safe casserole. Microwave for 6 to
   7 minutes at HIGH (100%), patting bag to separate vegetables halfway through cooking time. Set aside.
2. Mix bouillon-water, soy sauce, vinegar, fructose, and
   cornstarch in a 2-quart microwave-safe casserole until
   smooth. Cover with lid or vented plastic wrap. Microwave
   for 2 to 3 minutes at HIGH (100%), or until slightly
   thickened, stirring once.
3. Add onion and chicken strips to sauce mixture. Re-cover.
   Microwave for 12 to 13 minutes at MEDIUM (50%), or
   until chicken is tender and no longer pink, stirring once.
4. Using tongs, pull plastic bag off the vegetables. Stir vegetables into chicken mixture. Microwave for 2 to 3 minutes at HIGH (100%), or until heated through. Serve
   immediately.

Yield: 4 servings

——————— · ❄ · ———————

* Use unsalted variety for lowest sodium values, if desired.

Variation: For 2 servings of Oriental Chicken and Vegetables, cut ingredients in half. For step #1, empty ½ bag vegetables into a 1-quart microwave-safe casserole and cover with lid or vented plastic wrap. Microwave for 3 to 4 minutes at HIGH (100%), then set aside. Proceed with step #2 as directed. Decrease chicken to 8 ounces and microwave for 6 to 7 minutes at MEDIUM (50%) in step #3. Proceed with step #4.

Nutritional Analysis per Serving (¼ Recipe)

Calories: 185	Cholesterol: 72 mg
Carbohydrate: 9 g	Sodium: 172 mg
Fat: 3 g	Diabetic exchanges:
Protein: 28 g	Lean meat: 3
Fiber: N/A	Vegetables: 1.25

TIPS
· · · · · · · ·

Try serving Micro-Fry Chinese Chicken with heated bean sprouts (see Tip, page 152) or Parsleyed Rice (see page 239) and with a bowl of Egg Drop Soup (see page 273) as the appetizer.

MICRO-FRY CHINESE CHICKEN
—————— · · · · · ——————

2 teaspoons vegetable oil
1 pound boned and
    skinned chicken breasts,
    sliced into thin strips
    (1½ × ½-inch)
1 cup broccoli flowerets
½ cup celery, diagonally
    sliced
½ cup (2 ounces) sliced
    fresh mushrooms
4 ounces canned sliced
    bamboo shoots (½ cup),
    drained

½ cup sliced water
    chestnuts, fresh or
    canned, drained
2 teaspoons chicken
    bouillon granules*
    dissolved in ½ cup hot
    water
2 tablespoons garlic-wine
    vinegar or white wine
3 tablespoons reduced-
    sodium soy sauce
1 tablespoon cornstarch
1½ packets sugar
    substitute (equivalent to
    3 teaspoons sugar)

· ·
*Use unsalted variety for lowest sodium values, if desired.

1. Mix oil and chicken in a 2-quart microwave-safe casserole. Cover with lid or vented plastic wrap. Microwave for 5 to 6 minutes at MEDIUM HIGH (70%), or until chicken is no longer pink, stirring once. Transfer to serving bowl.
2. Place broccoli, celery, mushrooms, bamboo shoots, and water chestnuts in same casserole; microwave covered for 5 to 6 minutes at HIGH (100%), or until vegetables are tender-crisp, stirring twice. Drain and reserve juices for sauce in step #3. Set vegetables aside.
3. Mix bouillon-water, vinegar, soy sauce, vegetable juices, cornstarch, and sugar substitute in a 2-cup glass measure until smooth. Microwave covered for 2½ to 3 minutes at HIGH (100%) to thicken. Stir sauce and chicken into vegetables. Microwave, covered, for 2 to 3 minutes at HIGH (100%) to heat through. Serve immediately.

Yield: 4 servings

— · ❄ · —

Nutritional Analysis per Serving (¼ Recipe)

Calories: 222
Carbohydrate: 17 g
Fat: 6 g
Protein: 30 g
Fiber: N/A

Cholesterol: 74 mg
Sodium: 164 mg
Diabetic exchanges:
    Lean meat: 3
    Vegetables: 3

TIPS

You can substitute a 10½-ounce can of cream of mushroom or cream of chicken soup for the Cream Soup Substitute. Be sure to add 800 mg of sodium to your dietary total if you do make the substitution.

To make 1 can of cream soup, blend ⅓ cup dry Cream Soup Substitute (see page 259) with 1¼ cups water, and microwave for 2½ to 3½ minutes at HIGH (100%), or until thickened.

¼ cup chopped celery
¼ cup chopped onion
10-ounce package frozen chopped broccoli
10½ ounces Cream Soup Substitute (see page 259)
2 cups cooked Parsleyed Brown or White Rice (see page 239)

½ teaspoon Seasoned Salt Substitute #2 (see page 245) or store-bought alternative
1 cup cooked chicken or turkey, cubed (see page 180)

1. Place celery, onion, and broccoli in a 2-quart microwave-safe casserole. Cover with lid or vented plastic wrap. Microwave for 5½ to 6½ minutes at HIGH (100%), or until vegetables are tender.
2. Stir in Cream Soup Substitute, rice, Seasoned Salt Substitute, and chicken. Cover again. Microwave for 3 to 4 minutes at HIGH (100%), or until heated through, stirring once.

Yield: 4 servings

Nutritional Analysis per Serving (¼ Casserole)

Calories: 240
Carbohydrate: 34 g
Fat: 2 g
Protein: 20 g
Fiber: N/A
Cholesterol: 40 mg

Sodium: 84 mg
Diabetic exchanges:
Bread: 1
Lean meat: 2
Vegetable: 2

CHICKEN CHOW MEIN

· · · · ·

2 cups fresh pea pods or 8-ounce package frozen pea pods

2 stalks celery (1 cup), diagonally sliced

1 small onion (⅔ cup), chopped

4 teaspoons cornstarch dissolved in 1 cup cold water

2 teaspoons chicken bouillon granules*

4 teaspoons reduced-sodium soy sauce

1½ cups cooked chicken (see page 180), cut into strips

8-ounce can sliced water chestnuts or bamboo shoots, drained

1½ cup chow mein noodles, optional

1. Combine pea pods, celery, and onion in a 1½-quart microwave-safe casserole. Cover with lid or vented plastic wrap. Microwave for 5 to 6 minutes at HIGH (100%), or until tender-crisp. Set aside.
2. Combine cornstarch-water, bouillon granules, and soy sauce in a small bowl until dissolved. Pour over cooked vegetables. Add cooked chicken and water chestnuts. Cover again. Microwave for 4 to 6 minutes at HIGH (100%), or until mixture thickens, stirring twice.
3. Add chow mein noodles, if desired. Cover again. Microwave for 1 minute at HIGH (100%) to heat through.

Yield: 4 servings

——————— · ❄ · ———————

Variations: For Chow Mein, omit cooked chicken. Proceed as directed.

For Quick Chow Mein, omit pea pods. Decrease microwaving time in step #1 to 2 to 2½ minutes at HIGH (100%).

Substitute 2 cups (8 ounces) fresh sliced mushrooms for the celery. Proceed as directed.

....

*Use unsalted variety for lowest sodium values, if desired.

Pea pods are also called snow peas. Choose ones that are bright green, cold, and not too plump (if pods are warm, the sugar has turned to starch; large peas are often tough and old).

This low-fat, high-fiber, and high-protein main dish is popular with all ages.

Calories: 190

Carbohydrate: 16 g

Fat: 3 g

Protein: 20 g

Fiber: N/A

Cholesterol: 51 mg

Sodium: 250 mg

Diabetic exchanges:

Bread: 0.5

Lean meat: 2

Vegetable: 2

TIPS

To drain cottage cheese, place it in a strainer that rests over a bowl. Allow liquid to drain into bowl, pressing cottage cheese lightly with a spoon. Reserve liquid.

For a special treat, serve Stuffed Chicken Breasts drizzled with Slim Cheese Sauce (see page 247) on a plate with Sunshine Zucchini and Carrots (see page 328).

LITE BROCCOLI-AND-CHEESE – STUFFED CHICKEN BREASTS

—————— · · · · · ——————

10-ounce package frozen chopped broccoli

1 large egg white, slightly beaten

¾ cup low-fat cottage cheese, drained (reserve liquid)

½ medium onion (½ cup), chopped

1 tablespoon fresh basil, chopped, or 1 teaspoon dried basil

¼ teaspoon ground nutmeg

1½ pounds boned and skinned chicken breasts (about 6 pieces)

½ cup Seasoned Bread Crumbs (see page 243)

Fresh chopped basil to garnish, optional

1. Place broccoli package on a paper plate or paper towel–lined glass pie plate (remove any foil wrapping from box). Microwave 4 to 5 minutes at HIGH (100%), or until broccoli is thawed. Discard packaging and drain broccoli well using a strainer. Pat with paper towels to absorb excess liquid.

2. Combine drained broccoli, egg white, drained cottage cheese, onion, basil, and nutmeg in a bowl to make stuffing.

3. Pound chicken breasts flat using a mallet or side of a

saucer until ¼-inch thick. Place 2 tablespoons of the broccoli-cheese stuffing into the center of each breast. Roll up breasts, tucking under ends.

4. Brush chicken breasts with drained liquid from the cottage cheese; sprinkle each breast with Seasoned Bread Crumbs. Place in a flat 10-inch or 8 × 12-inch microwave-safe casserole. Cover with lid or vented plastic wrap. Microwave for 16 to 18 minutes at MEDIUM HIGH (70%),† or until chicken is no longer pink. Rotate casserole once and rearrange chicken halfway through microwaving time, if necessary, for even cooking. Serve garnished with fresh chopped basil, if desired.

Yield: 6 servings

———————— · ❄ · ————————

Variation: For Florentine Stuffed Breasts, substitute 10 ounces frozen chopped spinach for the chopped broccoli.

┌───┐

Nutritional Analysis per Serving

Calories: 220   Cholesterol: 76 mg
Carbohydrate: 8 g   Sodium: 249 mg
Fat: 5 g   Diabetic exchanges:
Protein: 31 g   Lean meat: 3.5
Fiber: N/A   Vegetable: 1.5

└───┘

† Compacts: Microwave 15 to 16 minutes at HIGH (100%) in step #4.

Save a few mandarin orange sections to garnish plates at serving time, if desired.

For a creamier salad, stir 1 tablespoon reduced-calorie mayonnaise into the yogurt mixture in step #2

CHICKEN-MANDARIN SALAD

· · · · ·

Cook the chicken in the microwave first!

2 cups Cooked (Poached) Chicken, cut into bite-size pieces (see page 180)

1 cup (2 stalks) thinly sliced celery

¼ cup sliced green onion

1 5½-ounce-can juice-packed mandarin oranges, drained

½ cup (4 ounces) plain nonfat yogurt

1 packet sugar substitute (equivalent to 2 teaspoons sugar) or 1½ teaspoons fructose

Dash each ground cinnamon and nutmeg

4 cups torn iceberg lettuce and romaine leaves

1. Combine cooled chicken pieces, celery, onion, and oranges in a large mixing bowl.
2. Mix together yogurt, sugar substitute, cinnamon, and nutmeg. Stir into chicken-orange mixture. Toss. Refrigerate until serving time.
3. At serving time, arrange lettuce and romaine leaves on 4 individual serving plates. Top with 2 scoops of chicken-orange mixture.

Yield: 4 servings

· ❄ ·

Variation: Substitute ½ cup orange nonfat yogurt for the plain yogurt and omit the sugar substitute.

Nutritional Analysis per Serving (¼ Recipe)

Calories: 195

Carbohydrate: 11 g

Fat: 3 g

Protein: 28 g

Fiber: N/A

Cholesterol: 74 mg

Sodium: 117 mg

Diabetic exchanges:

Lean meat: 3

Vegetable: 0.5

Fruit: 0.25

CURRIED CHICKEN SALAD

· · · · ·

1 cup Cooked (Poached)
   Chicken, cooled (see
   page 180)

1 cup (2 stalks) diced
   celery

1 small peach, diced

2 tablespoons reduced-
   calorie mayonnaise

1 tablespoon Dijon
   mustard

1 teaspoon curry powder

½ large cantaloupe, cut in
   half

Fresh parsley and paprika
   to garnish, optional

By using the micro-
waved chicken in this
recipe, you will have a
fast and delicious
whole-meal salad.

1. Mix chicken, celery, and diced peach in a mixing bowl.
   Combine mayonnaise, mustard, and curry powder in a
   small bowl. Stir into chicken mixture.
2. Place scoop of chicken salad in each piece of cantaloupe.
   Serve garnished with fresh parsley and a sprinkle of paprika, if desired.

Yield: 2 servings

· ❄ ·

Nutritional Analysis per Serving (½ Recipe)

Calories: 245

Carbohydrate: 18 g

Fat: 7 g

Protein: 24 g

Fiber: N/A

Cholesterol: 68 mg

Sodium: 290 mg

Diabetic exchanges:

   Lean meat: 3

   Fruit: 1.25

HOT CHICKEN AND ROQUEFORT-APPLE SALAD

—————— · · · · · ——————

4 cups fresh torn spinach
or romaine leaves
(washed, drained, and
trimmed)
1 pound boned and
skinned chicken breast,
cut into bite-size pieces
½ teaspoon Seasoned Salt
Substitute #1 (see page
244) or store-bought
alternative
3 tablespoons apple juice
or apple cider
1 cup (3 to 4 ounces) sliced
fresh mushrooms,
optional

1 medium carrot, thinly
sliced
1 large Golden Delicious
or Granny Smith apple,
peeled and cut into ½-
inch cubes
½ cup crumbled
Roquefort or bleu
cheese
2 teaspoons garlic-wine
vinegar
1 tablespoon grated onion

1. Line 4 salad plates with the spinach leaves. Set aside.
2. Place chicken in a 9- or 10-inch microwave-safe baking
   dish. Sprinkle with Seasoned Salt Substitute. Add apple
   juice. Cover with waxed paper. Microwave for 12 to 14
   minutes at MEDIUM (50%), or until no longer pink,
   stirring twice. Remove chicken to a plate, reserving juice
   in baking dish.
3. Add mushrooms and carrots to reserved juice. Cover with
   lid or vented plastic wrap. Microwave for 3 minutes at
   HIGH (100%). Stir in apples. Cover again. Microwave
   for 2 to 2½ minutes at HIGH (100%), or until apple
   cubes are tender. Drain, reserving 2 tablespoons juices.
4. Combine chicken with mushroom-carrot-apple mixture
   and Roquefort cheese. Set aside.
5. Combine 2 tablespoon juices with vinegar and onion in a
   small microwave-safe custard cup. Microwave for 1 to 1½
   minutes at HIGH (100%), or until boiling. Pour over

chicken mixture and toss. Serve chicken mixture over spinach-lined plates.

Yield: 4 servings

———————— · ❄ · ————————

Nutritional Analysis per Serving (¼ Recipe)

Calories: 210

Carbohydrate: 14 g

Fat: 7 g

Protein: 24 g

Fiber: N/A

Cholesterol: 62 mg

Sodium: 178 mg

Diabetic exchanges:

Fruit: 1

Lean meat: 3.5

Vegetable: Free

HOT CHICKEN AND RED RASPBERRY SALAD

——————— · · · · · ———————

···························· SALAD ····························

4 cups fresh torn spinach or romaine leaves (rinsed, dried, and trimmed)

1 pound boned and skinned chicken breast, cut into bite-size pieces

½ teaspoon Seasoned Salt Substitute #2 (see page 245) or store-bought alternative

1 cup fresh red raspberries, divided

1 cup (3 to 4 ounces) sliced fresh mushrooms

¼ red onion, thinly sliced into rings

¼ cup crumbled Roquefort or bleu cheese (1 ounce)

TIPS
········

To prepare ahead of time, follow steps #1 and #4 in advance; place mushrooms, onion rings, and crumbled Roquefort in a bowl in the refrigerator. Just before serving time, proceed with steps #2, #3, and #5.

For 2 servings, cut ingredients in half. Microwave chicken for 5 to 7 minutes at MEDIUM (50%) in step #2.

· · 216 · ·

1½ to 2 tablespoons vegetable oil or olive oil

2 tablespoons cider vinegar or garlic wine vinegar

3 packets sugar substitute or 2 tablespoons sugar

1 tablespoon grated Parmesan cheese

1 teaspoon dried chives

1. Line 4 salad plates with spinach leaves. Set aside.
2. Salad: Place chicken in a 9- or 10-inch microwave-safe baking dish. Sprinkle with Seasoned Salt Substitute. Add ¼ cup crushed red raspberries and juices. Cover with waxed paper. Microwave for 12 to 14 minutes at MEDIUM (50%), or until chicken is no longer pink, stirring twice. Drain slightly.
3. Mix cooked chicken with mushrooms, onion rings, and Roquefort cheese. Divide among spinach-lined plates.
4. Hot Dressing: Combine oil, vinegar, and sugar substitute in a microwave-safe custard cup or 1-cup glass measure. Microwave for 30 to 40 seconds at HIGH (100%), to heat. Stir in Parmesan cheese and chives.
5. Drizzle dressing over salads. Garnish with remaining raspberries. Serve immediately.

Yield: 4 servings

———— · ❄ · ————

Variation: For Cold Chicken and Red Raspberry Salad, chill microwaved chicken until cool after step #2. Proceed as directed through step #3. Omit hot dressing. Instead, mix ½ cup plain nonfat yogurt, 1 tablespoon skim milk, ¼ cup red raspberries, and dash sugar substitute. Drizzle over salads and garnish with remaining berries.

HAWAIIAN CHICKEN SALAD

· · · · ·

2 cups cooked chicken (see page 280), cooled and cut into bite-size pieces
¾ cup diced celery (1½ stalks)

8-ounce can juice-packed pineapple chunks, drained, reserving ¼-cup juice
¼ cup reduced-calorie mayonnaise
1 head curly leaf lettuce

1. Combine cooled chicken pieces, celery, and pineapple in a large bowl. Set aside.
2. Combine ¼ cup pineapple juice and mayonnaise in a small bowl. Pour over chicken mixture. Toss lightly. Serve chilled on 4 individual plates lined with curly leaf lettuce.

Yield: 4 servings

──────── · ❄ · ────────

TIPS
·······

To lighten the calorie and fat content of this recipe even more, use only 2 tablespoons reduced-calorie mayonnaise (instead of ¼ cup). Add 2 tablespoons plain or pineapple nonfat yogurt with the mayonnaise in step #2.

WALDORF CHICKEN SALAD

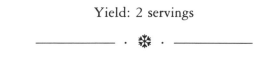

TIPS

Serve Waldorf Chicken Salad on a bed of romaine, curly endive, or other salad greens.

Adjust the sugar substitute to suit your taste. For a sweet salad, use up to ½ packet.

Leaving the apple unpeeled adds color to the salad, but you may peel it, if desired.

1 cup cooked chicken breast (see page 180), cut into cubes

¼ cup chopped celery (½ stalk)

1 cup coarsely chopped Red Delicious apple (see tip at left)

10 large seedless green grapes, cut lengthwise in half, optional

¼ cup plain nonfat yogurt

1 tablespoon reduced-calorie mayonnaise

Dash sugar substitute

Combine chicken breast cubes, celery, apple, and grapes in a 1-quart mixing bowl. Mix remaining ingredients. Pour over chicken mixture and toss to coat.

Yield: 2 servings

Variation: Substitute 1 cup chopped cooked turkey breast for the chicken.

Nutritional Analysis per Serving (½ Recipe)

Calories: 236

Carbohydrate: 16 g

Fat: 6 g

Protein: 28 g

Fiber: N/A

Cholesterol: 78 mg

Sodium: 140 mg

Diabetic exchanges:

Lean meat: 3

Fruit: 1.25

OVEN-ROASTED TURKEY

————— · · · · · —————

10- to 22-pound turkey
2 tablespoons vegetable oil
Dash poultry seasoning

Dash paprika or browning
powder for chicken*

1. Rinse and dry defrosted turkey. Stuff if desired. (If turkey is stuffed: add 1 pound to the weight of the turkey when calculating total cooking time.) Tie the legs together with a string or dental floss. Brush the bird with vegetable oil and sprinkle with seasoning and paprika. Shield the wings and legs (see shielding tips on pages 15–16). Place bird in a plastic cooking bag that has been dusted with 1 tablespoon flour. Tie the bag shut with the plastic tie, string, or dental floss, leaving a ½-inch opening for an air vent. Place bag of turkey breast side down on a microwave roasting rack or in a flat microwave-safe casserole.

2. Calculate total cooking time, allowing 9 to 12 minutes per pound.† Divide time in half. Microwave at HIGH (100%) for 10 minutes. Reduce power to MEDIUM HIGH (70%) and microwave remainder of first half of total time. Remove excess liquid and fat from cooking bag using a bulb baster.

3. Turn turkey breast side up. Microwave at MEDIUM HIGH (70%) for last half of total time or until probe registers 175° F. in the white meat. Let stand 15 to 20 minutes tented with foil or a kitchen towel. Cut open bag and carve.

Yield: 12 to 24 servings

————— · 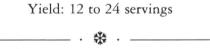 · —————

....
* Use salt-free variety for lowest sodium values, if desired.
† **Compacts:** Follow the same directions using a small (8- to 10-pound) turkey and microwave at HIGH (100%) instead of MEDIUM HIGH (70%) in steps #2 and #3.

When shopping, allow 8 to 12 ounces uncooked bone-in turkey per person.

Before cooking in a microwave oven, always defrost the turkey, remove the giblets and neck, rinse, and pat dry (with a paper towel). To defrost turkey, see general tips for poultry (page 177).

I have cooked up to a 22-pound turkey in a microwave oven. However, 12- to 14-pound turkeys work best.

The pop-out timer that comes with some turkeys will not work properly in microwave ovens. The turkey will be cooked before the timer pops out.

If a cooking bag is not available, place seasoned turkey on a microwave roasting rack or casserole and drape loosely with plastic wrap. Proceed as directed with step #2.

Variations: For Combination method to speed conventional oven baking: To enjoy the browning of your conventional oven and the speed of your microwave, prepare as directed in step #1. Microwave for 1 hour at MEDIUM HIGH (70%), turning over once. Transfer to a conventional oven (preheated to 350° F; bake for 1 to 1½ hours at 350° F.

For Convection Microwave: Prepare as directed in step #1. Low-Mix Bake at 350° (or Combination 2 or Code 2) for 10 to 12 minutes per pound. Let stand as directed in step #3.

Nutritional Analysis per Serving (3 Ounces, Skinned and Deboned)

Calories: 140

Carbohydrate: 0 g

Fat: 4 g

Protein: 26 g

Fiber: N/A

Cholesterol: 59 mg

Sodium: 55 mg

Diabetic exchanges:

    Lean meat: 3.5

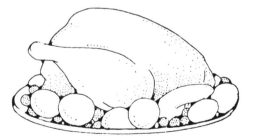

TURKEY BREAST

—————— · · · · · ——————

2½- to 4-pound turkey breast
2 tablespoons vegetable oil or margarine

Poultry seasoning
Paprika or browning powder for chicken*

1. Rinse and dry defrosted turkey breast, brush with oil, and sprinkle liberally with poultry seasoning and paprika or browning powder. Place skin side down on a microwave roasting rack. Cover loosely with plastic wrap or place in plastic cooking bag (see Variation and Tips).
2. Calculate total cooking time, allowing 14 to 16 minutes per pound. Divide time in half. Microwave for 5 minutes at HIGH (100%). Reduce power to MEDIUM (50%) and microwave remainder of first half of time. Remove excess liquid and fat from cooking bag using a bulb baster.
3. Turn skin side up. Microwave for last half of total time at MEDIUM (50%), or until a probe inserted in the meatiest area of the breast registers 175° F. Let stand 10 to 15 minutes tented with foil.

Yield: 6 to 8 servings

—————— · ❄ · ——————

Nutritional Analysis per Serving (3 Ounces, Skinned and Deboned)

Calories: 135
Carbohydrate: 0 g
Fat: 3 g
Protein: 26 g

Fiber: N/A
Cholesterol: 59 mg
Sodium: 63 mg
Diabetic exchanges:
  Lean meat: 3

....
* Use unsalted variety for lowest sodium values, if desired.

TIPS

To defrost turkey, see general tips for poultry (page 177).

Before cooking it in the microwave oven, always defrost the turkey breast, remove excess fat or tail piece, rinse and pat dry with paper towels.

The pop-out timer that comes with some turkey breasts usually will not pop out during the microwaving time.

Microwave-safe plastic cooking bags help ensure even cooking for turkey breasts. Instead of pricking holes in the plastic bag as the bag manufacturer often recommends, leave a ½-inch opening when tying the bag, for the air vent and easy removal of excess fat in step #2.

Serve Turkey Breast garnished with fresh parsley sprigs and sugared grapes (dip small clusters of green grapes first in beaten egg white and then in sugar).

Try serving micro-waved broccoli as a side dish to the Turkey Cutlets. Spoon a bit of lemon sauce over the broccoli too!

TURKEY CUTLETS WITH LEMON SAUCE

· · · · ·

4 turkey breast cutlets (3 ounces each)

2 egg whites, beaten

⅓ cup Seasoned Bread Crumbs (see page 243)

1 teaspoon chicken bouillon granules* dissolved in ½ cup water

1½ tablespoons lemon juice

2 teaspoons cornstarch

1 tablespoon chopped fresh parsley and chives

Lemon slices and parsley to garnish, optional

1. Using a meat mallet or side of a saucer, pound turkey cutlets between two layers of waxed paper until ¼-inch thick. Dip cutlets in egg white and then in Seasoned Bread Crumbs. Place in a 9- or 10-inch flat microwave-safe casserole. Cover loosely with waxed paper.

2. Microwave for 6 to 8 minutes at MEDIUM HIGH (70%), or until turkey is tender and no longer pink. Let stand 3 minutes.

3. Meanwhile, mix bouillon-water, lemon juice, and corn-starch in a 1-cup glass measure until smooth. Microwave for 2 to 3 minutes at HIGH (100%), or until thickened. Stir in parsley. Serve cutlets with lemon sauce, garnished with lemon slices and parsley sprigs, if desired.

Yield: 4 servings

· ❄ ·

Nutritional Analysis per Serving (1 Cutlet)

Calories: 131

Carbohydrate: 6 g

Fat: 2 g

Protein: 21 g

Fiber: N/A

Cholesterol: 20 mg

Sodium: 123 mg

Diabetic exchanges:

Bread: 0.25

Lean meat: 2.5

*Use unsalted variety for lowest sodium values, if desired.

TURKEY PARMESAN

Delicious served over spaghetti squash or whole wheat spaghetti.

16-ounce jar sugar-free
   spaghetti sauce*
2 cups (8 ounces) fresh
   mushrooms, cleaned
   and sliced
1 teaspoon Italian
   seasoning
1 tablespoon chopped
   fresh parsley or 1
   teaspoon dried parsley

4 turkey breast cutlets (3
   ounces each)
Dash browning powder
   for chicken*
1 tablespoon grated
   Parmesan cheese

1. Microwave spaghetti sauce in a covered 2-quart microwave-safe casserole for 4 to 5 minutes at HIGH (100%), or until boiling. Stir in mushrooms, Italian seasoning, and parsley. Place cutlets on top of sauce. Sprinkle with browning powder. Cover loosely with vented plastic wrap or waxed paper.
2. Microwave for 12 to 14 minutes at MEDIUM HIGH (70%), or until turkey is no longer pink, rearranging cutlets halfway through cooking time. Sprinkle with Parmesan cheese. Let stand 3 minutes. Serve ladled with sauce.

Yield: 4 servings

TIPS

For a low-calorie entree try serving Turkey Parmesan over Spaghetti Squash (see page 318). Add a green salad to complete the meal.

*Use unsalted variety for lowest sodium values, if desired.

Variation: Omit mushrooms. Substitute 16-ounce jar sugar-free spaghetti sauce with mushrooms for the plain spaghetti sauce. Proceed as directed.

Nutritional Analysis per Serving (1 Cutlet)	
Calories: 170	Cholesterol: 19 mg
Carbohydrate: 16 g	Sodium: 108 mg
Fat: 1 g	Diabetic exchanges:
Protein: 23 g	Lean meat: 2.5
Fiber: N/A	Vegetable: 2

TURKEY-VEGETABLE STEW

· · · · ·

A nutritious way to use leftover turkey or chicken.

2 tablespoons reduced-
  calorie margarine*
2 stalks (1 cup) celery,
  sliced
½ medium (½ cup) onion,
  chopped
1 large potato, peeled and
  cubed
1½ cups skim milk
2 tablespoons all-purpose
  flour

1 teaspoon chicken
  bouillon granules*
½ teaspoon Seasoned Salt
  Substitute #1 (see page
  244) or store-bought
  alternative
1½ cups cubed cooked
  turkey (see page 222)
10-ounce package frozen
  carrots and peas

TIPS
· · · · · · · ·

Try substituting 1½ cups of any of your favorite fresh or frozen vegetables for the frozen carrots and peas in step #2.

1. Mix margarine, celery, and onion in a 2-quart microwave-safe casserole. Cover with lid or vented plastic wrap. Microwave for 2 to 3 minutes at HIGH (100%), or until onion is tender. Stir in potato. Cover again. Microwave for 5 to 6 minutes at HIGH (100%).
2. Mix milk and flour in a small bowl until smooth. Stir in bouillon granules and Seasoned Salt Substitute. Pour over microwaved vegetables; add turkey and frozen carrots and peas. Stir. Cover again.
3. Microwave for 8 to 9 minutes at HIGH (100%), or until mixture comes to a boil and thickens, stirring twice.

Yield: 4 servings

——— · ❄ · ———

Variation: For Chicken Vegetable Stew, substitute 1½ cups cooked chicken (see page 180) for the cooked turkey. Proceed as directed.

· ·
*Use unsalted variety for lowest sodium values, if desired.

Nutritional Analysis per Serving ($\frac{1}{4}$ Recipe)

Calories: 239

Carbohydrate: 23 g

Fat: 7 g

Protein: 23 g

Fiber: N/A

Cholesterol: 41 mg

Sodium: 275 mg

Diabetic exchanges:

Lean meat: 2

Vegetable: 3.5

Fat: 1

PASTA, RICE, AND CASSEROLES

---   · ❄ ·   ---

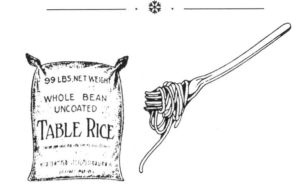

GENERAL TIPS FOR MICROWAVING RICE

- Microwaved rice never scorches or sticks to the pan. Some recipes start with uncooked rice; others specify cooked rice. Always follow the recipe.

- Combine water with rice in a 2-quart microwave-safe casserole. Cover with vented plastic wrap or a tight glass lid. (See the following chart for cooking times.)

GENERAL TIPS FOR MICROWAVING PASTA

- Microwaving pasta does not save much time over the conventional stove-top method, so always use the stove top to cook large batches.

- For small batches (2 cups or less) of noodles or macaroni, microwave water and 1 teaspoon vegetable oil until boiling. Stir in pasta. Cover with vented plastic wrap. (See the following chart for cooking times.)

PASTA AND RICE
MICROWAVING TIME CHART

TYPE/AMOUNT	AMOUNT OF WATER/PROCEDURE	TIME/POWER LEVEL
Speed Cook Elbow macaroni (small) or rotini, 2 cups dry (yields 4 cups cooked)	Mix 1 teaspoon vegetable oil with 4 cups very hot tap water and macaroni in a 2-quart microwave-safe bowl. Cover with vented plastic wrap.	Microwave for 7 to 8 minutes at HIGH (100%), or until tender (al dente), stirring twice. Drain.
Macaroni/Noodles 2 cups dry (7 to 8 ounces = 4 cups cooked)	Microwave 4 cups water (twice as much as pasta) in a 2-quart microwave-safe bowl covered with vented plastic wrap for 8 to 10 minutes at HIGH (100%), or until boiling. Add 1 teaspoon vegetable oil and pasta. Cover again.	Microwave pasta in boiling water for 3 to 4 minutes at HIGH (100%). Let stand covered 8 to 10 minutes. Drain.
White rice 1 cup	Mix 2 cups hot tap water with rice and 1 teaspoon margarine in a 2-quart microwave-safe bowl. Cover with vented plastic wrap.	Microwave 5 minutes at HIGH (100%) and 10 to 14 minutes at MEDIUM (50%). Let stand 5 minutes. Fluff with a fork.
Brown rice or wild rice 1 cup	Mix 2½ cups hot tap water with 1 cup rice and 1 teaspoon margarine in a 2-quart microwave-safe bowl. Cover with vented plastic wrap.	Microwave for 5 to 6 minutes at HIGH (100%) until bubbly. Then microwave 25 to 30 minutes at MEDIUM (50%) or 30 to 35 minutes at DEFROST (30%) until liquid is absorbed. Let stand 5 minutes.
Instant rice 1 cup	Follow directions on package, or mix equal amounts of rice and water with 1 teaspoon margarine in a 2-quart microwave-safe bowl. Cover with vented plastic wrap.	Follow directions on package or microwave 1 cup for 4 to 5 minutes at HIGH (100%). Let stand 5 minutes.

GENERAL TIPS FOR MICROWAVING CASSEROLES

- Often you do *not* have to precook the noodles for lasagna and other casseroles made with pasta. Most are microwaved at HIGH (100%).

- Remember to shield the corners of a square or rectangular pan to prevent overcooking (especially lasagna). If shielding is not recommended in your oven (check your owner's manual), lower the power level to MEDIUM HIGH (70%).

- If you use "no-boil" noodles, cut the cooking time of the lasagna and pasta casseroles by one-half.

LEAN MACARONI AND CHEESE
· · · · ·

1 cup elbow macaroni or rotini, uncooked
2½ cups hot water
1 teaspoon vegetable oil
1½ tablespoons reduced-calorie margarine*
2 tablespoons all-purpose flour
1½ cups skim milk

½ teaspoon Seasoned Salt Substitute #2 (see page 245) or store-bought alternative
1 cup (4 ounces) grated reduced-fat, mild cheddar cheese* (reserve 2 tablespoons for garnish)
¼ cup Dry Bread Crumbs (see page 53), optional

1. Combine macaroni, water, and oil in a 2-quart micro-wave-safe bowl. Microwave uncovered for 6 to 8 minutes at HIGH (100%), or until pasta is tender, stirring twice. Drain and rinse in cold water. Set aside in colander.

. . . .
*Use unsalted or reduced-sodium variety for lowest sodium values, if desired.

2. Microwave margarine in same bowl for 30 to 40 seconds at HIGH (100%), or until melted. Mix flour and milk until blended; stir into melted margarine. Add Seasoned Salt Substitute and blend well. Microwave for 3 to 4 minutes at HIGH (100%), or until thickened, stirring twice. Add cheese, stirring to help it melt.

3. Mix macaroni into thickened milk-cheese mixture. Sprinkle with bread crumbs. Microwave for 3 to 4 minutes at MEDIUM HIGH (70%), or until heated through. Serve garnished with sprinkle of grated cheese, if desired.

Yield: 6 servings

· ❄ ·

Nutritional Analysis per Serving (⅙ Recipe)

Calories: 180

Carbohydrate: 22 g

Fat: 6 g

Protein: 11 g

Fiber: N/A

Cholesterol: 1 mg

Sodium: 98 mg

Diabetic exchanges:

Bread: 1.25

Lean meat: 0.75

Skim milk: 0.25

Fat: 0.5

CHEESE-STUFFED MANICOTTI

· · · · ·

···························· SAUCE ····························

½ pound ground turkey, crumbled

½ medium onion (½ cup), chopped

2 cloves garlic, minced

3 cups (24 ounces) sugar-free spaghetti sauce*

1 teaspoon Italian seasoning

½ packet sugar substitute (equivalent to 1 teaspoon sugar), optional

*Use no-salt-added variety for lowest sodium values, if desired.

TIPS
········

I like to make manicotti the night before so all I have to do is pop it in the microwave oven when I get home from work. To make Cheese Stuffed Manicotti 4 to 24 hours in advance, omit microwaving sauce for 8 to 9 minutes at HIGH (100%) in step #2. Proceed with step #3 and step #4. Cover with vented plastic wrap. Refrigerate 4 to 24 hours. Forty-five minutes before serving time, microwave for 15 minutes at HIGH (100%). Turn over each manicotti; ladle again with sauce. Microwave 16 to 18 minutes at MEDIUM HIGH (70%). Let stand 10 to 15 minutes.

Omitting the turkey in the sauce will save 40 calories per manicotti: Microwave onion and garlic with 2 teaspoons water in the bowl for 2 to 3 minutes at HIGH (100%). Proceed with step #2.

.... FILLING ....

1 cup (8 ounces) low-fat cottage cheese, slightly drained
2 large egg whites, beaten
1 cup shredded part-skim mozzarella cheese

2 tablespoons grated Parmesan cheese
1 tablespoon chopped fresh parsley or 1 teaspoon dried parsley

.... PASTA ....

8 uncooked manicotti (noodles) (4–5 ounces)

1. Sauce: Combine turkey, onion, and garlic in a 2-quart microwave-safe bowl. Cover with vented plastic wrap. Microwave for 3 to 4 minutes at HIGH (100%), or until turkey is no longer pink, stirring once. Drain off grease.
2. Stir spaghetti sauce, Italian seasoning, and sugar substitute (optional) into the cooked turkey mixture. Cover again. Microwave for 8 to 9 minutes at HIGH (100%), or until hot and bubbly.
3. Filling: Meanwhile, mix filling ingredients in a bowl and fill uncooked manicotti using a fish fork, spoon, or knife.
4. Ladle 1/3 of the sauce into a 2-quart or 10-inch flat microwave-safe casserole. Place filled manicotti in the sauce. Ladle remainder of sauce over manicotti. Cover with vented plastic wrap.
5. Microwave for 10 minutes at HIGH (100%). Using tongs, turn each manicotti over. Ladle with sauce. Cover again. Microwave for 16 to 18 minutes at MEDIUM HIGH (70%). Let stand for 15 minutes to complete cooking.

Yield: 8 stuffed manicotti

———————— · ❄ · ————————

Variations: Substitute 1/2 pound ground veal or lean ground beef for the ground turkey.

For Manicotti Florentine, omit turkey from sauce. Microwave onion and garlic with 2 teaspoons water in a 2-quart microwave-safe bowl for 2 to 3 minutes at HIGH (100%). Proceed with step #2. Add 10-ounce package frozen chopped spinach, cooked and drained, to the filling in step #3. To cook spinach, microwave in the box (remove foil wrapper if necessary), on a paper plate or paper towel—lined plate for 5½ to 6½ minutes at HIGH (100%). Drain and pat dry with paper towels to absorb excess liquid. Proceed as directed.

Nutritional Analysis per serving (1 Manicotti)

Calories: 219
Carbohydrate: 22 g
Fat: 6 g
Protein: 18 g
Fiber: N/A
Cholesterol: 26 mg

Sodium: 264 mg
Diabetic exchanges:
  Bread: 1
  Lean meat: 2
  Vegetable: 1

If Italian seasoning is not available, substitute 1 teaspoon dried oregano and ½ teaspoon dried basil.

Place cottage cheese in a colander to drain off excess liquid.

To enhance serving size and attractiveness of rolls, cut each roll into 3 sections on individual serving plates.

Six "No-Boil Lasagna Noodles" may be substituted for the cooked lasagna noodles. Soak noodles for 5 minutes in hot tap water. (Use a large, 10- × 15-inch bar pan for soaking and do not overlap the noodles.)

Spinach and step #1 may be omitted, if desired.

You'll never miss the meat!

10-ounce package frozen chopped spinach
1 clove garlic, minced, or ¼ teaspoon garlic powder
½ medium onion (½ cup), chopped
½ cup (2 ounces) chopped mushrooms, optional
1 tablespoon water
2 large egg whites, slightly beaten
¼ teaspoon ground nutmeg
1 teaspoon Italian seasoning

1 cup (8 ounces) low-fat cottage cheese, lightly drained
¼ cup (1 ounce) shredded part-skim mozzarella cheese
¼ cup grated Parmesan cheese, divided
6 curly-edged 3 × 12-inch lasagna noodles, cooked according to package directions and drained
16-ounce jar sugar-free spaghetti sauce*
Parsley sprigs or chopped fresh parsley to garnish, optional

1. Place spinach package on a paper plate or paper towel–lined glass pie plate. (If box is wrapped in foil, remove wrapping.) Microwave for 6 to 7 minutes at HIGH (100%), or until spinach is cooked. Discard packaging and drain spinach well, using strainer. Pat with paper towels to absorb any liquid. Set aside.
2. Combine garlic, onion, mushrooms, and water in a 1-quart microwave-safe bowl or casserole. Cover with lid or vented plastic wrap. Microwave for 3 to 3½ minutes at HIGH (100%), or until tender.
3. Stir egg whites, nutmeg, Italian seasoning, cottage cheese, mozzarella cheese, 2 tablespoons Parmesan cheese, and spinach into cooked onion mixture; blend well. Spread ⅙ spinach mixture on each lasagna noodle. Start-

* Use no-salt-added variety for lowest sodium values, if desired.

ing with narrow end, carefully roll up each noodle, enclosing filling (like a jelly roll). Place seam side down in a 10-inch microwave-safe casserole that has been sprayed with vegetable coating.

4. Pour spaghetti sauce over rolls. Cover lightly with waxed paper. Microwave for 12 to 14 minutes at MEDIUM HIGH (70%), or until rolls are hot, gently rearranging rolls halfway through cooking time. Serve garnished with remaining 2 tablespoons Parmesan cheese and parsley sprigs, if desired.

Yield: 6 servings

——————— · ❄ · ———————

Variation: For Meat-Filled Lasagna Rolls, add ½ pound crumbled ground veal or ground turkey or lean ground beef with the onion in step #2. Microwave for 5 to 5½ minutes in step #2 (instead of 3 to 3½ minutes); drain grease. Proceed as directed.

Nutritional Analysis per Serving (1 Roll)

Calories: 218   Sodium: 339 mg
Carbohydrate: 31 g   Diabetic exchanges:
Fat: 3 g   Bread: 1
Protein: 16 g   Lean Meat: 1
Fiber: N/A   Vegetable: 3
Cholesterol: 9 mg

To defrost frozen shrimp, microwave 6 ounces for 2 to 3 minutes at DEFROST (30%), stirring once to separate clumps of shrimp. Rinse under cold water for 1 minute to complete thawing.

COLORFUL SHRIMP, PASTA, AND VEGETABLE SALAD

1 cup rotini or elbow
   macaroni, uncooked
4 cups hot tap water
1 teaspoon vegetable oil
16-ounce package frozen
   mixed vegetables
   (broccoli, carrots, and
   onions)
1 small zucchini or
   cucumber, peeled and
   chopped
1 medium tomato,
   chopped

1 large bunch (3 cups)
   romaine or spinach
   leaves, cleaned and torn
   into bite-size pieces
6 ounces frozen cooked
   shrimp, thawed
½ cup (4 ounces) plain
   nonfat yogurt
¼ cup reduced-calorie
   mayonnaise
1 tablespoon reduced-
   calorie ranch-style
   dressing mix, dry
Dash sugar substitute

1. Combine rotini, hot water, and oil in a 2-quart microwave-safe bowl. Microwave uncovered for 7 to 8 minutes at HIGH (100%), or until pasta is tender, stirring twice. Drain, rinse, and set aside in colander.
2. Cut a large "X" in the plastic bag of vegetables. Place cut side down in the same 2-quart casserole. Microwave for 6 to 7 minutes at HIGH (100%), or until tender-crisp. Using tongs, remove plastic bag. Drain and cool.
3. Combine rotini, cooked vegetables, fresh vegetables, and shrimp in a large salad bowl.
4. Mix yogurt, mayonnaise, dressing mix, and sugar substitute in a 1-cup measure. Pour over pasta and vegetables. Toss.

Yield: 6 servings

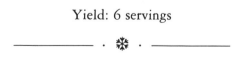

Variation: One-fourth cup bottled reduced-calorie ranch-style dressing may be substituted for the dry dressing mix and the mayonnaise.

Nutritional Analysis per Serving (⅙ Recipe)

Calories: 195
Carbohydrate: 26 g
Fat: 4 g
Protein: 13 g
Fiber: N/A
Cholesterol: 0 mg

Sodium: 372 mg
Diabetic exchanges:
  Bread: 1
  Lean meat: 1.5
  Vegetable: 1.5

SALMON (OR TUNA) AND MACARONI SALAD

——————— · · · · · ———————

2 cups rotini or elbow
  macaroni, uncooked
1 teaspoon vegetable oil
4 cups hot tap water
15 ounces canned salmon,
  drained, or 2 cans (6½
  ounces) water-packed
  tuna, drained
½ cup (1 stalk) diagonally
  sliced celery
½ cup (½ carrot) shredded
  carrots

½ packet sugar substitute
  (equivalent to 1
  teaspoon sugar) or 1
  teaspoon fructose
¼ cup reduced-calorie
  mayonnaise
½ cup plain nonfat yogurt
Sliced radishes,
  cucumbers, tomato, and
  iceberg lettuce to
  garnish, optional

1. Combine rotini, oil, and water in a 2-quart microwave-safe bowl. Microwave uncovered for 10 to 11 minutes at HIGH (100%), or until tender. Drain and rinse in cold water. Add salmon, celery, and carrots. Set aside.
2. In a small bowl, mix sugar substitute, mayonnaise, and yogurt until blended. Toss with salmon mixture. Serve garnished with sliced radishes, cucumbers and tomato, on a bed of lettuce if desired.

Yield: 6 servings

——————— · ❄ · ———————

TIPS
....

To prepare this salad ahead of time, mix sugar substitute, mayonnaise, and yogurt and refrigerate separately. Toss with salmon mixture just before serving time.

Variation: For Salmon Salad, substitute 1 head lettuce or romaine leaves, torn into bite-size pieces, for the pasta. Omit step #1. Proceed as directed. (Save 135 calories per serving.)

Nutritional Analysis per 1-Cup Serving

Calories: 248

Carbohydrate: 28 g

Fat: 8 g

Protein: 17 g

Fiber: N/A

Cholesterol: 27 mg

Sodium: 306 mg

Diabetic exchanges:

Bread: 1.5

Lean meat: 2

Fat: 0.5

TIPS

Two teaspoons dried parsley can be substituted for the 2 tablespoons chopped fresh parsley.

Two cups chicken broth can be substituted for the chicken bouillon granules and water.

PARSLEYED WHITE OR WILD RICE

· · · · ·

½ cup (1 stalk) chopped celery

½ cup (½ medium onion) chopped onion

2 teaspoons reduced-calorie margarine*

4-ounce can sliced mushrooms and juice*

3 teaspoons chicken bouillon granules, * dissolved in 2 cups hot water

1 cup raw long-grain white rice or mixed white and wild rice

2 tablespoons chopped fresh parsley

1. Combine celery, onion, and margarine in a 2-quart microwave-safe casserole. Cover with lid or vented plastic wrap. Microwave for 2½ to 3½ minutes at HIGH (100%), or until vegetables are tender.
2. Stir in mushrooms, bouillon-water, and rice. Cover again. Microwave for 5 to 6 minutes at HIGH (100%), or until boiling. Stir. Cover again. Microwave for 12 to 16 minutes at MEDIUM (50%), or until liquid is absorbed.

....

*Use no-salt-added variety for lowest sodium values, if desired.

3. Stir in parsley and fluff rice with a fork. Cover again. Let stand 5 minutes.

Yield: 6 servings

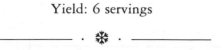

Variation: For Parsleyed Brown Rice, substitute brown rice for white rice and increase water by ½ cup. Proceed as directed, except microwave for 30 to 35 minutes at DEFROST (30%) instead of the 12 to 16 minutes at MEDIUM (50%) in step #2.

Nutritional Analysis per ½-Cup Serving

Calories: 139
Carbohydrate: 29 g
Fat: 1 g
Protein: 3 g
Fiber: N/A

Cholesterol: Trace
Sodium: 17 mg
Diabetic exchanges:
    Bread: 0.5

SAUCES,
SEASONINGS,
DRESSINGS, AND
PRESERVES

· ❆ ·

GENERAL TIPS FOR MICROWAVING SAUCES

- Use a 2-quart microwave-safe bowl for microwaving gravies and sauces.

- If sauces contain yogurt, cheese, or sour cream, microwave them at **MEDIUM HIGH** (70%) to prevent curdling. Otherwise, microwave sauces or gravies at HIGH (100%).

- Microwaved gravies and sauces never scorch (as stove-top ones can), which is a real plus.

- Stir gravies and sauces often. Leave a wooden or microwave-safe plastic spoon in the bowl while microwaving to make stirring easy.

- Flour and cornstarch work well as thickening agents for sauces when microwaving. However, cornstarch has fewer calories for its thickening power! For every 2 tablespoons of flour (60 calories), use 1 tablespoon of cornstarch (28 calories).

- Reheat 1 cup of sauce by stirring, covering with vented plastic wrap, and microwaving for 2 to 2½ minutes at HIGH (100%). If the sauce is made with milk, use MEDIUM HIGH (70%) instead.

- For sauces or gravies made with reduced-calorie margarine and cornstarch (or flour), first stir the cornstarch into the liquid (such as milk, water, or wine) until smooth. Then add the smooth liquid to the melted margarine. (Stirring the dry cornstarch or flour into melted margarine first will give lumpy results.)

- Yogurt can be substituted for sour cream in sauces. Mix 1 teaspoon cornstarch into every 1 cup of yogurt to help stabilize it when heated. Never bring a sauce made with yogurt to a full boil.

GENERAL TIPS ON MICROWAVING JAMS AND JELLIES

- Jellies and jams made in the microwave taste great and are very time-saving. If you have never tried to make homemade jam, please try it! You will be surprised at how easy it is. What a wonderful way to treat your family and friends.

- Always make only the amounts of jellies or jams listed in these recipes. Always use at least a 2-quart microwave-safe bowl. If you don't—in either case—the jam will boil over onto your microwave oven, which can be very messy.

- Use only conventional preservation methods for sealing jars and freezing foods. If jelly or jam will be eaten within a few weeks, it can just be refrigerated.

- If paraffin is used in sealing jam, do not microwave the paraffin.

- Powdered pectin has always worked best for me in these recipes.

- A 2-quart glass measuring bowl works great for making jellies because the handle will remain cool.

- Lemon juice is an important ingredient in causing your jam to gel. It helps balance the acid and sugar and the fruit and pectin. Do not eliminate it—it will not add a sour flavor.

GENERAL TIPS ON DEHYDRATING FRUITS AND VEGETABLES

- Use fresh or canned fruit or vegetables. (Use paper towels to remove excess liquid from canned produce.)

- Slice fruits or vegetables in uniform, ¼-inch-thick pieces.

- Place on a roasting rack. Do not overlap.

- Microwave 1 rack full for 12 to 15 minutes at MEDIUM (50%), or until limp and moist. Transfer to a wire rack and let stand overnight. (Try apples, bananas, pineapple, apricots, carrots, potatoes, or mushrooms).

TIPS
. . . .

Try doubling or tripling this recipe and freezing in a 2-quart freezer bag. Use as needed.

SEASONED BREAD CRUMBS OR SEASONED CORNFLAKES

——————— • • • • • ———————

The perfect light coating for fish, chicken, veal, or pork.

1 cup dry high-fiber
   reduced-calorie bread
   crumbs, finely crumbled
   (see page 54), or crushed
   cornflakes
1½ teaspoons paprika
½ teaspoon garlic powder
½ teaspoon onion powder
½ teaspoon Seasoned Salt
   Substitute # 1 (see page
   244) or store-bought
   alternative

¼ teaspoon ground white
   or black pepper
1 tablespoon parsley flakes
4 tablespoons grated
   Parmesan cheese
1 tablespoon vegetable oil

Combine bread crumbs, seasonings, and cheese in a small bowl. Toss oil into mixture until blended. Refrigerate and use as needed for 4 to 5 days, or freeze up to 6 months.

Yield: 1½ cups or eight 3-tablespoon servings

——————— · ❄ · ———————

Nutritional Analysis per 3-Tablespoon Serving

Calories: 52

Carbohydrate: 4 g

Fat: 3 g

Protein: 2 g

Fiber: N/A

Cholesterol: 2 mg

Sodium: 106 mg

Diabetic exchanges:

Bread: 0.25

Lean meat: 0.25

Fat: 0.5

SEASONED SALT SUBSTITUTE #1

——————— · · · · · ———————

An interesting blend of flavors. There's no salt in this recipe.

2 tablespoons dry mustard

1 tablespoon garlic powder

2 tablespoons onion powder

2 teaspoons ground white pepper

2 teaspoons crushed basil leaves

1 teaspoon ground turmeric, optional

1 teaspoon ground thyme

1 tablespoon paprika

Combine all the ingredients in a small bowl. Pour into a salt shaker and use in place of salt or seasoned salt.

Yield: ½ cup

——————— · ❄ · ———————

I set a shaker full of this recipe on my table at all times. My friends and family say it adds a nice flavor to almost any food.

Store-bought seasoned salt substitute that can be used in place of this recipe include Vegit and Mrs. Dash Original Blend.

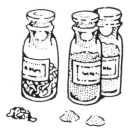

Nutritional Analysis per ¼-Teaspoon Serving

Calories: 2
Carbohydrate: Trace
Fat: Trace
Protein: Trace
Fiber: N/A

Cholesterol: 0 mg
Sodium: Trace
Diabetic exchanges: Free

TIPS
....

In place of this recipe, you may use Salt-It Seasoned Salt Substitute, or any brand of Seasoned Salt if sodium content is not important to your diet.

When making Seasoned Salt recipe #2, be sure to use a salt substitute that is approved by your doctor and measures the same as salt (ounce for ounce). If you prefer not to use a plain salt substitute in a recipe, use the seasoned salt substitute #1 (see page 244).

SEASONED SALT SUBSTITUTE #2
· · · · ·

Similar to seasoned salt, without the sodium.

1 teaspoon dry mustard
½ teaspoon garlic powder
½ teaspoon onion powder
½ teaspoon white pepper
2 teaspoons paprika
1 teaspoon ground allspice

1 teaspoon ground coriander
3 tablespoons salt substitute
Dash each dill weed and ground nutmeg, optional

Combine all the ingredients in a small bowl. Pour into a salt shaker and use in place of salt or seasoned salt.

Yield: ⅓ cup

————— · ❄ · —————

Nutritional Analysis per ¼-Teaspoon Serving

Calories: Less than 1
Carbohydrate: Trace
Fat: Trace
Protein: Trace

Fiber: N/A
Cholesterol: 0 mg
Sodium: 1 mg
Diabetic exchanges: Free

SOUR CREAM SUBSTITUTE

· · · · ·

Replaces sour cream!

1½ cups (12 ounces) low-
  fat cottage cheese
1½ tablespoons lemon
  juice

3 tablespoons skim milk or
  buttermilk

Using a food processor or blender, process all ingredients
until smooth. Refrigerate.

Yield: 1½ cups

· ❄ ·

T I P S

Serve this sauce cold
as a topping for any
vegetable or salad. If
you choose to add it to
a hot casserole, stir it in
the last minute of cook-
ing time and serve im-
mediately.

Nutritional Analysis per 2-Tablespoon Serving

Calories: 27
Carbohydrate: 1 g
Fat: 1 g
Protein: 4 g
Fiber: N/A

Cholesterol: 2 mg
Sodium: 116 mg
Diabetic exchanges:
  Skim milk: 0.33

BLEU CHEESE DRESSING OR DIP

· · · · ·

Delicious over salads or with vegetables.

1½ cups (12 ounces) low-
  fat cottage cheese
2½ tablespoons lemon
  juice
5 tablespoons water or
  skim milk

Dash each garlic powder
  and onion powder
½ cup (2 ounces)
  crumbled bleu cheese,
  divided

· · 246 · ·

Using a food processor or blender, process until smooth all ingredients except for 2 tablespoons crumbled bleu cheese. Stir in the remaining bleu cheese. Refrigerate.

Yield: 2 cups

———————— · ❄ · ————————

Nutritional Analysis per 2-Tablespoon Serving

Calories: 29   Cholesterol: 4 mg
Carbohydrate: 1 g   Sodium: 130 mg
Fat: 1 g   Diabetic exchanges: Skim
Protein: 3 g   milk: 0.33
Fiber: N/A

TIPS
· · · · · · · ·

Anytime a recipe calls for a medium white sauce, substitute this slim variation without the cheese. Three-fourths cup of standard medium white sauce has 305 calories—more than twice as many as this version.

A standard cheese sauce has about four times the number of calories in this slim sauce.

SLIM CHEESE SAUCE
WITH WHITE SAUCE VARIATION

———————— · · · · · ————————

2 teaspoons reduced-
    calorie margarine*
2 teaspoons all-purpose
    flour
½ cup skim milk
Dash Worcestershire sauce
Dash dry mustard

Dash Seasoned Salt
    Substitute #2 (see page
    245) or store-bought
    alternative
½ cup (2 ounces) grated
    reduced-fat cheddar
    cheese*

1. Microwave margarine in a 2-cup glass measure for 20 to 30 seconds at HIGH (100%), or until melted. Mix flour and milk in another measuring cup until thoroughly blended; stir into melted margarine. Add Worcestershire sauce, mustard, and Seasoned Salt Substitute; blend well.
2. Microwave for 1 to 2 minutes at HIGH (100%), or until

· ·
*Use unsalted or reduced-sodium variety for lowest sodium values, if desired.

thickened, stirring once. Add cheese, stirring to help it melt. Serve immediately. Or, to reheat, microwave for 30 to 40 seconds at MEDIUM HIGH (70%).

Yield: ¾ cup

——————— · ❊ · ———————

Variations: For Cheese Sauce without flour and margarine, mix ⅓ cup instant nonfat milk solids with the ½ cup skim milk, Worcestershire sauce, mustard, and salt substitute. Blend thoroughly. Proceed as directed in step #2.

For White Sauce, omit cheese. Proceed as directed.

Nutritional Analysis per 3-Tablespoon Serving

Calories: 64	Cholesterol: Trace
Carbohydrate: 3 g	Sodium: 58 mg
Fat: 3 g	Diabetic exchanges:
Protein: 5 g	Lean meat: 0.75
Fiber: N/A	Low-fat milk: 0.25

LIGHT GRAVY OR WINE SAUCE FOR CHICKEN OR VEGETABLES

——————— · · · · · ———————

1 teaspoon chicken
   bouillon granules, *
   dissolved in ½ cup hot
   water
1 tablespoon white wine
   or white grape juice

2 teaspoons cornstarch or
   1½ tablespoons all-
   purpose flour
⅓ cup skim milk
¼ teaspoon onion powder
Dash ground nutmeg

1. Microwave bouillon, water, and wine for 40 to 60 seconds at HIGH (100%), or until boiling. Mix cornstarch and

....
*Use unsalted variety for lowest sodium values, if desired.

This sauce is especially tasty served over any of the chicken and vegetable recipes or turkey or pork recipes.

milk in a small bowl until smooth. Stir into hot broth. Add onion powder and nutmeg.
2. Microwave for 1 to 2 minutes at HIGH (100%), or until bubbly. Serve over poultry or vegetables.

Yield: 1 cup sauce

——————— · ❄ · ———————

Nutritional Analysis per ¼-Cup Serving

Calories: 19
Carbohydrate: 3 g
Fat: Trace
Protein: Trace
Fiber: N/A

Cholesterol: Trace
Sodium: 12 mg
Diabetic exchanges: Bread: 0.25

TIPS
········

Use this recipe anytime you need 16 ounces of tomato sauce or spaghetti sauce. Covered and refrigerated, it will keep for about four days.

LEAN BLENDER TOMATO SAUCE

——————— · · · · · ———————

16-ounce can whole tomatoes* or stewed tomatoes,* lightly drained
1 teaspoon dried parsley flakes
½ teaspoon dried basil
2 teaspoons vegetable or olive oil

1 tablespoon chopped onion
1 clove garlic, peeled
Dash oregano
Dash Seasoned Salt Substitute #2 (see page 245) or store-bought alternative

1. Using food processor or blender, combine all ingredients until smooth.
2. Pour into a 2-quart microwave-safe bowl. Microwave uncovered for 5 minutes at HIGH (100%). Stir. Microwave

....
*Use no-salt-added variety for lowest sodium values, if desired.

again for 5 to 10 minutes at MEDIUM (50%), or until sauce thickens.

Yield: 2 cups

———————— · ❄ · ————————

Variation: If blender or food processor is not available, use crushed tomatoes, minced garlic, and minced onion. Omit step #1. Mix thoroughly and proceed as directed in step #2.

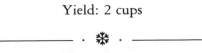

Nutritional Analysis per ½-Cup Serving	
Calories: 47	Cholesterol: 0 mg
Carbohydrate: 7 g	Sodium: 14 mg
Fat: 2 g	Diabetic exchanges:
Protein: 1 g	Vegetable: 1
Fiber: N/A	Fat: 0.5

FAVORITE VINAIGRETTE DRESSING

————— · · · · · —————

¼ cup garlic-wine vinegar
2 tablespoons water
2 tablespoons vegetable or
  olive oil

1 tablespoon Dijon
  mustard
Dash hot sauce, optional
Dash sugar substitute,
  optional

Combine all ingredients in a bowl (or jar with lid). Mix (or shake) until thoroughly blended.

Yield: ½ cup (8 servings)

———————— · ❄ · ————————

TIPS
....
Serve this light and delicious Vinaigrette over vegetables or cooked chicken and romaine salad.

TIPS
·······

Mock Ranch Dressing will keep for up to one week in the refrigerator. It can be substituted in any recipe that calls for ranch dressing.

MOCK RANCH DRESSING

· · · · ·

¾ cup plus 2 tablespoons (7 ounces) plain nonfat yogurt

2 tablespoons reduced-calorie mayonnaise

1 teaspoon dried chopped onion

½ teaspoon dried parsley

¼ teaspoon each onion powder, garlic powder, dill weed, and paprika

¼ teaspoon Seasoned Salt Substitute #2 (page 245) or store-bought alternative

Using a food processor or electric mixer and bowl, combine all ingredients until thoroughly blended. Refrigerate at least 2 hours.

Yield: 1 cup

——————— · ❄ · ———————

DIET FRENCH DRESSING

· · · · ·

1½ tablespoons cornstarch
1 cup water
¼ cup garlic-wine vinegar
   or cider vinegar
½ teaspoon dry mustard
½ teaspoon paprika

Dash each garlic powder,
   onion powder, and salt
   substitute
3 packets sugar substitute
   (equivalent to 6
   teaspoons sugar)

Mix cornstarch and water in a 2-cup glass measure until thoroughly blended. Microwave for 1½ to 2 minutes at HIGH (100%), or until thickened. Cool slightly. Stir in remaining ingredients. Refrigerate.

Yield: 1 cup

· ❄ ·

Nutritional Analysis per 2-Tablespoon Serving

Calories: 9
Carbohydrate: 2 g
Fat: Trace
Protein: Trace

Fiber: N/A
Cholesterol: 0
Sodium: Trace
Diabetic exchanges: Free

TIPS
· · · · · · · ·

Diet French Dressing will keep for two weeks in your refrigerator. Try using it as the dressing for Lean Taco Salad (see page 172).

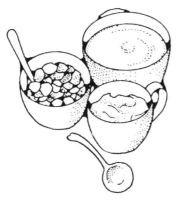

Start with washed fruit. Approximately 1 pound or 2½ cups before crushing will yield 1 cup crushed fruit.

SUGARLESS STRAWBERRY JAM

Less than 1 calorie per teaspoon—made with sugar substitute. Great for dieters and diabetics!

1 cup cleaned crushed strawberries or other berries

¾ cup sugar-free strawberry soda

2 packets sugar substitute (equivalent to 4 teaspoons sugar)

3-ounce package wild strawberry sugar-free gelatin, dry

1. Combine crushed fruit and strawberry soda in a 2-quart microwave-safe bowl. Microwave for 3 to 4 minutes at HIGH (100%), or until mixture comes to a boil and boils for 1 minute.
2. Stir in sugar substitute and gelatin. Blend until gelatin is dissolved.
3. Pour into hot sterilized jars. Cover lightly and let stand at room temperature to cool. Cover tightly and store in the refrigerator.

Yield: 1¼ cups

Nutritional Analysis per 2-Teaspoon Serving

Calories: 1

Carbohydrate: Trace

Fat: 0 g

Protein: 0 g

Fiber: 0 g

Cholesterol: 0 mg

Sodium: 0 mg

Diabetic exchanges: Free

RED RASPBERRY JAM

· · · · ·

1 tablespoon plus 1
   teaspoon quick tapioca
1 envelope (7 grams)
   unflavored gelatin, dry
½ cup unsweetened white
   grape juice concentrate,
   thawed

1 teaspoon lemon juice
2 cups cleaned crushed red
   raspberries

TIPS
·········

Be sure to read General Tips on Microwaving Jams and Jellies (page 242) before proceeding with this recipe.

1. Sprinkle tapioca and gelatin over the grape juice concentrate in a 2-quart microwave-safe bowl. Let stand 3 minutes. Stir until blended. Microwave for 1 to 1½ minutes at HIGH (100%), or until gelatin is dissolved, stirring once.
2. Stir in lemon juice and mashed berries. Microwave for 6 to 8 minutes at HIGH (100%), or until mixture comes to a boil and boils for 2 minutes.
3. Pour into hot sterilized jars. Cover lightly and let stand at room temperature to cool. Cover tightly and store in the refrigerator.

Yield: 2½ cups

——————— · ❄ · ———————

Nutritional Analysis per 1-Tablespoon Serving

Calories: 9	Fiber: N/A
Carbohydrate: 2 g	Cholesterol: 0 mg
Fat: Trace	Sodium: Trace
Protein: Trace	Diabetic exchanges: Free

Blender Apricot or Peach Butter does not need to be sealed as long as it is refrigerated and used within two weeks. See General Tips on Microwaving Jams and Jellies (page 242).

BLENDER APRICOT OR PEACH BUTTER

——————— · · · · · ———————

A tasty spread for bread or English muffins!

1 envelope (7 grams) unflavored gelatin, dry
½ cup apple juice
16-ounce can sliced apricots or peaches, packed in juice

¼ teaspoon ground cinnamon
Dash ground nutmeg
Dash sugar substitute, optional

1. Sprinkle gelatin over apple juice in a 2-cup glass measure. Let stand 1 minute. Stir until blended. Microwave for 40 to 60 seconds at HIGH (100%), or until very hot. Stir until gelatin is dissolved.
2. Using a food processor or blender, process apricots and juice, cinnamon, nutmeg, and gelatin-apple juice until smooth. Pour into hot sterilized jars. Cover lightly and let stand at room temperature to cool. Cover tightly and store in refrigerator.

Yield: 2½ cups

——————— · ❄ · ———————

Nutritional Analysis per 1-Tablespoon Serving

Calories: 3
Carbohydrate: 1 g
Fat: Trace
Protein: 6 g

Fiber: N/A
Cholesterol: 0 mg
Sodium: 14 mg
Diabetic exchanges: Free

DRIED CITRUS PEEL

———— · · · · · ————

Great to have on hand for garnishing and flavoring.

2 large citrus fruits
    (lemons, oranges,
    tangerines, or limes)

1. Finely grate the zest from the fruits. Spread zest on 2 layers of paper toweling. Microwave for 1 to 1½ minutes at HIGH (100%).
2. Stir and rearrange. Microwave again for 1 to 2 minutes at HIGH (100%), or until slightly dried. Let stand and cool until dry. Store in an airtight container. For flavoring, substitute 1 teaspoon dried peel for 1 tablespoon fresh peel in any recipe.

Nutritional Analysis per Serving

Calories: Cannot be calculated; no digestibility value for peel	Protein: Trace
	Fiber: N/A
	Cholesterol: 0 mg
	Sodium: 0 mg
Carbohydrate: 2 g	Diabetic exchanges: Free
Fat: 0 g	

Next time a recipe calls for 2 tablespoons of lemon peel, you can be prepared with the equivalent: 2 teaspoons dried peel!

Use a small sharp hand grater or "zester" to grate only the outer layer of the citrus peel, called the zest. Avoid using any of the bitter white pith beneath the zest.

SOUPS AND SANDWICHES

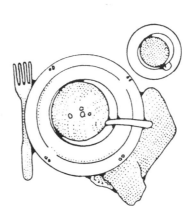

GENERAL TIPS FOR MICROWAVING SOUPS

- Soups cook quickly in the microwave.

- Microwave soups made with raw vegetables at HIGH (100%).

- Reduce liquids (used in conventionally cooked homemade soups) by one-quarter because very little evaporation occurs when microwaving.

- To prevent vegetables and meats from toughening, add salt, if you must, after microwaving soups. Most recipes in this book use a Seasoned Salt Substitute that can be added at any time.

- If using less tender cuts of meat in soups, microwave for half the time at HIGH (100%) and half the time at MEDIUM (50%) to tenderize the meats.

- Reheat leftover soup by stirring, covering with vented plastic wrap, and microwaving for 2 to 3 minutes at MEDIUM

HIGH (70%). (If you forget to stir, the air bubbles may cause an eruption.)

• Microwave a 10½-ounce can of soup, mixed with 1 can of liquid, in a 1-quart casserole for 5 to 6 minutes at MEDIUM HIGH (70%). (Use HIGH [100%] for a compact microwave.)

• Always cover soups with vented plastic wrap or a tight-fitting lid when microwaving.

GENERAL TIPS FOR MICROWAVING DRIED BEANS, PEAS, OR LENTILS FOR SOUPS

• Always soak dried beans or peas before cooking. Add 6 cups water and ¼ teaspoon baking soda (to soften beans) to 2 cups dried beans. Soak overnight for best results, or speed-soak.

• To speed-soak dried beans or peas, wash and sort 1 pound dried beans. Place beans in a 4- or 5-quart microwave-safe casserole and add hot water to cover. Cover with lid or plastic wrap and microwave for 8 to 10 minutes at HIGH (100%), or until boiling. Let stand at least 1 hour.

• To microwave soaked beans, peas, or dried lentils, see microwaving time chart (page 332).

GENERAL TIPS FOR MICROWAVING SANDWICHES

• Always use toasted breads as a base for sandwiches to prevent sogginess.

• Microwave sandwiches with filling at MEDIUM HIGH (70%) to prevent overcooking.

• To heat hard-taco shells, microwave six shells on two layers of paper towels for 30 to 45 seconds at HIGH (100%). For two shells, microwave 10 seconds at HIGH (100%).

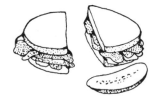

- To heat flour tortillas, wrap and roll each in two damp paper towels. Microwave six at a time for 45 to 50 seconds at HIGH (100%). Microwave two at a time for 20 to 30 seconds at HIGH (100%).

LOW-CALORIE "CREAM SOUP" MIX OR CREAM SOUP SUBSTITUTE

——————— • • • • • ———————

The perfect low-salt soup substitute when a casserole recipe calls for cream of mushroom, cream of chicken, or cream of celery soup.

¾ cup cornstarch
2 cups instant nonfat dry milk solids
¼ cup chicken bouillon granules*
½ teaspoon dried thyme

½ teaspoon dried basil
1 teaspoon onion powder or 2 tablespoons dried onion flakes
¼ teaspoon ground pepper

1. For dry Cream Soup Mix, mix all the ingredients together and store in an airtight container. (Yield: dry mix to make equivalent of nine 10½-ounce cans of cream soup.)
2. For Cream Soup Substitute (the equivalent to 10½-ounce can cream soup), blend ⅓ cup of the dry cream soup mix and 1¼ cups cold water in a 1-quart microwave-safe casserole until smooth. Microwave for 2½ to 3 minutes at HIGH (100%), or until thickened, stirring twice. Cool and use as a substitute for cream of chicken, cream of mushroom, or cream of celery soup in any casserole recipe.

Variation: Add ½ cup sliced Cooked (Poached) Chicken (see page 180), or ½ cup sliced cooked mushrooms, or ½ cup sliced cooked celery to the thickened soup for special flavor-

. . . .
*Use no-salt-added variety for lowest sodium values, if desired.

TIPS
. . . .

If a recipe in this book calls for 10½ ounces of cream soup, make up the soup as directed in step #2. If a recipe calls for cream soup mix, use the dry mix made in step #1.

Salt substitute to taste can be added to thickened soup, if desired.

One 10½-ounce can store-bought cream of mushroom soup contains 330 calories, 2,370 milligrams of sodium, and almost 24 grams fat. This recipe contains only 126 calories, 86 milligrams of sodium, and 1 gram fat, yet tastes almost the same. What a difference!

ing. To cook fresh mushrooms or celery, microwave ½ cup sliced vegetables in a custard cup, covered with vented plastic wrap, for 1½ to 2½ minutes at HIGH (100%), or until tender.

Nutritional Analysis per ⅓ Cup Dry or Equivalent to 1 10½-Ounce Can

Calories: 126
Carbohydrate: 22 g
Fat: 1 g
Protein: 5 g
Fiber: N/A

Cholesterol: 6 mg
Sodium: 86 mg
Diabetic exchanges:
  Skim milk: 1
  Bread: 0.25

QUICK "CREAM" OF MUSHROOM SOUP FOR TWO

· · · · ·

1 teaspoon reduced-calorie margarine*
2 cups (8 ounces) fresh mushrooms, cleaned and sliced

2 tablespoons chopped green onion, optional
⅓ cup Low-Calorie "Cream Soup" Mix, dry (see page 259)
1¾ cups water

1. Combine margarine, mushrooms, and chopped onion in a 1-quart microwave-safe casserole. Cover with waxed paper. Microwave for 3 to 4 minutes at HIGH (100%), or until vegetables are tender, stirring once. Set aside.
2. Combine dry soup mix and water in a small bowl until blended. Stir into mushrooms. Microwave for 3½ to 4 minutes at HIGH (100%), or until thickened, stirring twice.

Yield: 2 servings

———— · ❄ · ————

*Use unsalted variety for lowest sodium values, if desired.

TIPS
....

Mushrooms are high in potassium and niacin yet boast only 20 calories per cup of sliced or chopped pieces.

Choose mushrooms that are clean, white, and well shaped. Avoid any with deep dark spots.

Variation: For Quick "Cream" of Spinach Soup, omit step #1. Microwave 10-ounce box of frozen spinach on a paper plate for 5 to 6 minutes at HIGH (100%). (If package is wrapped in foil paper, remove foil before microwaving.) Empty cooked spinach into a 1-quart microwave-safe casserole and proceed with step #2.

Nutritional Analysis per 1-Cup Serving Soup

Calories: 95

Carbohydrate: 15 g

Fat: 2 g

Protein: 5 g

Fiber: N/A

Cholesterol: 3 mg

Sodium: 56 mg

Diabetic exchanges:

Bread: 0.25

Vegetable: 2

Fat: 0.25

TIPS
....

Seasoned Salt Substitute or Mrs. Dash Original can be added to the thickened soup, to taste, if additional seasoning is desired.

Canned cream of tomato soup has over 700 mg *more* sodium per serving than this homemade recipe has.

QUICK "CREAM" OF TOMATO SOUP FOR TWO

⅓ cup Low-Calorie "Cream Soup" Mix, dry (see page 259)

1¾ cups tomato juice*
Dash dried parsley to garnish, optional

Mix dry soup mix and tomato juice in a 1-quart microwave-safe casserole until blended. Microwave for 3½ to 4 minutes at HIGH (100%), or until thickened, stirring twice. Garnish with parsley if desired.

Yield: 2 servings

....
*Use unsalted variety for lowest sodium values, if desired.

LITE ASPARAGUS SOUP

2 tablespoons chopped
  onion
1 pound fresh asparagus,
  cleaned, tough ends and
  scales on spears
  removed, cut up
1¾ cups hot water,
  divided

2 teaspoons chicken
  bouillon granules*
½ teaspoon butter
  flavoring
Fresh minced parsley to
  garnish, optional

1. Combine onion, asparagus, and 1 cup hot water in a flat
   2-quart microwave-safe casserole. Cover with lid or vented
   plastic wrap. Microwave for 7 to 8 minutes at HIGH
   (100%), or until tender.
2. Mix remaining ¾ cup hot water, bouillon granules, and
   butter flavoring into asparagus. Transfer to a food processor or blender and process until smooth. Return to casserole. Microwave for 2 to 3 minutes at HIGH (100%) to
   heat through. Serve garnished with fresh minced parsley,
   if desired.

Yield: 4 servings

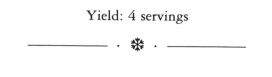

*Use unsalted variety for lowest sodium values, if desired.

Asparagus is at its peak
growing season and
most readily available
from March through
June.

Select firm, rich green
spears with pointed
compact tips that have
not flowered.

At only 3 calories per
stalk, asparagus is a
good source of vitamins
A and C as well as
niacin and potassium.
Asparagus also has a
natural diuretic effect.

Nutritional Analysis per ¾-Cup Serving

Calories: 29	Fiber: N/A
Carbohydrate: 4 g	Cholesterol: 1 mg
Fat: 1 g	Sodium: 6 mg
Protein: 2 g	Diabetic exchanges:
	Vegetable: 1

TIPS

Kidney beans add not only protein to your diet, but also dietary fiber, which has been linked to lower blood cholesterol and lower rates of heart disease.

For a smoother chili, blend tomatoes and tomato sauce (see variation) in a blender until desired consistency, then stir into meat in step #2.

CHILI CON CARNE

· · · · ·

1 pound ground turkey, veal, or lean ground beef, crumbled

1 medium onion (1 cup), chopped

1 clove garlic, minced, or ½ teaspoon garlic powder

3 16-ounce cans sliced stewed tomatoes, * undrained

½ teaspoon ground cumin

2 to 3 teaspoons chili powder

2 15½-ounce cans kidney beans, drained and rinsed with hot water

1. Combine ground meat, onion, and garlic in a 2-quart microwave-safe casserole. Cover with paper towel. Microwave 4 to 5 minutes at HIGH (100%), or until meat is no longer pink, stirring twice. Drain well.
2. Stir in remaining ingredients. Cover with casserole lid.
3. Microwave for 15 to 20 minutes at MEDIUM (50%), stirring once. Ladle into bowls and serve.

Yield: 8 servings

· ❄ ·

* Use no-salt-added variety for lowest sodium values, if desired.

Variations: For a thicker chili, add 8-ounce can tomato sauce with beans in step #2.

To lower the calorie content, substitute two 8-ounce cans sliced mushrooms, drained, for the kidney beans in step #2.

Nutritional Analysis per 1-Cup Serving

Calories: 239

Carbohydrate: 31 g

Fat: 5 g

Protein: 18 g

Fiber: 3 g

Cholesterol: 31 mg

Sodium: 103 mg

Diabetic exchanges:

  Bread: 1.5

  Lean meat: 2

  Vegetable: 1

BLENDER CUCUMBER SOUP

This doesn't require the microwave, but it's one of my favorite recipes to serve as an appetizer preceding any microwaved entree.

2 cups (16 ounces) plain low-fat yogurt

½ medium onion, cut up into chunks

2 teaspoons olive oil

2 teaspoons white vinegar

1½ teaspoons dried mint leaves

½ teaspoon dried dill weed

½ teaspoon Salt Substitute #2 (see page 245) or store-bought alternative

1 medium cucumber, peeled, seeded, and shredded

Chopped fresh parsley to garnish

1. Place all ingredients except cucumber and parsley in a food processor or blender. Process until smooth.
2. Stir in shredded cucumber. Cover and refrigerate. Serve

For your next special get-together, instead of serving the traditional green salad, try this wonderful summer appetizer.

very cold with an ice cube in the center of each bowl and garnish with chopped fresh parsley.

Yield: 4 servings

———————— · ❄ · ————————

Nutritional Analysis per ½-Cup Serving

Calories: 86

Carbohydrate: 11 g

Fat: 3 g

Protein: 6 g

Fiber: N/A

Cholesterol: 2 mg

Sodium: 93 mg

Diabetic Exchanges:

Vegetable: 1

Skim milk: 0.5

Fat: 0.5

T I P S

Instead of using evaporated skim milk, you can substitute 1¾ cups skim milk blended with 2 tablespoons cornstarch.

NEW ENGLAND CLAM CHOWDER
———— · · · · · ————

2 tablespoons water

2 teaspoons reduced-calorie margarine,*

½ medium onion (½ cup), chopped

1 stalk celery (½ cup), chopped

1 large potato (1½ cups), peeled and grated

13-ounce can evaporated skim milk

7-ounce can minced clams with liquid

4-ounce can mushroom pieces with liquid

Fresh snipped parsley to garnish, optional

1. Combine water, margarine (optional), onion, celery, and grated potato in a 3-quart microwave-safe casserole. Cover with lid or vented plastic wrap. Microwave for 7 to 9 minutes at HIGH (100%), or until vegetables are tender.
2. Stir in remaining ingredients except parsley. Cover. Mi-

....
*Use unsalted variety for lowest sodium values, if desired.

crowave for 7 to 8 minutes at MEDIUM HIGH (70%) until heated through and thickened, stirring once. Serve garnished with parsley, if desired.

Yield: 6 servings

———————— · ❄ · ————————

Variation: Two thin slices of cooked and crumbled bacon can be added in step #2. (To cook bacon, microwave bacon wrapped in two paper towels for 2 to 2½ minutes at HIGH (100%). Crumble bacon.

Nutritional Analysis per ¾-Cup Serving

Calories: 115
Carbohydrate: 17 g
Fat: 1 g
Protein: 9 g
Fiber: N/A

Cholesterol: 23 mg
Sodium: 111 mg
Diabetic exchanges:
  Lean meat: 0.5
  Vegetable: 2.5
  Skim milk: 0.25

"CREAM" OF BROCCOLI SOUP

——————— · · · · · ———————

2 teaspoons reduced-
  calorie margarine*
1 clove garlic, minced
¾ cup chopped onion
1 large potato, peeled and
  grated (to equal 1½
  cups)
1 pound fresh or frozen
  broccoli, thawed and
  cut into ½-inch pieces

2 cups hot water
1 tablespoon chicken
  bouillon granules*
2 tablespoons chopped
  fresh parsley or 1
  teaspoon dried parsley
1 cup low-fat or skim milk

....
*Use unsalted variety for lowest sodium values, if desired.

Broccoli is one of the vitamin A—rich foods that have been found to offer protection against cancer of the esophagus, lung, and stomach when eaten regularly.

1. In a 3-quart microwave-safe casserole, combine margarine, garlic, and onion. Cover with lid or vented plastic wrap. Microwave for 2 to 3 minutes at HIGH (100%). Stir in potato and broccoli. Cover again. Microwave for 7 to 9 minutes at HIGH (100%), or until vegetables are tender. Cool slightly.
2. In a small bowl, combine water and bouillon granules until dissolved. Mix into vegetables. Purée mixture in a food processor or blender, doing small batches at a time, if necessary.
3. Return puréed vegetables to casserole and stir in parsley and milk. Microwave for 6 to 7 minutes at HIGH (100%), or until heated through and thickened.

Yield: 6 servings

———————— · ❄ · ————————

Variations: For Broccoli Yogurt Soup, substitute 1 cup (8 ounces) plain low-fat yogurt for the milk in step #3. Microwave for 6 to 8 minutes at MEDIUM HIGH (70%) instead of HIGH (100%) in step #3.

For Creamy Broccoli Soup, omit potato in step #1. Dissolve 1 tablespoon flour in ¼ cup cold water. Decrease hot water to 1¼ cups in step #2. Mix flour-water with hot water and bouillon granules; blend with vegetables as directed in step #2. Substitute 13-ounce can evaporated skim milk for the 1 cup low-fat milk. Proceed as directed in step #3.

Nutritional Analysis per 1-Cup Serving

Calories: 97
Carbohydrate: 16 g
Fat: 1 g
Protein: 6 g
Fiber: N/A

Cholesterol: 1 mg
Sodium: 56 mg
Diabetic exchanges:
  Bread: 0.25
  Vegetable: 2
  Skim milk: 0.25

OLD-FASHIONED CABBAGE SOUP

1 medium head cabbage,
   shredded (to equal 5
   cups)
1 medium potato, peeled
   and thinly sliced
1 large onion, thinly sliced
   and separated in rings
1 cup water

½ teaspoon dried dill
   weed
¼ teaspoon caraway seeds
⅛ teaspoon ground pepper
2 cups skim milk
¼ cup (2 ounces) plain
   nonfat yogurt

1. Combine cabbage, potato, onion, and water in a 3-quart microwave-safe casserole. Cover with lid or vented plastic wrap. Microwave for 12 to 15 minutes at HIGH (100%), or until vegetables are tender.
2. Transfer to a food processor or blender. Add dill weed, caraway seeds, pepper, skim milk, and yogurt. Process until blended.
3. Return to casserole. Cover again. Microwave for 8 to 10 minutes at MEDIUM HIGH (70%) to heat through. Serve garnished with additional dill weed, if desired.

Yield: 6 servings

Nutritional Analysis per 1-Cup Serving

Calories: 79
Carbohydrate: 14 g
Fat: Trace
Protein: 5 g
Fiber: N/A

Cholesterol: 1 mg
Sodium: 65 mg
Diabetic exchanges:
   Bread: 0.25
   Vegetable: 0.5
   Skim milk: 0.5

TIPS

Cabbage is especially low in calories (only 18 per cup, shredded), yet high in vitamin C and potassium. Cabbage and other cruciferous vegetables may help reduce the risk of some kinds of cancer.

Cauliflower is another cruciferous vegetable that may help reduce the risk of some kinds of cancer when eaten regularly.

Choose a head of cauliflower that has fresh-looking green leaves attached and no brown spots.

"CREAM" OF CAULIFLOWER SOUP

WITH "CREAM" OF ASPARAGUS SOUP VARIATION

——————— · · · · · ———————

½ medium onion (¼ cup), minced

1 stalk celery (⅓ cup), minced

2 teaspoons margarine,* optional

3½ cups (1¼ pounds) fresh or frozen cauliflowerets

2 teaspoons chicken bouillon granules,* dissolved in 1¼ cups hot water

1 cup evaporated skim milk

1 cup (4 ounces) shredded reduced-fat cheddar cheese*

Parsley to garnish, optional

1. Combine onion, celery, and margarine in a 2-quart microwave-safe bowl. Microwave covered with a lid or vented plastic wrap for 4 to 5 minutes at HIGH (100%), or until vegetables are tender.
2. Stir in cauliflowerets. Cover. Microwave again for 7 to 8 minutes at HIGH (100%), or until tender.
3. Using a food processor, blender, or sieve, process cooked mixture until puréed.
4. Pour mixture back into bowl. Stir in remaining ingredients. Cover. Microwave for 5 to 7 minutes at MEDIUM HIGH (70%), or until heated, stirring twice. Ladle into soup bowls and garnish each serving with a sprig of parsley or a teaspoon of chopped parsley, if desired.

Yield: 4 servings

——————— · ❄ · ———————

* Use unsalted or reduced-sodium variety for lowest sodium values, if desired.

Variation: For "Cream" of Asparagus Soup, substitute 1 pound fresh asparagus, trimmed and chopped, for the califlower. (See Tip for preparing asparagus, page 293).

Nutritional Analysis per 1-Cup Serving

Calories: 177

Carbohydrate: 16 g

Fat: 6 g

Protein: 14 g

Fiber: N/A

Cholesterol: 3 mg

Sodium: 172 mg

Diabetic exchanges:

Lean meat: 1

Vegetable: 2.5

Skim milk: 0.5

Fat: 0.5

"CREAM" OF MUSHROOM SOUP

4 cups (1 pound) fresh mushrooms

¼ medium onion (¼ cup), finely chopped

4 cups low-sodium chicken broth (canned or made from bouillon)

13-ounce can evaporated skim milk

½ cup cold water

2 tablespoons cornstarch

Seasoned Salt Substitute #2 (see page 245) or store-bought alternative, to taste

Chopped fresh parsley, to garnish

T I P S
Use about 3 10¾-ounce cans low-sodium chicken broth plus ¼ cup water to equal 4 cups broth—or make your own (see Variation, page 181).

1. Remove and chop mushroom stems. Reserve caps. Combine stems, onion, and broth in a 2-quart microwave-safe casserole. Cover with vented plastic wrap or lid. Microwave for 9 to 10 minutes at HIGH (100%).

2. Using a slotted spoon, remove mushroom stems and discard. Slowly stir in milk.

3. In a small bowl, mix cold water and cornstarch until smooth. Stir into soup. Cover again. Microwave for 6 to 8 minutes at MEDIUM HIGH (70%), until soup just starts to boil, stirring twice to make smooth.

4. Thinly slice reserved mushroom caps and stir into soup. Cover again. Microwave for 1 to 2 minutes at MEDIUM HIGH (70%). Let stand covered for 5 minutes before serving. Add Seasoned Salt Substitute to taste, and serve garnished with fresh parsley.

Yield: 6 servings

---- · ❄ · ----

Nutritional Analysis per 1-Cup Serving

Calories: 97

Carbohydrate: 15 g

Fat: 1 g

Protein: 6 g

Fiber: N/A

Cholesterol: 3 mg

Sodium: 95 mg

Diabetic exchanges:

Vegetable: 2.0

Skim milk: 0.5

TIPS
....

Baking soda is added to the soaking water to help soften the beans.

For a thicker soup, simply remove one cup of beans, peas, or lentils after microwaving in step #2; mash; and stir back into soup during standing time.

Oops, you forgot to soak the beans last night! To speed-soak the beans, cover with 6 cups of hot water and

NAVY BEAN SOUP
WITH SPLIT PEA OR LENTIL SOUP VARIATION

---- · · · · · ----

1 pound (2 cups) dried navy beans, washed, sorted, and soaked overnight in a microwave-safe 5-quart casserole with 6 cups water mixed with ¼ teaspoon baking soda

7 cups hot water

½ cup each chopped onion, chopped carrot, chopped celery

3 teaspoons instant chicken bouillon granules*

1 cup (4 ounces) chopped 95% lean boiled ham, optional

1½ teaspoons dried thyme

1 bay leaf

....

*Use unsalted variety for lowest sodium values, if desired.

1. Drain beans and add 7 cups hot water, vegetables, and bouillon granules. Cover with lid or vented plastic wrap and microwave for 15 minutes at HIGH (100%), or until boiling.
2. Stir in ham, thyme, and bay leaf. Cover again. Microwave for 90 to 95 minutes at MEDIUM (50%), or until beans are tender, stirring twice. Let stand covered 10 minutes. Discard bay leaf and serve immediately.

Yield: 10 servings

———————— · ❄ · ————————

Variation: For Split Pea or Lentil Soup, substitute split peas or lentils for the beans. Soak peas as directed, but do not soak lentils. (Lentils do not need soaking.) Add peeled potato (cut into ¼-inch cubes) with the chopped vegetables in step #1. Proceed as directed in step #1. In step #2, microwave for only 60 to 70 minutes at MEDIUM (50%), or until tender. Let stand covered, for 10 minutes.

¼ teaspoon baking soda. Microwave for 8 to 10 minutes at HIGH (100%), or until water boils. Let stand one hour. Proceed with step #1.

If you want a more liquid soup, add up to 1 cup more water after microwaving 60 minutes in step #2.

Nutritional Analysis per ¾-Cup Navy Bean Soup

Calories: 184	Cholesterol: 6 mg
Carbohydrate: 30 g	Sodium: 115 mg
Fat: 1 g	Diabetic exchanges:
Protein: 12 g	Bread: 1.5
Fiber: 3 g	Lean meat: 0.75
	Vegetable: 1.5

TIPS
....

Egg Drop Soup makes
a delicious first course
to many chicken din-
ners (see pages 144
and 207).

EGG DROP SOUP

· · · · ·

10¾-ounce can chicken
  broth*
½ teaspoon garlic powder
1 teaspoon reduced-
  sodium soy sauce
½ cup (2 ounces) fresh
  mushrooms, sliced
4 cups hot water

2 teaspoons chicken
  bouillon granules*
½ cup Egg Substitute
  (see page 91) or Egg
  Beaters or 2 large eggs,
  beaten
Fresh chopped parsley to
  garnish, optional

1. Mix chicken broth, garlic powder, soy sauce, mushrooms, hot water, and bouillon granules in a 3-quart microwave-safe casserole. Cover with lid or vented plastic wrap. Microwave for 10 to 11 minutes at HIGH (100%), or until boiling.
2. Gradually pour Egg Substitute into heated broth, stirring constantly. Cover again. Let stand 5 minutes. Sprinkle with chopped parsley, if desired.

Yield: 8 servings

· ❄ ·

Variation: Add 2 green onions, thinly sliced, with the mushrooms in step #1, if desired.

Nutritional Analysis per ¾-Cup Serving

Calories: 36
Carbohydrate: 1 g
Fat: 2 g
Protein: 2 g
Fiber: N/A
Cholesterol: Trace

Sodium: 48 mg
Diabetic exchanges:
  Lean meat: 0.25
  Vegetable: 0.25
  Fat: 0.25

....

*Use unsalted variety for lowest sodium values, if desired.

GAZPACHO

· · · · ·

½ medium onion (½ cup), chopped

½ medium green bell pepper (½ cup), chopped

1 clove garlic, minced

1 small cucumber, peeled, seeded, and cut into chunks

6 cups (48 ounces) fresh chopped tomatoes or canned tomatoes*

¼ teaspoon ground black pepper

Dash ground cumin, optional

3 tablespoons olive oil

3 tablespoons wine or garlic-wine vinegar

2 cups tomato juice*

1. Microwave onion, green pepper, and garlic in a 2-cup glass measure, covered with vented plastic wrap, for 3 to 3½ minutes at HIGH (100%).
2. Using a blender or food processor, process microwaved vegetables and remaining ingredients except for tomato juice until puréed. Stir in tomato juice. Transfer to a covered container or glass jars and refrigerate until serving time. Serve cold.

Yield: 7 to 8 servings

· ❄ ·

Variation: For 3½ cups, cut ingredients in half. Microwave for 2 minutes at HIGH in step #1. Proceed as directed.

Nutritional Analysis per 1-Cup Serving	
Calories: 116	Cholesterol: 0 mg
Carbohydrate: 17 g	Sodium: 130 mg
Fat: 5 g	Diabetic exchanges:
Protein: 3 g	Vegetable: 3.25
Fiber: N/A	Fat: 1

*Use no-salt-added variety for lowest sodium values, if desired.

Choose tomatoes that are bright red, smooth, plump, and firm.

Gazpacho, the Spanish garden-fresh soup, is the perfect appetizer for a summer meal. Always serve chilled. Garnish with additional chopped cucumber, tomato, onions, or parsley and croutons, if desired.

Gazpacho will keep in your refrigerator for about two weeks.

The flour is optional, but it does help thicken the soup.

FRENCH ONION SOUP

· · · · ·

4 teaspoons reduced-calorie margarine*

2 medium onions, thinly sliced and separated into rings

2 teaspoons all-purpose flour, optional

½ teaspoon garlic powder

2 10¾-ounce cans beef broth,* undiluted

½ teaspoon Worcestershire sauce

2 slices reduced-calorie high-fiber whole wheat bread without crusts, toasted

¼ cup (1 ounce) shredded mozzarella cheese

1 tablespoon grated Parmesan cheese

1. Combine margarine and onion in a 2-quart casserole. Cover with lid or vented plastic wrap. Microwave for 9 to 10 minutes at HIGH (100%), or until onion is tender, stirring once.

2. Mix flour and garlic powder into onions until blended. Stir in beef broth and Worcestershire sauce. Cover again. Microwave for 7 to 8 minutes at HIGH (100%), or until slightly thickened and boiling, stirring twice.

3. Pour soup into 4 individual casseroles or serving bowls. Top each with ½ slice toasted bread, 1 tablespoon mozzarella cheese, and a sprinkle of Parmesan cheese. Microwave 4 bowls for 2 to 2½ minutes at HIGH (100%), or until cheese melts, rotating bowls once after 1 minute for even cooking. (Microwave 1 bowl for 30 to 40 seconds at HIGH [100%].) Serve immediately.

Yield: 4 servings

———— · ❄ · ————

....
*Use unsalted variety for lowest sodium values, if desired.

TRIM BLENDER VICHYSSOISE
("CREAM" OF POTATO SOUP)

3 large white potatoes, peeled and cut into ½-inch cubes (1½ pounds, or about 4 cups)
1 stalk celery, diced
½ cup diced green or yellow onion
10¾-ounce canned chicken broth,* or 1¼ cups homemade chicken broth (see page 181)
¼ teaspoon dried thyme
¼ teaspoon crushed rosemary
Dash ground cumin, optional
13-ounce can evaporated skim milk, or 1¼ cups skim milk
Salt Substitute or salt and pepper to taste, optional
2 tablespoons minced fresh chives or parsley to garnish

1. Combine potatoes, celery, onion, and chicken broth in a deep 2-quart microwave-safe casserole. Cover with lid or vented plastic wrap. Microwave for 12 to 15 minutes at HIGH (100%), or until vegetables are tender.
2. Process vegetables, chicken broth, thyme, rosemary, cumin, and milk in a food processor, blender, or sieve until smooth or slightly chunky. Return mixture to casserole dish.

....
* Use reduced-sodium variety for lowest sodium values, if desired.

TIPS

Vichyssoise is the traditional French potato and onion (or leek) soup that is served cold as an appetizer.

You may want to adjust the amount of skim milk according to desired thickness.

3. Microwave covered for 5 to 6 minutes at HIGH (100%), or until thickened, stirring once. Sprinkle with salt substitute and minced chives, if desired. Serve hot as a soup, or chill and serve as an appetizer.

Yield: 6 servings

—————— · ❄ · ——————

Variation: For Potato and Broccoli Vichyssoise, substitute ½ large bunch of broccoli (about 3 stalks, sliced ½ inch thick) for one of the potatoes in step #1. Proceed as directed above.

Nutritional Analysis per 1-Cup Serving

Calories: 158

Carbohydrate: 30 g

Fat: 1 g

Protein: 8 g

Fiber: N/A

Cholesterol: 3 mg

Sodium: 109 mg

Diabetic exchanges:

Bread: 1.5

Skim milk: 0.5

TIPS
....

Always refrigerate cooked deboned turkey and the turkey carcass within two hours of cooking time to prevent bacterial growth. Lean and Trim Turkey Soup can be made from a refrigerated carcass within four days of the time it was cooked.

LEAN AND TRIM TURKEY SOUP

—————— · · · · · ——————

Serve this one on the days following Thanksgiving.

1 meaty turkey carcass (if carcass has little meat, add 1½ cups diced turkey)

2 quarts water

Dash ground nutmeg

¼ teaspoon ground pepper

2 bay leaves

2 teaspoons chicken bouillon granules*

1 large (1¼ cups) onion, chopped

1½ cups (3 stalks) thinly sliced celery

2 cups (3 to 4 carrots) thinly sliced carrots

Dash salt substitute* or salt, optional

....

*Use unsalted variety for lowest sodium-values, if desired.

1. Combine all ingredients except the salt substitute in a 4-quart microwave-safe casserole. Cover with lid or vented plastic wrap; microwave for 30 minutes at HIGH (100%). Stir and microwave again for 15 minutes at MEDIUM (50%).
2. Cool to room temperature. Refrigerate until fat hardens. Strain soup; discard fat and bay leaf, but reserve broth and vegetables. Remove carcass and separate meat from bones. Discard bones.
3. Cut meat into bite-size pieces. Stir meat and vegetables into remaining broth. Microwave covered for 7 to 8 minutes at HIGH (100%), or until soup is heated. Add salt substitute to taste, if desired. Serve immediately.

Yield: 8 servings

———————— · ❄ · ————————

Variations: For Lean and Trim Chicken Soup, substitute chicken carcass for turkey carcass.

For Lean and Trim Turkey or Chicken Broth, strain soup, reserving broth in step #2; discard remainder.

For Lean and Trim Turkey Rice Soup, add ⅔ cup uncooked rice with meat and vegetables in step #3. Increase microwaving time to 10 minutes in step #3.

Nutritional Analysis per 1¼-Cup Serving

Calories: 77
Carbohydrate: 6 g
Fat: 2 g
Protein: 9 g
Fiber: N/A

Cholesterol: 20 mg
Sodium: 46 mg
Diabetic exchanges:
  Lean meat: 1
  Vegetable: 1

QUICK VEGETABLE SOUP

2 teaspoons beef-flavored bouillon granules* (or 2 bouillon cubes)

2 cups hot water

1 cup frozen vegetables (carrots, broccoli, and onions, or your choice)

½ teaspoon dried parsley

This is a quick way to enjoy a warm nutritious soup on a cold winter day. Add a turkey sandwich on whole wheat bread to complete your luncheon menu.

Use any mixture of frozen vegetables you have handy—be sure to adjust the calorie value if you add other starchy vegetables, such as corn or potatoes.

1. Combine bouillon granules and water in a 1-quart microwave-safe bowl until blended. Stir in vegetables and parsley.
2. Microwave for 5 to 6 minutes at HIGH (100%), or until heated.

Yield: 2 servings

Nutritional Analysis per 1½-cup Serving

Calories: 45

Carbohydrate: 8 g

Fat: 1 g

Protein: 2 g

Fiber: N/A

Cholesterol: 1 mg

Sodium: 20 mg

Diabetic exchanges:

Vegetable: 1.5

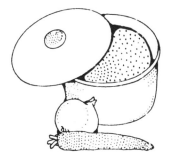

* Use unsalted variety for lowest sodium values, if desired.

CHILLED WATERCRESS SOUP

—————— · · · · · ——————

1 medium onion (1½ cups), thinly sliced

2 tablespoons reduced-calorie margarine*

3 teaspoons chicken bouillon granules*

2½ cups hot water

8 ounces watercress, thick stems removed

1 medium (1 cup) potato, peeled and cubed

3 cups (24 ounces) plain nonfat yogurt, divided

1. Microwave onion and margarine in a covered 2-quart microwave-safe bowl or casserole for 5 to 6 minutes at HIGH (100%), stirring once.
2. Dissolve bouillon in the hot water. Add to onions with the potato and blend. Cover again. Microwave for 8 to 10 minutes at HIGH (100%), or until potato is tender.
3. Stir in watercress and microwave 2 minutes at HIGH (100%). Let stand 15 minutes to cool.
4. Transfer soup to a food processor or blender and process to purée. Stir in 2 cups yogurt. Transfer to a storage dish. Chill. Serve in small soup bowls as an appetizer, topping each with a dollop of yogurt.

Yield: 6 to 8 servings

—————— · ❄ · ——————

Nutritional Analysis per 1-Cup Serving

Calories: 69

Carbohydrate: 10 g

Fat: 1 g

Protein: 5 g

Fiber: N/A

Cholesterol: 2 mg

Sodium: 79 mg

Diabetic exchanges:

Vegetable: 2

Skim milk: 0.25

---

* Use unsalted variety for lowest sodium values, if desired.

Watercress is rich in vitamins A and C, yet has only 7 calories per cup. It also is a natural diuretic.

Choose watercress leaves that are a healthy green in color and crisp. Avoid bunches of leaves with yellow tinges or a slimy texture.

At home, unwrap watercress, rinse under cold water, and dry thoroughly using paper towels. Use immediately or refrigerate, wrapped in plastic wrap, up to three days.

This delicious, low-cal-
orie sandwich is high in
fiber and vitamins. If
pitas are not available,
place filling between
two slices of reduced-
calorie   high-fiber
wheat bread instead.

SAUCY CHEDDAR-AND VEGETABLE-STUFFED PITAS

· · · · ·

1 clove garlic, minced
½ medium onion (½ cup),
   chopped
1 cup (3 to 4 ounces) fresh
   mushrooms, sliced
2 teaspoons olive oil
1 teaspoon Italian
   seasoning
1 cup alfalfa sprouts
1 small cucumber, seeded
   and chopped (1 cup)

½ cup (4 ounces) plain
   nonfat yogurt
½ cup (2 ounces) shredded
   reduced-fat cheddar
   cheese*
1 small tomato, seeded
   and chopped
2 whole wheat pita
   rounds, cut in half to
   form 4 pockets
2 teaspoons reduced-
   calorie ranch-style
   dressing mix, dry

1. Combine garlic, onion, mushrooms, and olive oil in a
   small microwave-safe dish. Microwave for 2 to 2½ minutes at HIGH (100%), or until tender. Stir in remaining
   ingredients except pitas.
2. Open pita pockets. Spoon ¼ mixture into each pocket.
   Arrange all on serving plate. Microwave for 2 to 3 minutes at MEDIUM HIGH (70%), or until warm and
   cheese is melted.

Yield: 4 servings

——————— · ❄ · ———————

Nutritional Analysis per ½-Pita Serving

Calories: 184
Carbohydrate: 24 g
Fat: 6 g
Protein: 10 g
Fiber: N/A
Cholesterol: 1 mg

Sodium: 252 mg
Diabetic exchanges:
   Bread: 1
   Lean meat: 0.5
   Vegetable: 1.5
   Fat: 1

···

*Use reduced-sodium variety for lowest sodium values, if desired.

FAST PITA PIZZA SLICES

· · · · ·

2 tablespoons tomato
   sauce *
Dash garlic powder
Dash oregano or Italian
   seasoning
6-inch whole wheat pita
   pocket, split and toasted

2 tablespoons diced onion
1 tablespoon chopped
   green bell pepper or
   mushrooms (optional)
2 tablespoons shredded
   mozzarella cheese

1. Mix tomato sauce, garlic powder, and oregano in a small
   dish. Spread one tablespoon sauce over each toasted pita
   half. Top each with half the onion, green pepper or mushrooms, and cheese.
2. Place both halves on a paper plate that has been lined
   with 2 paper towels. Microwave for 45 to 50 seconds at
   MEDIUM HIGH (70%),† or until cheese melts. Enjoy!

Yield: 2 servings

——————— · ❄ · ———————

Variations: For 4 slices, double recipe. Microwave 4 pita
halves for 1½ to 2 minutes at MEDIUM HIGH (70%) in
step #2.

For Pizza Bagelettes, substitute 2 miniature bagels
(bagelettes), split in half, for the pita pocket. Divide sauce
and vegetables among 4 bagelette halves. Microwave for 35
to 45 seconds at MEDIUM HIGH (70%) in step #2. For 8
bagelettes, double recipe and microwave for 1 to 1½ minutes
at MEDIUM HIGH (70%) in step #2.

For Hamburger Pita Pizza Slices or Bagelettes, stir 2 tablespoons cooked hamburger (or ground turkey) into the tomato
sauce in step #1. Proceed as directed.

* Use no-salt-added variety for lowest sodium values, if desired.
† **Compacts:** Microwave for same length of time at HIGH (100%) in step #2.

TIPS
· · · · · · · ·

The Fast Pizza
Bagelettes also make
delicious appetizers
(see the variations).

Bagelettes, or miniature
bagels, are found in
the frozen bread sec-
tion of the grocery
store.

Nutritional Analysis per Serving (1 Slice)	
Calories: 108	Cholesterol: 4 mg
Carbohydrate: 17 g	Sodium: 226 mg
Fat: 2 g	Diabetic exchanges:
Protein: 5 g	Bread: 1
Fiber: N/A	Vegetable: 0.5

VEGETABLES, SALADS, AND ACCOMPANIMENTS

· ❄ ·

GENERAL TIPS FOR MICROWAVING
VEGETABLES

- Microwaving vegetables retains as many nutrients or more than any other cooking method.

- Microwave all vegetables at HIGH (100%).

- All vegetables should be microwaved covered with a tight-fitting lid or vented plastic wrap.

- Arrange whole vegetables like spokes on a wagon wheel and place tender tips or flowerets to the center of casseroles for even cooking.

- To prevent dehydration and resulting toughness, do not salt vegetables before cooking.

- Always let vegetables stand for 2 to 3 minutes after microwaving to complete cooking.

- For a quick and easy cheese sauce for any vegetable, cover microwaved vegetables with 1 or 2 slices (or ½ cup grated) reduced-calorie cheese during standing time.

Fresh Vegetables

- *Do not add water to most fresh vegetables when microwaving, unless indicated (see the chart on page 330). Always rinse vegetables in water, but do not shake or dry off. This provides enough water for microwaving most vegetables.*

- Microwave vegetables whole whenever possible—such as cauliflower, potatoes, squash, corn on the cob, peas in the pods (shell after cooking). Vegetables will retain more nutrients and will cook more evenly.

- Pierce or prick whole vegetables such as potatoes and squash to prevent explosions and allow steam to escape.

- Microwave 1 pound of most fresh vegetables for 6 to 10 minutes at HIGH (100%) (see the following chart).

- Sauté chopped fresh vegetables such as onions, celery, and peppers with 2 teaspoons water or margarine for 2 to 3 minutes per cup.

Frozen Vegetables

- *Do not defrost frozen vegetables before cooking them.*

- Microwave frozen vegetables in the box or slit bag for convenience (remove any foil wrapping from package). The packages will hold in enough steam so no additional liquid is needed.

- Microwave a 10-ounce box on a paper plate or two layers of paper towels for 5 to 6 minutes at HIGH (100%), or follow the package directions.

- Microwave a 16-ounce bag, slit twice with a knife to form an "X" on one side and placed in a microwave-safe casserole, "X" side down, for 9 to 10 minutes at HIGH (100%), or follow the package directions.

Canned Vegetables

- Microwave canned vegetables in a microwave-safe covered casserole on MEDIUM HIGH (70%) to prevent overcooking. Microwave a 15-ounce can of vegetables, drained or undrained, for 3 to 4 minutes at MEDIUM HIGH (70%).

To Shorten Outdoor Grilling Time

- Precook potatoes by microwaving for 2 to 2½ minutes per medium-size potato before grilling. Wrap in foil and place on a hot grill for 15 to 20 minutes.

- Precook corn on the cob by microwaving in the husk for 2 minutes per ear (remove all but two layers of husk before microwaving). After microwaving, brush with margarine under husks, if desired. Wrap in foil and place on a hot grill for 10 to 12 minutes.

GENERAL TIPS FOR MICROWAVING PRESERVING

- Do not try to "can" in a microwave oven. It is not safe for you or the food you will eat. (A special microwave canner accessory is available in most department stores, but it is not efficient: You can do only one jar at a time.)

- Blanching vegetables before freezing is essential in order to preserve the quality, texture, and color of garden produce.

- Blanching is easy in the microwave oven. Follow the blanching chart and directions on page 329. Prepare only small amounts of vegetables at a time.

- Always clean vegetables and cut them into uniform pieces before blanching.

- A rule of thumb for microwave blanching: Blanch for half the microwave cooking time.

- Do not salt vegetables before blanching, as salt tends to dry out and toughen them.

- Always blanch vegetables by microwaving at HIGH (100%) power.

FRESH VEGETABLE MEDLEY WITH PARMESAN-LEMON SAUCE

· · · · ·

·················· VEGETABLE MEDLEY ····················

1 pound head cauliflower (about 1½ cups), cut into 1-inch flowerets
1 pound fresh broccoli (about 2 cups), cut into 1-inch flowerets
1 large carrot, cleaned and cut into sticks
1 small zucchini and/or small yellow squash, peeled and thinly sliced

·················· PARMESAN-LEMON SAUCE ····················

½ stick (¼ cup) reduced-calorie margarine, melted
2 teaspoons lemon juice
¼ teaspoon garlic powder
¼ teaspoon onion powder
1 teaspoon dried basil
¼ cup grated Parmesan cheese

1. Using a 10-inch glass pie plate or microwave-safe serving dish, arrange cauliflower around the outer edge.
2. Arrange broccoli inside the cauliflower ring, with the stems pointing toward outer edge of plate.
3. Place carrot sticks between broccoli stems. Pile zucchini slices in the center.
4. Mix Lemon Sauce ingredients except for the grated cheese in a small bowl. Pour over vegetables. Sprinkle with Parmesan cheese. Cover loosely with plastic wrap. Microwave

for 8 to 10 minutes at HIGH (100%).† Let stand 3 minutes.

Yield: 8 servings

————————— · ❄ · —————————

Nutritional Analysis per Serving (⅛ Recipe)

Calories: 76   Sodium: 131 mg
Carbohydrate: 5 g   Diabetic exchanges: Lean
Fat: 5 g   meat: 0.25
Protein: 4 g   Vegetable: 1
Fiber: N/A   Fat: 0.5
Cholesterol: 5 mg

SUMMER FRESH VEGETABLE AND FRUIT SALAD

————————— · · · · · —————————

2 tablespoons vegetable oil
2 cups (6 ounces) fresh
  mushrooms, sliced
2 packets sugar substitute
  (equivalent to 4
  teaspoons sugar)
¼ cup white or cider
  vinegar

4 cups torn romaine
½ cup seedless green or
  red grapes
¼ cup green onion, sliced
11-ounce can juice-packed
  mandarin orange
  segments, drained

1. Microwave oil and mushrooms in a 1-quart microwave-safe bowl or casserole for 3 to 4 minutes at MEDIUM HIGH (70%), or until tender.
2. In a large serving bowl, combine mushrooms and oil with the sugar substitute and vinegar. Refrigerate at least one hour.

. . . .
†**Compacts:** Microwave for 10 to 12 minutes at HIGH (100%) in step #4.

3. Just before serving, add remaining ingredients and toss to combine.

Yield: 6 servings

──────────── · ❋ · ────────────

Nutritional Analysis per 1¼-Cup Serving

Calories: 92   Sodium: 6 mg
Carbohydrate: 13 g   Diabetic exchanges:
Fat: 5 g   Vegetable: 0.5
Protein: 1 g   Fruit: 0.75
Fiber: N/A   Fat: 1
Cholesterol: 0 mg

GARDEN FRESH MARINADE

──────── · · · · · ────────

···················· VEGETABLES ··························

1 pound fresh broccoli
   (about 2 cups), cut into
   1-inch flowerets
1 pound head cauliflower
   (about 1½ cups), cut
   into 1-inch flowerets

3 carrots, cleaned and
   sliced diagonally
10-ounce package frozen
   artichoke hearts
12 cherry tomatoes

···················· MARINADE ··························

⅓ cup cider vinegar
⅔ cup water
½ teaspoon garlic powder
½ teaspoon dry mustard
2 packets sugar substitute
   (equivalent to 4
   teaspoons sugar)

1 teaspoon dried chives
1 teaspoon dried marjoram
1 teaspoon dried rosemary

TIPS
········

In a hurry? Substitute 1 cup reduced-calorie Italian salad dressing for the marinade.

Artichoke hearts can be omitted, if desired. Decrease microwaving time in step #2 to 3 to 4 minutes at HIGH (100%).

1. Place broccoli, cauliflower, and carrots in a 3-quart microwave-safe casserole. Cover. Microwave for 10 minutes at HIGH (100%).
2. Stir in artichoke hearts. Cover again and microwave for 6 to 8 minutes at HIGH (100%), or until vegetables are tender-crisp. Stir in tomatoes.
3. Mix marinade ingredients in a small bowl. Pour marinade over vegetables and toss to combine. Cover. Refrigerate overnight.

Yield: 8 servings

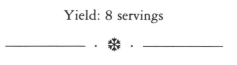

Variations: 2 tablespoons vegetable oil or olive oil can be added to make a thicker marinade, if desired.

For Garden and Pasta Salad, combine 2 cups elbow macaroni or rotini, uncooked, with 4 cups hot water and 1 teaspoon vegetable oil in a 2-quart microwave-safe bowl. Microwave for 8 to 10 minutes at HIGH (100%), or until pasta is tender. Drain and rinse in cold water. Add macaroni to the salad with the marinade in step #3. Cover and refrigerate as directed.

Nutritional Analysis per 1-Cup Serving

Calories: 197   Cholesterol: 0 mg
Carbohydrate: 12 g   Sodium: 42 mg
Fat: Trace   Diabetic exchanges:
Protein: 3 g   Vegetable: 2.25
Fiber: N/A

ITALIAN STUFFED ARTICHOKES

2 medium artichokes
¼ to ½ cup grated
   Parmesan cheese
1 medium tomato, seeded
   and chopped
1 tablespoon chopped
   parsley

1 tablespoon olive oil
1 clove garlic, minced
½ teaspoon Seasoned Salt
   Substitute #2 (see page
   245) or store-bought
   alternative

1. Slice off stem and ½ inch of top of each artichoke. Using kitchen scissors, snip off tips of leaves. Rinse under running water.
2. Wrap each artichoke in plastic wrap, tucking plastic wrap ends under bottom. Place bottom side up in 2 microwave-safe custard cups. Microwave for 7 to 8 minutes at HIGH (100%), rotating position halfway through cooking time. Let stand 10 minutes. Remove purple area at the base of each artichoke.
3. Mix remaining ingredients together in a small bowl to make filling. Then stuff filling between leaves of artichokes; work from outside to the center until leaves are too dense to be filled.
4. Place on microwave-safe serving tray or individual serving dishes. Microwave for 3 to 4 minutes at HIGH (100%) to heat through. Let stand 2 minutes.

Yield: 2 servings

❋

Variation: For 4 servings, double recipe. Increase microwaving time to 12 to 13 minutes at HIGH (100%) in step #2 and to 4 to 5 minutes at HIGH (100%) in step #4.

If eating artichokes is new to you, simply remove a leaf from the head and scrape the flesh across your top front teeth.

Artichokes are commonly served as an appetizer, but the stuffed versions are becoming popular entrees.

Artichokes add phosphorous, calcium, potassium, and dietary fiber to your diet.

Nutritional Analysis per Serving (1 Artichoke)

Calories: 190

Carbohyrate: 15 g

Fat: 12 g

Protein: 9 g

Fiber: N/A

Cholesterol: 10 mg

Sodium: 378 mg

Diabetic exchanges:

Lean meat: 1

Vegetable: 2

Fat: 2

SWISS ASPARAGUS

1 pound fresh asparagus,
   prepared (see tips at left)
2 teaspoons reduced-
   calorie margarine*
3 teaspoons cornstarch
1 teaspoon chicken
   bouillon granules*

Dash ground nutmeg
1 cup skim milk
½ cup (2 ounces) shredded
   reduced-fat Swiss
   cheese*
2 tablespoons wheat
   crackers, crumbed

1. Place asparagus (stem ends toward the outside) in a 10-inch flat microwave-safe casserole or 2-quart microwave-safe baking dish. Cover with lid or vented plastic wrap. Microwave for 5 to 6 minutes at HIGH (100%), or until asparagus is crisp-tender. Set aside.
2. Microwave margarine in a 1-quart microwave-safe bowl for 30 to 40 seconds at HIGH (100%). Set aside. Combine cornstarch, bouillon granules, nutmeg, and skim milk in a small bowl until well blended. Stir into melted margarine.
3. Microwave uncovered for 2 to 3 minutes at HIGH (100%), or until thickened, stirring once. Blend in cheese, stirring until cheese melts. Pour over asparagus. Sprinkle with cracker crumbs and microwave for 1 to 1½ minutes at HIGH (100%) to heat. Serve immediately.

Yield: 4 servings

* ❄ *

Nutritional Analysis per Serving (¼ Recipe)

Calories: 120
Carbohydrate: 11 g
Fat: 5 g
Protein: 9 g
Fiber: N/A
Cholesterol: 12 g

Sodium: 85 g
Diabetic exchanges: Lean
   meat: 0.5
Vegetable: 1.5
Skim milk: 0.25
Fat: 0.5

*Use unsalted or low-sodium variety for lowest sodium values, if desired.

Choose asparagus spears with bright green or white ends that are brittle, not limp. Stalks should be about three-quarters green.

Prepare asparagus by rinsing with water (do not dry) and removing the white portion and tough outer peel at the stem end (use a small knife or vegetable peeler).

Place asparagus in the casserole with the tips toward the center and stems toward the out-side, to promote even microwaving.

Asparagus is a source of vitamins A and C, iron, and potassium. It also has a natural di-uretic effect.

Students in my cooking classes often complain that carrots turn out tough when cooked in the microwave oven. I find that fresh carrots often are tender if they are microwaved first, refrigerated until serving time, and then reheated.

Carrots and broccoli, rich in vitamin A, have been found to reduce the risk of some types of cancer when eaten regularly, according to the American Cancer Society.

CARROTS AND BROCCOLI TARRAGON

· · · · ·

5 medium carrots, cleaned and sliced diagonally (about 2 cups)

2 tablespoons water

1 teaspoon dried tarragon

1 pound fresh broccoli (about 2 cups), cut into flowerets

2 teaspoons reduced-calorie margarine*

1. Mix carrot slices, water, and tarragon in a 2-quart microwave-safe casserole. Cover with lid or vented plastic wrap. Microwave for 6 to 8 minutes at HIGH (100%). Set aside.
2. Microwave broccoli in a 1-quart microwave-safe covered casserole for 3 to 4 minutes at HIGH (100%), or until tender-crisp.
3. Mix cooked broccoli and margarine into the cooked carrots. Cover again. Refrigerate until serving time. Just before serving, microwave vegetables for 2 to 3 minutes at HIGH (100%), or until tender and heated through.

Yield: 4 servings

_____ · ❄ · _____

Nutritional Analysis per 1-Cup Serving

Calories: 65

Carbohydrate: 12 g

Fat: 1 g

Protein: 3 g

Fiber: N/A

Cholesterol: 0 mg

Sodium: 45 mg

Diabetic exchanges:

Vegetable: 2.5

* Use unsalted variety for lowest sodium values, if desired.

BRUSSELS SPROUTS IN GARLIC SAUCE

—————— · · · · · ——————

1 pound (about 30) fresh
   brussels sprouts, rinsed
¼ cup water
1 tablespoon reduced-
   calorie margarine*
2 cloves garlic, minced

½ teaspoon cornstarch,
   dissolved in ⅓ cup
   evaporated skim milk
Dash each nutmeg and
   pepper

1. Cut an "X" in the bottom of each brussels sprout. Place in a 1½-quart microwave-safe casserole. Add the water. Cover with lid or vented plastic wrap. Microwave for 6 to 7 minutes at HIGH (100%), or until tender-crisp. Drain liquid and set sprouts aside.
2. Microwave margarine and garlic in the casserole for 1 to 1½ minutes at HIGH (100%), or until tender. Stir in cornstarch-milk and nutmeg. Microwave for 1 to 1½ minutes at MEDIUM HIGH (70%), or until milk mixture thickens, stirring once. Add sprouts to sauce and stir gently. Let stand covered for 2 minutes.

Yield: 4 servings

—————— · ❄ · ——————

Nutritional Analysis per ¾-Cup Serving

Calories: 92
Carbohydrate: 17 g
Fat: 2 g
Protein: 6 g
Fiber: N/A
Cholesterol: 1 mg

Sodium: 58 mg
Diabetic exchanges:
   Vegetable: 2
   Skim milk: 0.5
   Fat: 0.25

---

* Use unsalted variety for lowest sodium values, if desired.

Brussels sprouts are another of the cruciferous vegetables, high in vitamins A and C. They have been found to reduce the risk of some kinds of cancer.

Always choose brussels sprouts that are bright green, tightly closed, and fairly firm.

To save calories you can use as little as 1 teaspoon mayonnaise to brush the cooked cauliflower with. Omit the tangy mustard sauce. Sprinkle with grated cheese. (The mayonnaise helps the cheese cling to the cauliflower.)

Figure exact microwaving time in step #1 by allowing approximately 7 minutes per pound of cauliflower.

LITE TANGY-CHEESY CAULIFLOWER

· · · · ·

Makes a beautiful accompaniment to any meal.

1 medium to large head cauliflower

2 tablespoons reduced-calorie mayonnaise or yogurt

½ teaspoon prepared mustard

½ cup (2 ounces) shredded reduced-fat cheddar cheese*

1. Prepare cauliflower by removing stem and greens. Rinse under water but do not shake to dry. Place in a microwave-safe dish. Cover loosely with plastic wrap.
2. Microwave for 8 to 9 minutes at HIGH (100%),† or until tender.
3. Meanwhile, combine mayonnaise and mustard to make the tangy sauce.
4. Immediately spoon mustard sauce on top of cauliflower. Sprinkle with cheese.
5. Let stand 5 minutes until cheese melts.

Yield: 8 servings

———— · ❄ · ————

Nutritional Analysis per Serving (⅛ Recipe)

Calories: 50
Carbohydrate: 5 g
Fat: 3 g
Protein: 4 g
Fiber: N/A
Cholesterol: 1 mg

Sodium: 54 mg
Diabetic exchanges: Lean meat: 0.25
Vegetable: 1
Fat: 0.25

* Use unsalted or reduced-sodium variety for lowest sodium values, if desired.
† **Compacts:** Microwave for 10 to 12 minutes at HIGH (100%).

COMPANY GLAZED CARROTS WITH APPLES

——————— · · · · · ———————

4 large carrots (4 to 5
  cups), cleaned and
  sliced
1 medium Red or Golden
  Delicious apple, peeled
  and chopped

1 packet sugar substitute
  or brown sugar
  substitute (equivalent to
  2 teaspoons sugar)
1 teaspoon reduced-calorie
  margarine*
2 teaspoons water

1. Combine all ingredients in a 1-quart microwave-safe casserole. Cover loosely with vented plastic wrap or lid.
2. Microwave for 5 to 6 minutes at HIGH (100%).
3. Stir. Microwave again for 3 to 4 minutes at HIGH (100%),† or until tender.
4. Let stand 5 minutes before serving.

Yield: 4 servings

——————— · ❄ · ———————

Variation: For Company Orange-Glazed Carrots, omit apple. Increase water to ¼ cup. Proceed as directed in steps #1 and #2. Mix ¼ cup orange juice and 1 teaspoon cornstarch in a 1-cup measure until smooth. Stir into carrots. Microwave for 2 to 3 minutes at HIGH (100%), or until carrots are tender.

Nutritional Analysis per ½-Cup Serving	
Calories: 60	Cholesterol: 0 mg
Carbohydrate: 13 g	Sodium: 26 mg
Fat: 1 g	Diabetic exchanges:
Protein: 1 g	Vegetable: 2
Fiber: N/A	Fruit: 0.25

* Use unsalted variety for lowest sodium values, if desired.
† **Compacts:** Microwave in step #3 for 5 to 6 minutes at HIGH (100%).

Company Glazed Carrots can be microwaved in advance, refrigerated, and reheated for 3 to 4 minutes at HIGH (100%) at serving time. (Carrots often become more tender if prepared this way.)

This is a light yet delicious salad to serve for a luncheon or brunch. Leave the peel on the apple to add color, texture, and dietary fiber.

MOLDED WALDORF SALAD

· · · · ·

¾ cup hot water

.3-ounce package sugar-free cherry gelatin, dry

½ cup cold water

Approximately ¾ cup ice cubes

1 large Red Delicious apple, cored and chopped (1½ cups)

½ cup diced celery (about 1 stalk)

1 small head Bibb lettuce or romaine

1. Microwave water in a 1-quart microwave-safe bowl for 1 to 1½ minutes, or until boiling. Stir in gelatin.
2. Mix cold water and ice cubes to make 1¼ cups. Stir into gelatin; keep stirring until gelatin thickens slightly. Remove any unmelted cubes. Mix in apple and celery.
3. Chill in bowl or pour into 6 small custard cups that have been sprayed with vegetable coating. Refrigerate at least 2 hours. Serve unmolded on a bed of lettuce on a serving plate or on individual salad plates.

Yield: 6 servings

———— · ❄ · ————

Nutritional Analysis per Serving (1 Small Mold or ⅙ Large Mold)

Calories: 27

Carbohydrate: 6 g

Fat: Trace

Protein: 1 g

Fiber: N/A

Cholesterol: 0 mg

Sodium: 23 mg

Diabetic exchanges:

　Vegetable: 0.5

　Fruit: 0.25

SUGAR-FREE CRANBERRY SAUCE

2 cups (8 ounces) fresh
  cranberries
1 cup water

15 packets sugar substitute
  (equivalent to ⅔ cup
  sugar)

1. Combine cranberries and water in a 1-quart microwave-safe casserole. Cover with waxed paper.
2. Microwave for 3 minutes at HIGH (100%). Stir. Cover again. Microwave for 4 to 5 minutes at HIGH (100%), or until skins pop.
3. Stir in sugar substitute. Strain, if desired. Pour into serving container and refrigerate.

Yield: 6 servings

❄

Variation: For Cranapple Sauce, add 1 small cored, peeled, and grated apple to the cranberries in step #1. Increase total microwaving time by 1 minute in step #2.

Nutritional Analysis per ½-Cup Serving

Calories: 25
Carbohydrate: 6 g
Fat: Trace
Protein: Trace

Fiber: 0 g
Cholesterol: 0 mg
Sodium: 10 mg
Diabetic exchanges: Fruit: 0.5

TIPS

For a large batch of Cranberry Sauce, double ingredients; use a 3-quart microwave-safe casserole. In step #2, microwave for 6 minutes at HIGH (100%); stir; and microwave for 8 to 10 minutes at HIGH (100%).

Cranberries are usually available in grocery stores only October through December, but they freeze well for up to nine months, so buy extra bags and freeze them to enjoy all year.

Select firm, plump berries. Rinse before using and remove any dark, shriveled ones.

SUGAR-FREE CRANBERRY-APPLE SAUCE

——————— · · · · · ———————

A diabetic recipe that all will enjoy!

2 cups apple juice
½ cup frozen apple juice concentrate, slightly thawed
2 tablespoons orange juice concentrate
¼ cup cornstarch

2 cups (8 ounces) fresh cranberries, cleaned and rinsed
1 medium Red or Golden Delicious apple, peeled, cored, and grated, optional

1. Mix apple juice, fruit juice concentrates, and cornstarch in a 2-quart microwave-safe bowl until blended. Stir in cranberries and apple. Cover with waxed paper.
2. Microwave for 3 minutes at HIGH (100%). Stir. Cover again. Microwave again for 6 to 7 minutes at HIGH (100%), or until skins on cranberries pop.
3. Strain if desired. Pour into serving container and refrigerate.

Yield: 10 servings

——————— · ❄ · ———————

Nutritional Analysis per ½-Cup Serving

Calories: 79
Carbohydrate: 19 g
Fat: Trace
Protein: Trace

Fiber: N/A
Cholesterol: 0 mg
Sodium: 1 mg
Diabetic exchanges:
    Fruit: 1.25

BAKED POTATOES
—————— • • • • • ——————

1–6 white potatoes
1–6 red potatoes, peeled
  and scrubbed†

1. Scrub potatoes and pierce with a fork. Microwave on a paper plate or two layers of paper towels. (For drier skins, stand pierced potatoes on end in microwave muffin cups.)
2. Microwave for 3 to 4½ minutes at HIGH (100%)† per 8 ounces of potato. Part of the potato will still feel firm to the touch, but will finish cooking during standing time. For 2 medium potatoes (12 ounces), microwave for 5 to 6 minutes at HIGH (100%). For 2 large potatoes (1 pound), microwave for 6 to 8 minutes at HIGH (100%). For 4 potatoes (2 pounds), microwave for 12 to 14 minutes at HIGH (100%). For 6 potatoes (2½–3 pounds), microwave for 15 to 18 minutes at HIGH (100%). Times will vary according to size, type, and moisture content.
3. Let stand 10 to 15 minutes wrapped in foil (shiny side toward potato) or covered with a casserole dish to complete cooking.

TIPS
....

If baking more than 2 potatoes, arrange them in the microwave like spokes on a wagon wheel to achieve even cooking.

Be sure to pierce baking potatoes before cooking to keep them from exploding, and be sure to let them stand after microwaving in order to complete cooking.

Microwaving potatoes on paper towels will help prevent them from becoming moist or soggy on the bottom.

For best results, weigh your potatoes and calculate cooking time as directed in step #2.

Nutritional Analysis per 5-Ounce Serving		
	Red Potato	White Potato
Calories:	116	163
Carbohydrate:	27 g	36 g
Fat:	Trace	Trace
Protein:	2 g	3 g
Fiber:	2 g	2 g
Cholesterol:	0	0
Sodium:	7 mg	1 mg
Diabetic exchanges:		
Bread:	1.5	2

† **Compacts:** Microwave for 4 to 5½ minutes at HIGH (100%) per 8 ounces of potato in step #2.

BOILED POTATOES

— · · · · · —

**1– 6 red potatoes, peeled
and scrubbed**

1. Place 2 pounds peeled and quartered potatoes in a 1- or 2-quart microwave-safe casserole. Add ½ to 1 cup water to cover potatoes.
2. Cover with lid or vented plastic wrap. Microwave as directed in step #2 under baked potatoes (see page 302) until fork tender, stirring once. If potatoes overcook easily in your microwave, microwave for half the time at HIGH (100%) and the remaining time at MEDIUM (50%).
3. Let stand, covered, for 5 minutes. Drain and mash or use as desired.

Nutritional Analysis per 5-Ounce Serving

Calories: 116
Carbohydrate: 27 g
Fat: Trace
Protein: 2 g
Fiber: 2 g

Cholesterol: 0 mg
Sodium: 7 mg
Diabetic exchanges:
  Bread: 1.5

SLIM AU GRATIN POTATOES

· · · · ·

TIPS

For best results, use long white potatoes in this recipe.

3 medium potatoes, thinly sliced (about 3½ cups)
½ medium onion (about ½ cup), chopped
½ cup water
¼ cup evaporated skim milk
1 teaspoon dried chives

1 teaspoon Seasoned Salt Substitute #1 (see page 244) or store-bought alternative
¾ cup (3 ounces) grated reduced-calorie cheddar cheese,* divided

1. Combine potatoes, onion, and water in a 1-quart microwave-safe casserole. Cover with lid or vented plastic wrap. Microwave for 9 to 10 minutes at HIGH (100%), or until almost tender, stirring once.
2. Stir in remaining ingredients except for ¼ cup cheese. Sprinkle remaining ¼ cup cheese on top of potato mixture. Microwave uncovered for 3 to 4 minutes at MEDIUM HIGH (70%),† or until cheese is melted and potatoes are tender.

Yield: 6 servings

——————— · ❄ · ———————

Variation: You can substitute ½ cup skim milk for the evaporated skim milk. Decrease water to ⅓ cup.

Nutritional Analysis per Serving (⅙ Recipe)

Calories: 104
Carbohydrate: 15 g
Fat: 3 g
Protein: 6 g
Fiber: N/A

Cholesterol: Trace
Sodium: 52 mg
Diabetic exchanges:
  Bread: 0.75
  Lean meat: 0.75
  Vegetable: 0.25

---

* Use reduced-sodium variety for lowest sodium values, if desired.
† Compacts: Microwave for 3 to 4 minutes at HIGH (100%) instead of MEDIUM HIGH (70%) in step #2.

To keep from slicing through the bottom of the potato, place one wood-handled spoon on each side of the potato before cutting. When the knife hits the handles, it stops.

Recipe can be doubled or tripled, if desired. Figure microwave cooking time by allowing 3 to 4 minutes per 5-ounce potato.

EASY PARMESAN POTATO FANS

2 medium white potatoes (5 ounces each), washed
1½ tablespoons reduced-calorie margarine*
¼ teaspoon each garlic powder, onion powder, and paprika

1 teaspoon lemon juice
2 tablespoons grated Parmesan cheese
Parsley flakes or lemon slices to garnish, optional

1. Cut each potato at ¼-inch intervals, cutting to within ¼ inch of the bottom of the potato but not through. Place potatoes in ice water for at least 10 minutes to help slices fan out.
2. Microwave margarine in a small microwave-safe dish for 20 seconds at HIGH (100%) to melt. Stir in garlic powder, onion powder, paprika, and lemon juice. Set aside.
3. Remove potatoes from ice water; pat dry with paper towels. Place potatoes in a small microwave-safe casserole dish; brush top and sides of potatoes with seasoned margarine. Cover loosely with plastic wrap. Microwave for 6 to 8 minutes at HIGH (100%),† or until tender. Sprinkle with Parmesan cheese. Let stand, covered, 5 minutes. Garnish with parsley flakes and/or lemon slices, if desired.

Yield: 2 servings

Nutritional Analysis per Serving (1 Potato Fan)

Calories: 169
Carbohydrate: 25 g
Fat: 7 g
Protein: 5 g
Fiber: N/A

Cholesterol: 4 mg
Sodium: 102 mg
Diabetic exchanges:
  Bread: 1.5
  Lean meat: 0.5
  Fat: 0.75

*Use unsalted variety for lowest sodium values, if desired.
†Compacts: Microwave for 8 to 9 minutes at HIGH (100%) in step #3.

PARSLEY AND MINT POTATOES

5 medium red potatoes
(about 2 pounds), peeled
and quartered
½ cup water
2 tablespoons finely
chopped onion
2 tablespoons finely
chopped fresh parsley or
2 teaspoons dried
parsley

2 tablespoons finely
chopped fresh mint or 1
teaspoon mint flakes
3 tablespoons plain nonfat
yogurt
2 tablespoons lemon juice
1 teaspoon sugar or ½
packet sugar substitute
½ teaspoon dried basil
¼ teaspoon dry mustard

1. Place potatoes and water in a 2-quart microwave-safe casserole. Cover with lid or vented plastic wrap. Microwave
for 12 to 15 minutes at HIGH (100%), or until fork-
tender, stirring halfway through cooking time. Let stand
5 minutes. Drain.
2. Meanwhile, mix remaining ingredients in a small bowl,
stirring until blended. To serve warm, pour yogurt mixture over potatoes and toss to coat. Microwave for 1 to
1½ minutes at MEDIUM HIGH (70%) and serve immediately. To serve cold, refrigerate potato mixture for at
least 2 hours. Just before serving time, stir yogurt mixture into potatoes.

Yield: 8 servings

Nutritional Analysis per Serving (⅛ Recipe)

Calories: 90
Carbohydrate: 20 g
Fat: Trace
Protein: 2 g

Fiber: N/A
Cholesterol: Trace
Sodium: 13 mg
Diabetic exchanges:
Bread: 1.25

TIPS

To enhance the color
of Parsley and Mint Po-
tatoes, use red onion
or add 2 tablespoons
chopped red pepper
with the onion.

If skins tear or crack while removing pulp, simply push them back in place after filling and they will again hold their shape.

Baked potatoes are naturally low in sodium and virtually fat-free but high in numerous trace minerals and vitamins.

TWICE-BAKED POTATOES

——————— · · · · · ———————

2 medium white potatoes (approximately 6 ounces each), baked and hot (see page 302)

¼ cup (2 ounces) plain nonfat yogurt

2 tablespoons reduced-calorie bleu cheese salad dressing*

1 teaspoon very finely grated onion

Snipped chives or paprika to garnish

1. Cut a ¼-inch horizontal slice from the top of each hot potato. Discard slice. Scoop out the potato pulp using a small spoon and leaving the skins intact. Using an electric mixer and bowl, mash potato pulp, yogurt, dressing, and onion. Beat until fluffy. Divide mixture between reserved shells.

2. Place filled potatoes on a microwave-safe plate lined with 2 paper towels. Microwave for 1½ to 2 minutes at HIGH (100%), or until heated. Sprinkle with chives or paprika to garnish and serve immediately.

Yield: 2 servings

——————— · ❈ · ———————

Variation: To make 4 or 6 servings, double or triple the recipe. Proceed as directed. In step #2, microwave for 3 to 4 minutes for 4 potatoes and 5 to 6 minutes for 6 potatoes.

Nutritional Analysis per Serving (1 Potato)

Calories: 155
Carbohydrate: 33 g
Fat: 1 g
Protein: 6 g

Fiber: N/A
Cholesterol: 6 mg
Sodium: 42 mg
Diabetic exchanges:
  Bread: 2.0
  Skim milk: 0.25

---

* Use reduced-sodium variety for lowest sodium values, if desired.

GERMAN POTATO SALAD

3–4 medium potatoes (1½ pounds), peeled and cubed

¾ cup water, divided

2 teaspoons vegetable oil

½ small onion (⅓ cup), finely chopped

1 tablespoon all-purpose flour

3 tablespoons cider vinegar

½ teaspoon dry mustard

½ stalk (⅓ cup) diced celery

2 tablespoons pickle relish

2 tablespoons finely chopped fresh chives

If you prefer a sweeter, less tangy dressing, add sugar substitute or fructose (equal to 1 teaspoon sugar) after microwaving in step #2.

1. Place potatoes and ½ cup water in a 2-quart flat microwave-safe casserole. Cover with lid or vented plastic wrap. Microwave for 10 to 12 minutes at HIGH (100%), or until tender, stirring once. Drain. Transfer to a bowl and let stand, covered.

2. Mix oil and onion in the 2-quart casserole. Cover with lid or vented plastic wrap. Microwave for 2½ to 3 minutes at HIGH (100%), or until onion is tender. Mix flour, vinegar, dry mustard, and ¼ cup water in a small bowl until smooth. Pour over onion, cover, and microwave for 1½ to 2 minutes at HIGH (100%), or until thickened.

3. Mix celery, pickle relish, and chives with the potatoes. Add hot dressing and toss. Serve hot. (If prepared ahead of time, refrigerate and then microwave for 2 to 3 minutes at HIGH [100%] to reheat.)

Yield: 6 servings

* ❄ *

Variation: Substitute 16 ounces frozen southern-style hash browns for fresh potatoes. Omit ½ cup water. Microwave as directed in step #1.

Nutritional Analysis per Serving ($\frac{1}{6}$ Recipe)

Calories: 94

Carbohydrate: 19 g

Fat: 2 g

Protein: 2 g

Fiber: N/A

Cholesterol: 0 mg

Sodium: 45 mg

Diabetic exchanges:

Bread: 1.25

Vegetable: 0.25

Fat: 0.25

EASY PARMESAN POTATO WEDGES

1½ tablespoons reduced-
   calorie margarine*
1 teaspoon lemon juice
¼ teaspoon each garlic
   powder, onion powder,
   and paprika
2 tablespoons grated
   Parmesan cheese

2 medium white potatoes
   (5 ounces each), washed
   and cut into 6 wedges
   each
Parsley flakes to garnish,
   optional

1. Microwave margarine in a small microwave-safe dish or custard cup for 20 seconds at HIGH (100%) to melt. Stir in lemon juice. Set aside.
2. Mix seasonings with Parmesan cheese in a small dish.
3. Dip each potato wedge in the lemon-margarine and then into the cheese mixture. Place wedges in an 8-inch microwave-safe casserole and microwave for 6 to 8 minutes at HIGH (100%),† or until potatoes are almost tender. Let stand 5 minutes. Serve garnished with parsley flakes, if desired.

Yield: 2 servings

* ❄ *

Nutritional Analysis per Serving (1 Potato)

Calories: 167
Carbohydrate: 25 g
Fat: 7 g
Protein: 5 g
Fiber: N/A

Cholesterol: 4 mg
Sodium: 102 mg
Diabetic exchanges:
   Bread: 1.5
   Fat: 1

* Use unsalted variety for lowest sodium values, if desired.
† Compacts: Microwave for 8 to 9 minutes at HIGH (100%) in step #3.

TIPS

Microwaved potatoes will not feel soft until after standing time in step #1.

Be sure to prick skins of sweet potatoes with a fork before microwaving so the buildup of steam doesn't cause them to explode while microwaving.

Sweet potatoes and yams are especially high in vitamins A and C as well as potassium. Be sure to choose firm, unblemished ones with smooth skins and no soft spots, cracks, or wrinkles.

4 medium yams or sweet potatoes (about 2 pounds)

1½ tablespoons reduced-calorie margarine *

2 tablespoons orange juice or skim milk

2 tablespoons brown sugar (or equivalent brown sugar substitute)

1. Wash sweet potatoes. Prick skins with a fork. Microwave on a paper towel, 1 inch apart, for 12 to 15 minutes at HIGH (100%), turning and rearranging halfway through cooking time. Let stand 10 minutes covered with foil (shiny side in) or a casserole dish to soften.

2. Scoop out centers of potatoes into a 2-quart bowl; discard skins. Add margarine, juice, and brown sugar. Using an electric mixer, mash ingredients until smooth. Spoon into a 1-quart microwave-safe casserole that has been sprayed with vegetable coating.

3. Microwave for 5 to 6 minutes at HIGH (100%) to heat through. Serve immediately.

Yield: 8 servings

Nutritional Analysis per ½-Cup Serving

Calories: 82
Carbohydrates: 17 g
Fat: 1 g
Protein: 1 g

Fiber: 1 g
Cholesterol: 0 mg
Sodium: 7 mg
Diabetic exchanges:
  Bread: 1

....
*Use unsalted variety for lowest sodium values, if desired.

CREAMY CUCUMBERS

· · · · · ────────

½ cup (4 ounces) plain
  nonfat yogurt
5 teaspoons lemon juice
½ teaspoon sugar or
  equivalent sugar
  substitute

Dash dry mustard
2 small cucumbers (2
  cups), peeled and thinly
  sliced

Combine yogurt, lemon juice, sugar, and mustard in a 1-
quart bowl until smooth. Add cucumbers and toss to coat.
Refrigerate until serving time.

Yield: 4 to 6 servings

──────── · ❄ · ────────

┌───┐
│   *Nutritional Analysis per ½-Cup Serving*   │
│   │
│ Calories: 13   Fiber: N/A   │
│ Carbohydrate: 2 g   Cholesterol: Trace   │
│ Fat: 0 g   Sodium: 15 mg   │
│ Protein: 1 g   Diabetic exchanges: │
│   Vegetable: Free   │
└───┘

TIPS
· · · · · · · ·

This is not a microwave
recipe, but it makes a
nice accompaniment
to many microwave
dishes.

To prepare corn for cooking in the husk, remove outer husks and silks, leaving two layers of light-green inner husks and silks on ear. (You can turn back inner husks and rinse corn under water, but it is not necessary. You can also brush each corn with 1 teaspoon reduced-calorie margarine under husks before microwaving, if desired.)

To remove husks after microwaving, stand ear on base and, using a hot pad glove or paper towel, pull the husks and silks down and off the ear. Rinse with hot water and cut off stem.

One medium ear of yellow sweet corn is a source of vitamin A, niacin, potassium, and fiber, and has only 70 calories.

CORN ON THE COB

Once you've tried it in the microwave oven, you'll never boil it again!

1–6 ears corn on the cob

1. Cook corn in the husk (see tip at left) or remove husks, rinse, and place in a microwave-safe casserole so cobs are not layered. Cover with casserole lid or vented plastic wrap.
2. Microwave for 2½ to 3 minutes per large ear at HIGH (100%),† rearranging ears and turning over halfway through cooking time. (You can microwave up to 6 ears at one time: 2 ears for 5 to 6 minutes; 4 ears for 10 to 11 minutes; and 6 ears for 12 to 15 minutes.)
3. Let stand 5 minutes. Remove husks (see tip at left).

Yield: 1 to 6 servings

Nutritional Analysis per Serving (1 Ear)

Calories: 120
Carbohydrate: 29 g
Fat: 1 g
Protein: 4 g

Fiber: 6 g
Cholesterol: 0 mg
Sodium: 4 mg
Diabetic exchanges:
    Vegetable: 2

† **Compacts:** Microwave each ear for 4 to 5 minutes at HIGH (100%).

QUICK MANDARIN VEGETABLES AND TOFU

—————— · · · · · ——————

Tofu makes this tasty meal high in protein but low in cholesterol.

16-ounce package frozen mixed vegetables (broccoli, carrots, and water chestnuts)
2 teaspoons cornstarch
2 tablespoons reduced-sodium soy sauce
4 tablespoons water

2 teaspoons garlic-wine vinegar, optional
1 teaspoon chicken bouillon granules*
Dash ground ginger
8 ounces firm tofu, cut into ½-inch cubes

1. Using a sharp knife, cut an "X" into the back side of the bag of vegetables. Place "X" side down in a 2-quart microwave-safe casserole. Microwave for 7 to 9 minutes at HIGH (100%), or until tender-crisp. Let stand 2 minutes.
2. Meanwhile, combine cornstarch, soy sauce, water, vinegar, bouillon granules, and ginger in a 2-cup glass measure until mixed and cornstarch is completely dissolved. Microwave uncovered for 1 to 1½ minutes at HIGH (100%) until mixture comes to a boil, stirring once.
3. Using tongs, pull plastic bag off the vegetables. Pour soy sauce mixture onto vegetables in the casserole, add tofu, and toss. Cover with lid or vented plastic wrap. Microwave for 3 to 4 minutes at HIGH (100%), until heated through.

Yield: 4 servings

—————— · ❄ · ——————

————————————————————————————————
*Use unsalted variety for lowest sodium values, if desired.

Tofu is the solid soy-milk food that is high in protein and virtually free of cholesterol.

Serve Mandarin Vegetables and Tofu sprinkled with sesame seeds or with a side dish of brown rice to increase the protein value in the tofu (and make it a complete protein source).

TIPS

To thaw shrimp for the variation, see tip on page 107.

This recipe will serve two or three as an entree. Add shrimp or chicken as directed in the variations.

MICRO STIR-FRY VEGETABLES

2 teaspoons vegetable oil
½ clove garlic, minced
4 green onions, diagonally sliced
2 stalks celery (1 cup), diagonally sliced

16 ounces mixed frozen vegetables (broccoli, carrots, and water chestnuts)

.... SAUCE ....

¼ cup water
3 teaspoons cornstarch
2 tablespoons white wine
1 teaspoon chicken bouillon granules

2 tablespoons reduced-sodium soy sauce
Dash ground ginger

1. Stir oil, garlic, onions, and celery into a 1-quart microwave-safe casserole. Cover with lid or vented plastic wrap. Microwave for 2 minutes at HIGH (100%). Stir in frozen vegetables. Cover. Microwave for 6 to 7 minutes at HIGH (100%), or until vegetables are tender-crisp. Stir and set aside.

2. Mix sauce ingredients together in a small bowl until smooth. Pour over vegetables. Microwave for 1 to 1½ minutes at HIGH (100%), until vegetables are tender-crisp and sauce has thickened.

Yield: 4 servings

Variations: For Micro Stir-Fry Vegetables and Chicken, stir in 1 cup cooked chicken breast (see page 180), skinned, boned, and diced with the sauce in step #2.

For Micro Stir-Fry Shrimp and Vegetables, stir in 6 ounces frozen cooked shrimp, thawed, with the sauce in step #2.

Nutritional Analysis per ¾-Cup Serving

Calories: 75

Carbohydrate: 12 g

Fat: 3 g

Protein: 3 g

Fiber: N/A

Cholesterol: 0 mg

Sodium: 73 mg

Diabetic exchanges:

Vegetable: 2

Fat: 0.5

RATATOUILLE

· · · · ·

A French casserole, made from fresh garden vegetables, that can be served either hot or cold.

1 medium onion, thinly sliced into rings

1 clove garlic, minced

1 small eggplant, peeled and cut into ½-inch cubes

2 small zucchini (2 cups), thinly sliced

½ green bell pepper, cut into strips

2 small tomatoes, seeded and chopped

½ teaspoon dried basil

½ teaspoon dried oregano

1 tablespoon grated Romano or Parmesan cheese

Combine all ingredients in a 2-quart microwave-safe casserole. Cover with lid or vented plastic wrap. Microwave for 8 to 10 minutes at HIGH (100%), or until vegetables are tender and eggplant is transparent, stirring twice. Let stand 2 minutes. Serve hot or refrigerate and serve chilled.

Yield: 8 servings

——— · ❄ · ———

Ratatouille also can be served as a hot topping for Parmesan Chicken Breasts (see page 183), Cajun Catfish (see page 112), or many other chicken or fish entrees.

Variation: Traditional ratatouille often calls for sautéing the vegetables in olive oil. Therefore, you can add 2 tablespoons olive oil with the onion in step #1, if desired.

Nutritional Analysis per Serving (⅛ Recipe)

Calories: 32   Fiber: N/A
Carbohydrate: 6 g   Cholesterol: 1 mg
Fat: Trace   Sodium: 17 mg
Protein: 2 g   Diabetic exchanges:
                                              Vegetable: 1.25

TIPS
....

Be sure to use a sweet-tasting apple, such as Granny Smith, Golden Delicious, or Jonathan to produce a sweet filling.

For added color and fiber, do not peel the apple.

SWEET APPLE-FILLED SQUASH

————— · · · · · —————

1 medium acorn squash (about 1 pound)

1 medium apple, peeled, cored, and thinly sliced

2 teaspoons reduced-calorie margarine*

2 teaspoons brown sugar or brown sugar substitute

½ teaspoon ground cinnamon

1. Prick squash with a fork a few times to allow steam to escape while cooking. Microwave whole squash in a 9-inch glass casserole for 3 to 4 minutes at HIGH (100%), turning squash over halfway through cooking time.
2. While squash is microwaving, combine remaining ingredients in a small bowl to make apple filling.
3. Slice partially cooked squash in half lengthwise and scoop out seeds. Fill squash cavities with apple filling. Cover with waxed paper. Microwave for 5 to 6 minutes at HIGH (100%), or until filling is tender.

Yield: 2 servings

————— · ❄ · —————

....
*Use unsalted variety for lowest sodium values, if desired.

Variations: For Stuffed Acorn Squash, omit cinnamon and brown sugar. Add 2 tablespoons each diced celery and diced onion with the apple in step #2. Proceed as directed.

For 4 to 6 servings, double recipe, using 2 pounds squash (2 to 3 small) and a large flat casserole. Microwave for 7 to 8 minutes at HIGH (100%) in step #1. Microwave for 6 to 7 minutes at HIGH (100%) in step #3.

Nutritional Analysis per Serving (½ Recipe)

Calories: 169   Cholesterol: 0 mg
Carbohydrate: 39 g   Sodium: 9 mg
Fat: 2 g   Diabetic exchanges:
Protein: 2 g   Bread: 1
Fiber: N/A   Fruit: 1
                       Fat: 0.5

SPAGHETTI SQUASH

· · · · ·

The perfect substitute for pasta!

2-pound spaghetti squash

1. Place squash on a glass pie plate or shallow microwave-safe casserole. Pierce rind with a knife or ice pick to make 3 or 4 steam outlets. Microwave for 12 to 14 minutes at HIGH (100%), or until squash feels soft and yields slightly to pressure. Let stand 5 minutes.
2. Cut squash in half. Remove seeds. Using a fork, scrape pulp from rind, shredding and separating into strands. Serve immediately.

Yield: 4 servings

──── · ❄ · ────

TIPS
....

What a calorie saver! Spaghetti squash has only 35 calories per cup while pasta has about 195 calories per cup.

Serve spaghetti squash with Quick Spaghetti Sauce and Meatballs (see page 164).

Don't discard the seeds. They taste great microwaved and lightly salted for snacks. To microwave squash seeds, wash, pat dry, and place on paper towels. Microwave ½ cup for 2 to 3 minutes at HIGH (100%). Salt lightly, store, and enjoy.

Variations: For larger squash, microwave approximately 6 minutes per pound.

For cooked pumpkin, microwave as directed for squash. Mash pulp.

Nutritional Analysis per 1¼-Cup Serving

Calories: 45
Carbohydrate: 10 g
Fat: Trace
Protein: 1 g

Fiber: N/A
Cholesterol: 0 mg
Sodium: 28 mg
Diabetic exchanges:
Vegetable: 2

TIPS

This is a very flavorful and nutritious dish, yet it takes only minutes to prepare. Try serving it as a side dish with Company Round Steak (see page 150), or Easy Crumb-Coated Snapper (see page 138), or Diet Barbecue Chicken (see page 198).

NUTRITIOUS CONFETTI SPAGHETTI SQUASH

——————— · · · · · ———————

½ medium onion, thinly sliced

2 cloves garlic, minced

2 medium tomatoes, seeded and chopped

2 small zucchini (2 cups), unpeeled and julienned or thinly sliced

2 teaspoons olive oil

1 tablespoon garlic-wine vinegar

1 teaspoon basil leaves

1 small spaghetti squash (about 2 pounds), cooked and separated into strands (see page 318)

⅓ cup crunchy bran cereal to garnish, optional

1. Combine all ingredients except squash and cereal in a flat 2-quart microwave-safe casserole. Cover with lid or vented plastic wrap. Microwave for 7 to 9 minutes at HIGH (100%), or until vegetables are tender-crisp.
2. Toss cooked vegetables with cooked spaghetti squash strands. Serve immediately, garnished with bran cereal, if desired.

Yield: 6 servings

——————— · ❄ · ———————

Variation: Add 1 red bell pepper, julienned, with the onion in step #1 and microwave for 8 to 10 minutes at HIGH (100%) instead of 7 to 9 minutes.

Nutritional Analysis per Serving (⅙ Recipe)

Calories: 89
Carbohydrate: 18 g
Fat: 2 g
Protein: 3 g
Fiber: N/A

Cholesterol: 0 mg
Sodium: 86 mg
Diabetic exchanges:
  Bread: 1
  Vegetable: 0.5

SUMMER SQUASH MEDLEY

· · · · ·

2 small zucchini (2 cups), sliced in ¼-inch rounds
2 small yellow squash (2 cups), sliced in ¼-inch rounds
½ teaspoon chicken bouillon granules* dissolved in 2 tablespoons hot water

¼ teaspoon dried basil
Dash ground pepper
1 teaspoon reduced-calorie margarine*
Parsley flakes and ¼ cup (2 ounces) plain nonfat yogurt to garnish, optional

1. Microwave zucchini, yellow squash, bouillon-water, basil, and pepper in a 1-quart covered microwave-safe casserole for 5 to 6 minutes at HIGH (100%).
2. Stir in margarine. Cover again and let stand 5 minutes. Serve garnished with parsley and a dollop of yogurt, if desired.

Yield: 2 servings

—————— · ❄ · ——————

....

*Use unsalted variety for lowest sodium values, if desired.

TIPS
....

Any summer squash
will work in this recipe.
Try using 1 zucchini
and 1 yellow squash.
Peeling the eggplant is
optional. Unpeeled, the
color will add to the at-
tractiveness of the dish.

GARDEN VEGETABLE AND SQUASH CASSEROLE

———— · · · · · ————

A delicious no-meat dish for a warm summer evening

1 clove garlic, minced

1 small onion (⅔ cup), chopped

2 teaspoons vegetable or olive oil

2 small summer squash (about 2 cups), rinsed and sliced

2 small eggplants (about 6 cups), rinsed and cut into cubes

1 medium tomato, chopped

½ teaspoon dried basil

1 teaspoon Seasoned Salt Substitute #2 (see page 245) or store-bought alternative

¼ cup grated Parmesan cheese

Chopped chives or parsley to garnish, optional

1. Combine garlic, onion, and vegetable oil in a 2-quart microwave-safe casserole. Cover with lid or vented plastic wrap. Microwave for 3 to 3½ minutes at HIGH (100%), or until tender.

2. Stir in squash and eggplant. Cover again. Microwave for 10 to 12 minutes at HIGH (100%), or until eggplant is tender, stirring twice. Stir in tomato, basil, and Seasoned Salt Substitute.

3. Microwave for 1 to 2 minutes at HIGH (100%), or until heated. Sprinkle with Parmesan cheese and chives or parsley to garnish, if desired.

Yield: 6 servings

———————— · ❄ · ————————

Variation: One medium green bell pepper, cored and seeded, can be added with the eggplant.

Nutritional Analysis per Serving (⅙ Recipe)

Calories: 83

Carbohydrate: 11 g

Fat: 2 g

Protein: 4 g

Fiber: N/A

Cholesterol: 3 mg

Sodium: 83 mg

Diabetic exchanges:

  Lean meat: 0.25

  Vegetable: 2

  Fat: 0.25

GARLIC AND LEMON SWISS CHARD

———————— · · · · · ————————

2 teaspoons vegetable or olive oil

2 cloves garlic, minced

1 pound Swiss chard leaves, stalks removed, cleaned and cut into strips

1 tablespoon lemon juice

Dash Seasoned Salt Substitute #1 (see page 244) or store-bought alternative

1. Microwave oil and garlic in a 1-quart microwave-safe casserole for 1 to 1½ minutes at HIGH (100%). Stir in Swiss chard leaves. Cover with vented plastic wrap or lid. Microwave for 4½ to 5½ minutes at HIGH (100%), or until tender-crisp.

TIPS

If you like spinach, you'll like Swiss chard. Like spinach, it's high in vitamins A and C as well as fiber, potassium, iron, and even some protein.

2. Let stand 5 minutes. Add lemon juice and Seasoned Salt Substitute, toss and serve.

Yield: 4 servings

———————— · ❄ · ————————

┌───┐
│   *Nutritional Analysis per Serving (¼ Recipe)*   │
│   │
│ Calories: 41   Cholesterol: 0 mg   │
│ Carbohydrate: 4 g   Sodium: 159 mg   │
│ Fat: 2 g   Diabetic exchanges: │
│ Protein: 2 g   Vegetable: 1   │
│ Fiber: N/A   Fat: 0.5   │
└───┘

TIPS
·······

This recipe is my favorite way to serve zucchini. It also is a perfect way to use zucchinis from your garden. The tomato adds vitamins A and C as well as some potassium, niacin, iron, and protein to your diet.

ZUCCHINI BOATS

———————— · · · · · ————————

2 medium zucchini (about 1 pound)

1 medium tomato, seeded and chopped

½ medium onion (½ cup), chopped

¼ cup Dry Bread Crumbs (see page 54)

½ cup (2 ounces) grated reduced-fat cheddar cheese *

½ teaspoon Seasoned Salt Substitute #2 (see page 245) or store-bought alternative

2 tablespoons reduced-calorie mayonnaise

1 tablespoon grated Parmesan cheese

Dash paprika, to garnish

1. Pierce skin of zucchini and place zucchini on a paper towel in microwave oven. Microwave for 4 to 5 minutes at HIGH (100%), or until hot. Cool 5 minutes. Slice off stem ends. Cut in half lengthwise; scoop out pulp, leav-

···
* Use reduced-sodium variety for lowest sodium values, if desired.

ing ¼-inch shell. Chop pulp coarsely. Invert zucchini shells on a 10-inch or 8 × 12-inch flat microwave-safe casserole to keep warm. Set aside.

2. Combine zucchini pulp, tomato, and onion in a 1-quart microwave-safe casserole. Microwave for 4 to 5 minutes at HIGH (100%), or until tender, stirring once. Drain.

3. Add bread crumbs, cheddar cheese, Seasoned Salt Substitute, and mayonnaise; toss. Turn zucchini shells hollow side up, mound ¼ filling in each shell. Sprinkle with Parmesan cheese and paprika.

4. Microwave uncovered for 3 to 4 minutes at HIGH (100%), or until zucchini is hot and tender.

Yield: 4 servings

— · ❄ · —

Variation: Add 1 cup chopped fresh mushrooms with the zucchini pulp and onion in step #2. Proceed as directed and increase mayonnaise to 3 tablespoons.

Nutritional Analysis per Serving (1 Boat)

Calories: 100
Carbohydrate: 8 g
Fat: 6 g
Protein: 6 g
Fiber: N/A

Cholesterol: 4 mg
Sodium: 136 mg
Diabetic exchanges:
  Lean meat: 0.5
  Vegetable: 1.5
  Fat: 0.75

To make soft bread crumbs quickly, place 2 slices reduced-calorie wheat bread or any bread in a food processor and process into crumbs.

Do not substitute reduced-calorie margarine for the regular margarine. If you do, the topping on the tomatoes will become soggy.

PARMESAN-TOPPED TOMATOES
———— · · · · · ————

An attractive garnish on any plate.

2 large vine-ripened
   tomatoes
1 tablespoon regular
   polyunsaturated
   margarine*
⅓ cup soft bread crumbs
   (made from reduced-
   calorie wheat bread) (see
   tip at left)

2 tablespoons grated
   Parmesan cheese
½ teaspoon Seasoned Salt
   Substitute #2 (see page
   245) or store-bought
   alternative, optional

1. Cut tomatoes in half crosswise and then arrange in a circle on a microwave-safe plate.
2. In a small microwave-safe bowl or custard cup, microwave margarine for 20 to 30 seconds at HIGH (100%) to melt. Toss in bread crumbs. Microwave for 1 to 1½ minutes at HIGH (100%) to toast, stirring twice. Stir in Parmesan cheese and Seasoned Salt Substitute.
3. Sprinkle crumb-cheese mixture on each tomato half. Microwave for 2½ to 3 minutes at HIGH (100%), or until hot. Let stand 1 minute.

Yield: 4 servings

———— · ❄ · ————

Variation: For Italian Tomatoes, substitute 2 tablespoons reduced-calorie mayonnaise for the margarine. Substitute ⅔ cup (3 ounces) shredded mozzarella cheese for the bread crumbs. Cut each tomato half in half again and place all pieces in a circle on a microwave-safe plate. Omit step #2. Mix mayonnaise, mozzarella cheese, Parmesan cheese, and dash each basil and onion powder. Proceed as directed in step #3.

···
*Use unsalted variety for lowest sodium values, if desired.

Nutritional Analysis per Serving (½ Tomato)

Calories: 64
Carbohydrate: 5 g
Fat: 42 g
Protein: 2 g
Fiber: N/A

Cholesterol: 2 mg
Sodium: 82 mg
Diabetic exchanges:
    Lean meat: 0.25
    Vegetables: 0.5
    Fat: 0.75

CHEESE-TOPPED ZUCCHINI-TOMATO CASSEROLE

· · · · ·

3 teaspoons reduced-calorie margarine*
1 clove garlic, minced
1 medium onion, thinly sliced
2 medium zucchini, thinly sliced
2 medium tomatoes, sliced

½ teaspoon each dried basil and Seasoned Salt Substitute #1 (see page 244) or store-bought alternative
¼ cup (1 ounce) shredded part-skim mozzarella cheese
¼ cup Seasoned Bread Crumbs (see page 243)

1. Place margarine, garlic, onion, and zucchini in a 10-inch flat microwave-safe casserole. Cover with lid or vented plastic wrap. Microwave for 3 to 4 minutes at HIGH (100%).
2. Stir in tomatoes, basil, and Seasoned Salt Substitute. Cover again. Microwave for 3 to 4 minutes at HIGH (100%), or until tomatoes and vegetables are tender. Immediately sprinkle with cheese and bread crumbs. Cover. Let stand 3 minutes to allow cheese to melt.

Yield: 4 servings

———— · ❄ · ————

* Use unsalted variety for lowest sodium values, if desired.

TIPS
· · · · · · · ·

This casserole is a wonderful way to use your garden produce. The mozzarella cheese adds enough protein so that doubling the serving would make a nice entree on a hot summer day.

Variations: Yellow squash can be substituted for all or part of the zucchini.

Shredded reduced-calorie cheddar cheese can be substituted for the mozzarella cheese. Use the same amount or double it for a tasty entree.

Nutritional Analysis per Serving (¼ Recipe)

Calories: 85	Cholesterol: 5 mg
Carbohydrate: 9 g	Sodium: 75 mg
Fat: 4 g	Diabetic exchanges:
Protein: 4 g	Bread: 0.25
Fiber: N/A	Vegetable: 2
	Fat: 0.5

T I P S
....

Sliced zucchini contains only 25 calories per cup and is a good source of vitamins A and C as well as potassium.

Three large carrot, peeled and sliced, may be substituted for the 10-ounce package of frozen carrots.

SUNSHINE ZUCCHINI AND CARROTS
· · · · ·

1 medium zucchini (1 cup), cut into ¼-inch slices
10-ounce package frozen sliced carrots
¼ cup orange juice

½ stalk celery (⅓ cup), finely chopped
1 tablespoon onion, finely chopped, optional
Orange slices to garnish, if desired

Combine all ingredients except orange slices in a 1-quart microwave-safe casserole. Cover loosely with plastic wrap or lid. Microwave for 8 to 10 minutes at HIGH (100%),† or until carrots are tender-crisp and zucchini is tender, stirring once. Let stand 2 minutes. Serve garnished with orange slices, if desired.

Yield: 4 servings

——— · ❄ · ———

† **Compacts:** Microwave for 9 to 11 minutes at HIGH (100%) in step #1.

Variation: For Sunshine Zucchini and Carrots with Orange Sauce, proceed as directed above. Combine 2 teaspoons cornstarch with ½ cup additional orange juice in a small dish until blended. Stir into cooked vegetables. Cover and microwave for 2 to 2½ minutes longer at HIGH (100%), or until thickened, stirring once. (Stir in sugar substitute equivalent to 2 teaspoons sugar to sweeten sauce, if desired.) Serve immediately.

Nutritional Analysis per ½-Cup Serving

Calories: 39
Carbohydrate: 9 g
Fat: Trace
Protein: 1 g
Fiber: N/A

Cholesterol: 0 mg
Sodium: 47 mg
Diabetic exchanges:
   Vegetable: 1.25
   Fruit: 0.25

BLANCHING VEGETABLES FOR FREEZING

1. Prepare vegetables as for conventional cooking (wash, peel, slice, etc.)
2. Use only the amount of vegetable specified in the following chart and place in a microwave-safe dish.
3. Add water as indicated. Do not add salt. Cover with lid or plastic wrap.
4. Cook on HIGH (100%) for the time listed.
5. Stir halfway through cooking time.
6. Check for doneness. Vegetables should have an evenly bright color throughout. Using tongs, transfer vegetables to a freezer bag. Add a dash of salt if desired. Seal.
7. Plunge sealed bag into ice water at once until cool.
8. Label, date, and freeze bags quickly.

TIPS

Vegetables tend to dry out if microwaved with salt. You can add salt when you place the vegetables in the freezer bag.

The microwave oven is perfect for blanching small batches. It is not only quick, but it helps retain much of the vitamin C in vegetables. However, when blanching large batches you will save more time by using the conventional stove-top method.

TIME CHART FOR BLANCHING VEGETABLES

VEGETABLE	AMOUNT	MICROWAVE-SAFE DISH	WATER	MINUTES
Asparagus	1 pound cut into 1-inch pieces	2 quart	¼ cup	3 to 4
Beans	1 pound	1½ quart	½ cup	4 to 6
Broccoli	1 bunch, 1¼–1½ pounds	2 quart	½ cup	4 to 5½
Carrots	1 pound, sliced	1½ quart	¼ cup	4 to 6
Cauliflower	1 head, cut into flowerets	2 quart	½ cup	4 to 5½
Corn, cut	4 cups	1½ quart	¼ cup	4 to 5
Corn on Cob	6 ears	12x8-inch dish	none	5½
Onions	4 medium, quartered	1 quart	½ cup	3 to 4½
Parsnips	1 pound, cubed	1½ quart	¼ cup	2½ to 4
Peas	2 pounds, shelled	1 quart	¼ cup	3½ to 5
Spinach	1 pound, washed	2 quart	none	2½ to 4
Squash, yellow	1 pound, sliced or cubed	1½ quart	¼ cup	3 to 4½
Turnips	1 pound, cubed	1½ quart	¼ cup	3 to 4½
Zucchini	1 pound, sliced or cubed	1½ quart	¼ cup	3 to 4½

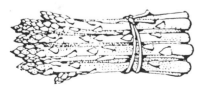

FRESH VEGETABLE
MICROWAVING TIME CHART

Follow General Tips for Microwaving Vegetables (see page 285) or see specific recipes in this section.

VEGETABLE/AMOUNT	PREPARATION†	MICROWAVING TIME AT HIGH (100%)
Artichokes, 1 medium	Cut off top ½ inch. Snip off prickly tips. Wrap in plastic wrap.	4 to 5 minutes
Asparagus, 1 pound	Remove tough peel at stem ends or, for tender tips only, break spears by hand where they snap easily. Arrange tip end toward the center in casserole.	6 to 8 minutes
Beans (green or wax) 1 pound	Trim or snap off tips and cut into 2-inch pieces (optional). Add ½ cup water.	8 to 10 minutes
Beet greens 1 pound, rinsed	Clean and remove stems from leaves. Add 2 tablespoons water.	4 to 5 minutes
Beets 2-inch diameter with short stem	Remove greens, leaving 1-inch stem. Add ½ cup water. After standing time, trim stems and slip off skins.	15 to 20 minutes
Broccoli 1 pound or 2 cups flowerets	Remove tough stem. Split stalks lengthwise into quarters or use flowerets only.	6 to 8 minutes
Brussels sprouts, 25 to 30 small heads	Trim and cut an "X" in bottom of each stem. Add ¼ cup water.	6 to 8 minutes
Cabbage 1 pound wedges (or 4½ cups, shredded)	Cut into 4 wedges (or shred). Add ¼ cup water.	11 to 13 minutes (8 to 10 minutes)
Carrots 1 pound	Remove tops, trim ends, and peel or scrub. Add ¼ cup water.	8 to 10 minutes
Cauliflower 1-pound head or flowerets	Remove leaves and core. Cook whole or cut into small flowerets.	6 to 8 minutes
Corn kernels 2 cups	Run a sharp knife down ear of corn to remove kernels.	5 to 6 minutes
Corn on the cob 1 ear	Remove silks and outer husks. Cook in inner husks or wrapped in plastic wrap.	2½ to 3 minutes per ear

VEGETABLE/AMOUNT	PREPARATION†	MICROWAVING TIME AT HIGH (100%)
Eggplant 1 pound whole or sliced	Pierce skin and cook whole, or peel and slice ¼-inch thick.	5 to 7 minutes
Kohlrabi 1 pound, sliced	Peel, cut in half, and slice ¼-inch thick. Add ¼ cup water.	5 to 7 minutes
Mushrooms 1 pound (6 cups), whole or sliced	Brush to remove dirt or grit. Slice if desired. Add 1 tablespoon water.	3 to 6 minutes
Onions, 1 pound	Peel and cut into quarters.	6 to 8 minutes
Peas 2 cups shelled or unshelled	Add 2 tablespoons water if cooked in shells.	5 to 6 minutes
Potatoes, 1 pound	For baked, scrub and pierce skin. Let stand wrapped in foil for 10 to 15 minutes after microwaving. For boiled, peel, quarter, and add ½ cup water. Let stand in water for 5 minutes after microwaving; drain.	6 to 8 minutes
Pumpkin 4 to 5 pounds	Cut in half. Remove seeds after cooking.	16 minutes (4 minutes per pound)
Rutabagas 1 pound	Peel and slice or cube. Add ¼ cup water.	7 to 9 minutes
Spinach 1 pound	Remove tough ends and trim.	4 to 6 minutes
Squash 1 pound whole		
winter: acorn, butternut, pumpkin, spaghetti	Pierce skin, turn over twice during cooking time.	6 to 8 minutes
summer: zucchini, yellow	Scrub or peel, slice ¼-inch thick.	4 to 6 minutes
Tomatoes 1 pound	Peel and cut into quarters or wedges.	3 to 4 minutes
Turnips 1 pound	Trim ends. Peel and slice or cube. Add ¼ cup water.	6 to 9 minutes

. . . .
†Use a 1½- to 2-quart microwave-safe casserole covered with vented plastic wrap unless otherwise instructed.

DRIED BEANS, PEAS, AND LENTILS MICROWAVING TIME CHART

TYPE/AMOUNT	PREPARATION/INSTRUCTIONS	TIME/POWER LEVEL
Dried beans (navy, northern, kidney, pinto, black), 2 cups	Soak overnight in 6 cups water or speed-soak (see General Tips, page 258). Add minced garlic, chopped onion, and bay leaf. For soup, drain beans after soaking. Add water and vegetables (see recipes this section.)	Microwave for 10 to 12 minutes at HIGH (100%) or until boiling and microwave for 45 to 60 minutes at MEDIUM (50%), or to desired doneness, stirring twice. Let stand 5 to 10 minutes. Microwave as directed in recipe.
Dried lentils or split peas	Same as for beans. (Lentils do not need to be soaked.) For soup, drain lentils after soaking. Add water and vegetables (see recipes this section).	Microwave for 10 to 12 minutes at HIGH (100%) or until boiling and microwave for 30 to 60 minutes at MEDIUM (50%), or to desired doneness, stirring twice. Let stand 5 to 10 minutes. Microwave as recipe directs.

SUBSTITUTIONS
AND EQUIVALENTS

· ❄ ·

SUGAR SUBSTITUTE EQUIVALENCY TABLE

SUGAR (SUCROSE), GRANU-LATED	EQUAL OR NUTRA-SWEET (ASPAR-TAME), POWDERED	FRUCTOSE (FRUIT SUGAR), POWDERED	SPRINKLE SWEET (SAC-CHARIN), GRANU-LATED	SUGAR TWIN (SAC-CHARIN), GRANU-LATED	SWEET'N LOW, WHITE OR BROWN (SAC-CHARIN), GRANU-LATED	SWEET 10 (SAC-CHARIN) LIQUID
1 teaspoon (16 calories)	½ packet (2 calories)	¾ teaspoon (9 calories)	1 teaspoon (2 calories)	1 teaspoon (1.5 calories)	dash (or use the spoon in package) (2 calories)	10 drops (2 calories)
¼ cup (192 calories)	6 packets (24 calories)	3 tablespoons (108 calories)	¼ cup (24 calories)	¼ cup (18 calories)	1 teaspoon (17 calories)	1½ teaspoons (24 calories)
½ cup (385 calories)	12 packets (48 calories)	⅓ cup (192 calories)	½ cup (48 calories)	½ cup (36 calories)	2 teaspoons (34 calories)	1 tablespoon (48 calories)
1 cup (770 calories)	24 packets (96 calories)	⅔ cup (384 calories)	1 cup (96 calories)	1 cup (96 calories)	4 teaspoons (68 calories)	2 tablespoons (96 calories)

SUBSTITUTIONS—IN A PINCH

FOR	YOU CAN USE...
1 ounce baking chocolate square	3 tablespoons cocoa or carob powder plus 1 tablespoon margarine
1 cup (6 ounces) chocolate chips	⅓ cup cocoa or carob powder, plus ¼ cup fructose (or ⅓ cup sugar) and ¼ cup margarine
1 cup cocoa	1 cup carob powder (plus 1 teaspoon chocolate flavoring, optional)
1 tablespoon cornstarch	2 tablespoons flour or 1½ tablespoons tapioca
1 cup milk	½ cup evaporated milk plus ½ cup water
1 cup buttermilk	1 tablespoon lemon juice or vinegar plus enough milk to make 1 cup
1 cup half-and-half	⅞ cup milk plus 3 tablespoons margarine
1 cup heavy cream	¾ cup milk plus ⅓ cup margarine
1 cup sour cream	1 cup yogurt plus 1 teaspoon cornstarch
1 teaspoon baking powder	¼ teaspoon baking soda and 1 teaspoon cream of tartar
1 cup miniature marshmallows	10 large marshmallows cut up
1 cup brown sugar	1 cup white sugar mixed with 1 tablespoon dark molasses
1 tablespoon sugar	2 teaspoons fructose (See Sugar Substitute chart, page 333)
1 cup sugar	⅔ cup fructose (see Sugar Substitute chart, page 333)
1 whole egg	2 egg whites or ¼ cup Egg Substitute (see page 91)
1 tablespoon fresh herbs	1 teaspoon dried herbs (parsley, dill, and so on)
1 clove garlic	⅛ teaspoon to ¼ teaspoon garlic powder

COMMON FOOD EQUIVALENTS

¼ pound butter or margarine	1 stick or ½ cup
1 cup shredded cheese	4 ounces
1 cup cottage cheese	8 ounces
1 cup chocolate chips	6 ounces
1⅓ cups coconut	4 ounces
1 pound flour	3½ cups
1 pound brown sugar, packed	2¼ cups
1 pound powdered (confectioner's) sugar	3¾ cups
1 pound granulated sugar	2¼ cups
1 medium lemon	2½ tablespoons lemon juice and 1 teaspoon peel
1 medium orange	⅓ cup juice and 1 tablespoon peel
1 pound bananas (3–4 medium)	2 cups mashed
1 pint berries	2 cups
1 pound apples (3 large)	3 cups pared and sliced
1 pound bread	12 to 16 slices
1 slice fresh bread	½ cup fresh crumbs
1 pound macaroni	5 cups uncooked or 8 to 10 cups cooked
2 ounces spaghetti	1 cup cooked
1 cup small pasta	1¾ cups cooked
1 cup raw rice	3 cups cooked
1 cup wild rice	4 cups cooked
1 cup dry bread crumbs	2–3 slices bread
1 pound dates	2 cups chopped
1 quart strawberries	4 cups sliced
1 medium peach/pear	½ cup sliced
1 pound walnuts or pecans	3¾ to 4 cups chopped
1 pound raisins	2¾ cups
1 pound dried beans	2 to 2½ cups uncooked or 5½ cups cooked
1 cup dried beans	2 to 3 cups cooked
1 large egg	2 tablespoons
13-ounce can evaporated milk	1½ cups
1 pound carrots	2 cups cooked
1¼ pounds bunch celery	3 cups raw sliced
1 large clove garlic	1 teaspoon minced
1 pound zucchini	3 cups raw
1 pound winter squash, raw	1 cup mashed

INDEX

—— · ❄ · ——

American Diabetic Association, Exchange
Lists for Meal Planning, 25–27
American Dietetic Association, Exchange
Lists for Meal Planning, 25–27
American Heart Association, dietary
guidelines of, 2, 22, 24–25
Appetizers, 29
California Stuffed Mushrooms, 34
Chicken Kabobs, 204–205
Fast Pizza Bagelettes, 282–283
Low-Calorie Guacamole Dip, 35
Mock Marinated Herring, 36
Party Cheese Ball—Hawaiian Style, 37
Spinach Dip in Rye Bread, 38
Warm Citrus Appetizer, 33
Zucchini-Stuffed Mushrooms, 39–40
Apples
Applesauce, 66
Blender Apple–Oat Bran Muffins, 45–46
Cinnamon Apple Bars, 60
Delicious Baked Apples, 68
High-Fiber Apple-Bran Muffins, 48–49
Hot Chicken and Roquefort-Apple Salad,
215–216
Miniature Apple Crisps, 69
Slim Apple Pie, 76
Sugar-Free Cranberry-Apple Sauce, 301
Sweet Apple-Filled Squash, 317–318
Applesauce, 66
Apricot butter, 255
Artichokes, 292
Italian Stuffed Artichokes, 292
Asparagus, 262, 293

Asparagus (cont'd)
Lite Asparagus Soup, 262–263
Swiss Asparagus, 293
Au Gratin Potatoes, 304
Avocadoes, tips about, 35

Bagelettes, tips about, 282
Baked apples, 68
Baked chicken and mushrooms, 194
Baked goods, tips for microwaving, 55–56
Baked Potatoes, 302–303
Banana "Cream" Pie, 77
Barbecue chicken, 198–199
Bars, 55–56
Carob and Oat Bran Cake Brownies,
57–58
Cinnamon Apple Bars, 60
Oat Bran–Date Bars, 58–59
Bean curd. See Tofu
Bean soup, 271–272
Beans
microwaving time chart, 332
tips about soaking, 271–272
Beef
Beef Burgundy, 146–147
Beef Stroganoff, 148–149
Cajun Meat Loaf, 157
Cheesy Meat Loaf Florentine, 158–159
Chinese Beef and Vegetable Stir Fry,
144–145
Company Round Steak, 151
Homemade Spaghetti Meat Sauce, 162–163

Beef (*cont'd*)
   Italian Pizza Burgers, 168
   Lasagna Rolls with Meat Filling, 170
   Lean Taco Salad, 172
   Lite Lasagna, 160–161
   Low-Calorie Round Steak Royal,
     149–150
   Marinated Beef Kabobs, 152–153
   Marinated Teriyaki Steak, 145–146
   Meat Loaf for One or Two, 155
   Quick Spaghetti Meat Sauce, 163–164
   Sloppy Joes, 154
   Stuffed Green Peppers, 171–172
   Swiss Mushroom Meat Loaf, 159
   Trim Microwave Meat Loaf or Turkey
     Loaf, 156–157
Beef Burgundy, 146–147
Beef Stroganoff, 148–149
Berries, tips about, 79
Beverages, 30
   Citrus Cooler, 31–32
   Coffee Olé, 32–33
   Low-Cal Tomato Cocktail, 30
   Mock Champagne, 31–32
   Sparkling Rosé, 31–32
Blanching vegetables for freezing, 328–329
Blender Apple–Oat Bran Muffins, 45–46
Blender Apricot or Peach Butter, 255
Blender Berry Cheesecake, 61–62
Blender Chocolate "Cream" Pie, 78
Blender Cucumber Soup, 264–265
Blender Strawberry Sorbet, 86–87
Bleu Cheese Dressing or Dip, 246–247
Blueberries
   Blender Blueberry Cheesecake, 61–62
   Blueberry-Apple Crisps, 69
   Blueberry Sorbet, 87
   Frozen Blueberry Yogurt, 84–85
Boiled Potatoes, 303

Bran muffins (low-calorie), 44
Bread crumbs
   dry, 54
   seasoned, 243–244
   soft, 325
Breads, 41–42
   recipes
     Cranberry-Oat Bran Bread, 50
     Melba Toast, 47
     Nutritious English Muffin Bread with
       Raisins, 51–52
     Slim Corn Bread, 52–53
   tips
     checking for doneness, 50
     defrosting, 43
     reheating, 43
Breakfast sausage, 176
Broccoli, 266
   Broccoli Yogurt Soup, 267
   Broccoli and carrots tarragon, 295
   "Cream" of Broccoli Soup, 266–267
   Curried Chicken and Broccoli Casserole,
     191
   Cheddar, Broccoli, and Tortilla Brunch
     Pie, 104–105
   Chicken-Broccoli Divan, 192–193
   Lite Broccoli-and-Cheese Unstuffed
     Chicken Breasts, 211–212
Brownies, carob and oat bran, 57–58
Browning meats, tips about, 144–145
Browning powder, tips about, 170, 187
Brussels sprouts, 296
   Brussels Sprouts in Garlic Sauce, 296
Burgers, Italian pizza-style, 170
Burgundy sauce for beef, 146–147

Cabbage, 268
   Old-Fashioned Cabbage Soup, 268

Cafix, 32
Cajun Catfish or Redfish, 112
Cajun Chicken, 202–203
Cajun Meat Loaf, 157
Cakes, tips for microwaving, 55–56
Calico Frittata, 101
California Stuffed Mushrooms, 34
Calories and daily requirements, 20–21
Canned vegetables, tips for microwaving, 287
Cantaloupe Boats, 71–72
Carbohydrates, 21
Carob powder, 57
    Carob and Oat Bran Cake Brownies, 57–58
Carrots, 294
    Carrots and Broccoli Tarragon, 295
    Company Glazed Carrots with Apples, 298
    Sunshine Zucchini and Carrots, 327–328
Casseroles, 229–230
    Garden Vegetable and Squash Casserole, 321–322
    Chicken and Rice Casserole, 209
    Cheese-Topped Zucchini-Tomato Casserole, 326–327
    Curried Chicken and Broccoli Casserole, 191
Catfish, 112
    Cajun Catfish or Redfish, 112
Cauliflower, 269
    "Cream" of Cauliflower Soup, 269–270
    Lite Tangy-Cheesy Cauliflower, 296–297
Celery and onion stuffing for chicken, 182–183
Cereals, tips about, 91, 106
Champagne Sorbet, 88
Cheddar, Broccoli, and Tortilla Brunch Pie, 104–105

Cheddar-and-vegetable-stuffed pitas, 281
Cheese
    Cheese-Stuffed Manicotti, 232–234
    Cheese-Topped Zucchini-Tomato Casserole, 326–327
    Cheesy Meat Loaf Florentine, 158–159
    Lite Tangy-Cheesy Cauliflower, 296–297
    Mock Lasagna Rolls with Cheese Filling, 169–170
    Party Cheese Ball—Hawaiian Style, 37
    Slim Cheese Sauce, 247–248
Cheesecakes, 61–63, 83
Cherry-glazed ham, 167
Chicken, 177–180
    Cajun Chicken, 202–203
    Chicken Breasts Parmesan, 183–184
    Chicken-Broccoli Divan, 192–193
    Chicken Cacciatore, 189
    Chicken Chow Mein, 210–211
    Chicken Fajitas, 199–200
    Chicken Kabobs, 204–205
    Chicken Kiev, 188
    Chicken-Mandarin Salad, 213
    Chicken, Onion, and Tomato Kabobs, 205
    Chicken à l'Orange, 196–197
    Chicken Parmigiana, 195
    Cooked (Poached) Chicken, 180–181
    Chicken Portuguese, 189
    Chicken and Red Raspberry Salad, 216–217
    Chicken and Rice Casserole, 209
    Chicken and Roquefort-Apple Salad, 215–216
    Chicken soup, 278
    Chicken and Vegetables Rosemary for Two, 200–201
    Curried Chicken and Broccoli Casserole, 191

Chicken (*cont'd*)
Curried Chicken Salad, 214
Diet Barbecue Chicken, 198–199
Hawaiian Chicken Salad, 218
Juicy Baked Chicken and Mushrooms, 194
Lemon Chicken Breasts with Vegetables, 203
Lemon Chicken in Wine Sauce, 184–185
Light Gravy or Wine Sauce for Chicken or Vegetables, 248–249
Lite Broccoli-and-Cheese Unstuffed Chicken Breasts, 211–212
Mexican Chicken, 196
Micro-Fry Chinese Chicken, 207–208
Oriental Chicken à l'Orange, 197
Oriental Chicken and Vegetables, 206–207
Quick Saucy Chicken, 190–191
Trim Chicken Cordon Bleu, 186–187
Waldorf Chicken Salad, 219
Whole Roasted Chicken Stuffed with Celery and Onion, 182–183
Chili con Carne, 263–264
Chilled Watercress Soup, 280
Chinese Beef and Vegetable Stir Fry, 144–145
Chinese chicken, 207–208
Chinese Pork and Vegetables, 164–165
Chocolate Cheesecake, 63
Chocolate "cream" pie, 78
Chocolate pudding, 74
Cholesterol, 24, 121, 123, 132–133
Chowder (clam), New England–style, 265–266
Chow Mein (chicken), 210–211
Cinnamon Apple Bars, 60
Citrus appetizer (warm), 33
Citrus Cooler, 31–32

Citrus peel, dried, 256
Clam chowder, New England–style, 265–266
Cocktail sauce for shrimp, 126
Cod, 110
Cod Italiano, 110–111
Coffee Olé, 32–33
Colombard wine, salmon poached in, 132
Colorful Shrimp, Pasta, and Vegetable Salad, 237–238
Combination cooking, 17
Common Food Equivalents, 335
Compact microwaves, adjustments for, 14
Company Glazed Carrots with Apples, 298
Company Round Steak, 151
Convection microwave oven, 17–18
Cooked (Poached) Chicken, 180–181
Cookies, 65
Cooking times, 12
Cookware to use in microwave ovens, 9–11
Cordon Bleu–style chicken, 186–187
Corn
Corn on the Cob, 313
tips about grilling, 287
Corn Bread, Slim, 52–53
Cornflakes, seasoned, 243–244
Cottage cheese, tips about draining, 61, 211
Covering foods in the microwave, 11–12
Crabmeat Frittata, 99–100
Cranberries, tips about, 50, 301
Cranberry-Grape Sorbet, 88
Cranberry–Oat Bran Bread, 50
Sugar-Free Cranberry-Apple Sauce, 301
Sugar-Free Cranberry Sauce, 300
Cream cheese, substitute for, 37
"Cream" pies, 77–78
Cream sauce for mackerel and mushroom loaf, 121–122

"Cream" soups
   "Cream" of Broccoli Soup, 266–267
   "Cream" of Cauliflower Soup, 269–270
   "Cream" of Mushroom Soup, 270–271
   "Cream" of Potato Soup, 276–277
   Creamy Broccoli Soup, 267
   Low-Calorie "Cream Soup" Mix or Cream
      Soup Substitute, 259–260
   Quick "Cream" of Mushroom Soup for
      Two, 260–261
   Quick "Cream" of Tomato Soup for Two,
      261–262
Cream of Wheat, 106
Creamy Cucumbers, 312
Crumb-coated snapper or pike, 138
Cucumber sauces
   for fish fillets, 120
   for lemon salmon, 133–134
Cucumber soup, 264–265
Cucumbers, creamy, 312
Curried Chicken and Broccoli Casserole, 191
Curried Chicken Salad, 214
Curried orange chicken, 196–197
Custard cups, 75

Date–oat bran bars, 58–59
Defrosting tips
   breads, 43
   fruit, 64, 66, 87
   meat, 139–141
   scallops, 130
   shrimp, 237
Dehydrating fruits and vegetables, tips for,
   243
Delicious Baked Apples, 68
Desserts, tips for microwaving, 56
Diabetic exchanges, 25–27
Dietary fiber, 23–24, 45

Diet Barbecue Chicken, 198–199
Diet French Dressing, 252
Dips
   Bleu Cheese, 246–247
   Watercress, 280
Dishes to use in microwave ovens, 9–11
Divan of chicken and broccoli, 192–193
Dressings
   Bleu Cheese Dressing, 246–247
   Diet French Dressing, 252
   Favorite Vinaigrette Dressing, 250–251
   Mock Ranch Dressing, 251
Dried Beans, Peas, and Lentils Microwaving
   Time Chart, 332
Dried beans, tips for microwaving, 258
Dried Citrus Peel, 256
Dried fruits, tips for microwaving, 57
Drinks, 30
   Citrus Cooler, 31–32
   Coffee Olé, 32–33
   Low-Cal Tomato Cocktail, 30
   Mock Champagne, 31–32
   Sparkling Rosé, 31–32
Dry Bread Crumbs, 54

Easy Blender Cheesecake, 62–63
Easy Crumb-Coated Snapper or Pike, 138
Easy Parmesan Potato Fans, 305
Easy Parmesan Potato Wedges, 310
Egg Drop Soup, 273
Eggs, 89–90, 92
   Egg Drop Soup, 273
   Egg Salad Deluxe for One, 97
   Egg Substitute, 92
   Egg Substitute Scrambled Eggs, 92
   Fast Egg and Potato Frittata, 100–101
   Italian Omelet, 95
   Low-Calorie Cheesy Omelet, 93

Eggs (*cont'd*)

"No Cholesterol" Omelet for Two, 94

No-Cholesterol Scrambled Eggs, 92

Poached Eggs, 96

Scrambled Eggs or Egg Omelet in a
Styrofoam Cup, 93

See also Frittatas; Quiche

Egg Salad Deluxe for One, 97

Egg Substitute, 92

English muffin bread with raisins, 51–52

English Pumpkin Pudding Wedges, 80

Evaporated skim milk, substitute for, 265

Exchange Lists for diabetics, 26–27

Fajitas, chicken, 199–200

Fast Blueberry Sauce, 61–64

Fast Egg and Potato Frittata, 100–101

Fast Pita Pizza Slices, 282–283

Fast Pizza Bagelettes, 283

Fast Raspberry Sauce, 61–64

Fast Strawberry Sauce, 61–64

Fats, 22

Favorite Vinaigrette Dressing, 250–251

Fiber, 23–24, 45

Fish recipes

Cajun Catfish or Redfish, 112

Cod Italiano, 110–111

Easy Crumb-Coated Snapper or Pike, 138

Fish Fillets in Cucumber Sauce, 120

Halibut in Lemon Sauce, 117

Lemon Flounder or Sole, 116

Lemon Salmon with Cucumber Sauce,
133–134

Lobster Tails and Lemon or Orange Sauce,
119–120

Mackerel and Mushroom Loaf with Cream
Sauce, 121–122

Micro-Steamed Shrimp, 126

Fish recipes (*cont'd*)

Orange-Baked Swordfish Fillets, 123–124

Orange Roughy Almondine, 122–123

Poached Salmon Colombard and
Vegetables, 132

Quick Fish Creole, 137

Rolled Red Snapper Kiev, 135

Saucy Vegetable Fish Fillets, 136

Sautéed Garlic Scallops, 129

Scallops in Wine Sauce, 130–131

Shrimp Creole, 127

Shrimp Primavera, 124–125

Shrimp Salsa, 128

Stuffed Flounder, 114–115

Yogurt-Baked Flounder, 113

Fish tips

about buying, 118

about microwaving, 107–108

Fish Microwaving Time Chart,
108–109

Florentine Stuffed (Chicken) Breasts, 212

Flounder, 113

Lemon Flounder, 116

Stuffed Flounder, 114–115

Yogurt-Baked Flounder, 113

Food Equivalents, 335

Freezing and blanching vegetables, 328

French dressing, 252

French Onion Soup, 275–276

Fresh vegetables

Fresh Vegetable Medley with Parmesan-
Lemon Sauce, 288–289

microwaving time chart, 330–331

tips for microwaving, 286

Frittatas, 98–101

Frozen foods

breads, defrosting, 43

fruit, defrosting, 64, 66, 87

meat, defrosting, 139–141

Frozen foods (*cont'd*)

  scallops, defrosting, 130

  shrimp, defrosting, 237

  vegetables, tips about, 124–125, 286

  yogurt, 84–85

Frozen Blueberry Yogurt, 84–85

Fruit, tips

  for dehydrating, 243

  for microwaving, 57

  for thawing when frozen, 64, 66, 87

Fruit-Flavored Yogurt, 86

Fruit Pizza Pie, 70–71

Fruit and vegetable salad, 289–290

Garden Fresh Marinade, 291

Garden and Pasta Salad, 291

Garden Vegetable and Squash Casserole,
  321–322

Garlic and Lemon Swiss Chard, 322–323

Garlic sauce for Brussels sprouts, 296

Gazpacho, 274

Gelatin Cookies, 65

General tips for microwaving

  appetizers, 29

  baked goods, 55–56

  beverages, 30

  breads, 41–43

  cereals, 91

  defrosting breads, 43

  defrosting meats, 139–140

  dehydrating fruits and vegetables, 243

  dried beans, peas, or lentils for soups,
    258

  dried fruits, 57

  eggs, 89

  fish, 107–108

  fruits, 57, 243

  jams and jellies, 242–243

General tips for microwaving (*cont'd*)

  meats, 139–141

  pasta, rice, and casseroles, 229–231

  pies and desserts, 56

  poultry, 177–178

  preserving food, 287–288

  quick breads and muffins, 41–42

  reheating breads, 43

  sandwiches, 258–259

  sauces, 241–242

  soups, 257–258

  vegetables, 285–287

  yeast breads, 42

German Potato Salad, 308–309

Glazed carrots with apples, 298

Graham cracker crust, 82–83

Gravy, 241–242

  Light Gravy or Wine Sauce for Chicken or
    Vegetables, 248–249

Green peppers, stuffed, 171–172

Grilling, tips about, 287

Ground meat, tips about microwaving, 168

Guacamole dip (low-calorie), 35

Halibut, 117

  Halibut in Lemon Sauce, 117

Ham, Lite Cherry-Glazed, 167

Hard-cooked eggs, 90

Hawaiian Chicken Salad, 218

Hawaiian-style party cheese ball, 37

Herring, mock marinated, 36

High-Fiber Apple-Bran Muffins, 48–49

Homemade Spaghetti Meat Sauce, 162–163

Homemade Spaghetti Sauce with Meatballs,
  161–163

Homemade Yogurt, 85–86

Honeydew Boats, 71–72

Hot Chicken and Red Raspberry Salad,
    216–217
Hot Chicken and Roquefort-Apple Salad,
    215–216

Insoluble fiber, 23–24
Italian Omelet, 95
Italian Pizza Burgers, 168
Italian seasoning, tips about, 235
Italian Stuffed Artichokes, 292
Italian Tomatoes, 325

Jams and jellies, 242–243
    Blender Apricot or Peach Butter, 255
    Red Raspberry Jam, 254
    Sugarless Strawberry Jam, 253
Juicy Baked Chicken and Mushrooms, 194

Kabobs, marinated
    beef, 152–153
    chicken, 204–205
Kidney beans, tips about, 263
Kiev-style chicken, 188
Kiev-style rolled red snapper, 135

Lamb, Leg of, with Sherry-Mushroom
    Sauce, 174–175
Lasagna, 160–161, 231
    Lasagna Rolls with Meat Filling, 170
    Lite Lasagna, 160–161
    Meatless Lasagna Rolls, 235–236
    Meatless Lite Lasagna, 161
    Mock Lasagna Rolls with Cheese Filling,
        169–170

Lean Blender Tomato Sauce, 249–250
Lean Breakfast Sausage, 176
Lean Macaroni and Cheese, 231–232
Lean Sausage Breakfast Frittata, 98
Lean Taco Salad, 172–173
Lean and Trim Chicken Soup, 278
Lean and Trim Turkey or Chicken Broth,
    278
Lean and Trim Turkey Rice Soup, 278
Lean and Trim Turkey Soup, 277–278
Leg of Lamb with Sherry-Mushroom Sauce,
    174–175
Lemon Cheesecake, 63
Lemon Chicken Breasts with Vegetables,
    203
Lemon Chicken in Wine Sauce, 183–184
Lemon Flounder or Sole, 116
Lemon and Garlic Swiss Chard, 322–323
Lemon peel, tips about, 256
Lemon Salmon with Cucumber Sauce,
    133–134
Lemon sauces
    for halibut, 117
    for lobster tails, 118–119
    for turkey cutlets, 223–224
    for vegetables, 288–289
Lemon zest, tips about, 203
Lentils, 258, 332
    Lentil Soup, 272
Light Gravy or Wine Sauce for Chicken or
    Vegetables, 248–249
Lite Asparagus Soup, 262–263
Lite Broccoli-and-Cheese Unstuffed Chicken
    Breasts, 211–212
Lite Cherry-Glazed Ham, 167
Lite Chocolate Pudding, 74
Lite Lasagna, 160–161
Lite Tangy-Cheesy Cauliflower, 296–297
Lobster, 118

Lobster (*cont'd*)
    Lobster Tails and Lemon or Orange Sauce,
        118–119
Low-Cal Graham Cracker Crust, 82–83
Low-Calorie Bran Muffins, 44
Low-Calorie Cheesy Omelet, 93
Low-calorie cocktail sauce for shrimp, 126
Low-Calorie "Cream Soup" Mix or Cream
    Soup Substitute, 259–260
Low-Calorie Guacamole Dip, 35
Low-Calorie Round Steak Royal, 149–150
Low-Cal Tomato Cocktail, 30

Macaroni
    Lean Macaroni and Cheese, 231–232
    Salmon (or Tuna) and Macaroni Salad,
        238–239
    See also Pasta
Mackerel, 121
    Mackerel and Mushroom Loaf with Cream
        Sauce, 121–122
Mandarin Mousse, 72–73
Mandarin vegetables and tofu, 314–315
Manicotti, cheese-stuffed, 232–234
Margarine, tips about melting, 288
Marinated Beef Kabobs, 152–153
Marinated chicken kabobs, 204–205
Marinated Teriyaki Steak, 145–146
Marinated vegetables, 291
Meat
    browning tips, 144–145
    defrosting tips, 139–141
    microwaving tips, 140–143
    slicing tips, 144
    See also Beef; Pork; Veal
Meatballs, 161–163, 164
Meat Defrosting Time Chart, 141
Meat-Filled Lasagna Rolls, 236

Meatless Lasagna Rolls, 235–236
Meatless Lite Lasagna, 161
Meat loaf recipes, 155–159
Meat Microwaving Time Chart, 142–143
Meat sauces for spaghetti, 162–164
Melba Toast, 47
Melons, 71–72
    Honeydew or Cantaloupe Boats, 71–72
    Melon Sorbet, 87
Mexican Chicken, 195
Micro-Baked Custard Cups, 75
Micro-Fry Chinese Chicken, 207–208
Micro-Steamed Shrimp, 126
Micro Stir-Fry Vegetables, 315–316
Microwave browning skillet, 144
Microwave cooking
    benefits of, 5–6
    general tips
        appetizers, 29
        baked goods, 55–56
        beverages, 30
        breads, 41–43
        cereals, 91
        defrosting breads, 43
        defrosting meats, 139–140
        dehydrating fruits and vegetables, 243
        dried beans, peas, or lentils for soups,
          258
        dried fruits, 57
        eggs, 89
        fish, 107–108
        fruits, 57, 243
        jams and jellies, 242–243
        meats, 139–141
        pasta, rice, and casseroles, 229–231
        pies and desserts, 56
        poultry, 177–178
        preserving food, 287–288
        quick breads and muffins, 41–42

Microwave cooking (*cont'd*)
    reheating breads, 43
    sandwiches, 258–259
    sauces, 241–242
    soups, 257–258
    vegetables, 285–287
    yeast breads, 42
  principles of, 7–8
  questions about, 7–18
Microwave Cookware Test, 10
Microwave ring, making your own, 52, 80
Milk, evaporated skim, substitute for, 265
Miniature Apple or Pear Crisps, 69
Mint and parsley potatoes, 306
Mock Champagne, 31–32
Mock Lasagna Rolls with Cheese Filling,
    169–170
Mock Marinated Herring, 36
Mock Ranch Dressing, 251
Mock Sour Cream Topping, 63
Molded Waldorf Salad, 299
Monounsaturated fats, 22
Mornay sauce for asparagus, 293
Mousse, Mandarin, 72–73
Muffins, 41–42
  Blender Apple–Oat Bran Muffins, 45–46
  High-Fiber Apple-Bran Muffins, 48–49
  Low-Calorie Bran Muffins, 44
  Strawberry–Oat Bran Muffins, 46–47
Mushrooms, 260
  California Stuffed Mushrooms, 34
  "Cream" of Mushroom Soup, 270–271
  Juicy Baked Chicken and Mushrooms,
    194
  Leg of Lamb with Sherry-Mushroom
    Sauce, 174–175
  Mackerel and Mushroom Loaf with Cream
    Sauce, 121–122

Mushrooms (*cont'd*)
  Tofu-Mushroom Quiche, 102–103
  Zucchini-Stuffed Mushrooms, 39–40

National Cancer Institute, fiber intake
    recommendations of, 24
Navy Bean Soup, 271–272
Neufchâtel cheese as substitute for cream
    cheese, 37
New England Clam Chowder, 265–266
"No Cholesterol" Omelet for Two, 94
No-Cholesterol Scrambled Eggs, 92
Nonalcoholic beverages, 30
  Citrus Cooler, 31–32
  Coffee Olé, 32–33
  Low-Cal Tomato Cocktail, 30
  Mock Champagne, 31–32
  Sparkling Rosé, 31–32
Nonalcoholic Champagne Sorbet, 88
Nutritional analysis, 19–28
Nutritious Confetti Spaghetti Squash,
    319–320
Nutritious English Muffin Bread with
    Raisins, 51–52

Oat bran, 45, 50
  Blender Apple–Oat Bran Muffins, 45–46
  Carob and Oat Bran Cake Brownies,
    57–58
  Cranberry–Oat Bran Bread, 50
  Oat Bran–Date Bars, 58–59
  Strawberry–Oat Bran Muffins, 46–47
Oatmeal, 106
Old-Fashioned Cabbage Soup, 268
Omega-3 fatty acid, 121, 123, 132–133

Omelets
    Egg Omelet in a Styrofoam Cup, 93
    Italian Omelet, 95
    Low-Calorie Cheesy Omelet, 93
    "No Cholesterol" Omelet for Two, 94
Orange-Baked Swordfish Fillets, 123–124
Orange curried chicken, 196–197
Orange Roughy Almondine, 122–123
Orange sauce for lobster tails, 119–120
Oriental Chicken à l'Orange, 197
Oriental Chicken and Vegetables, 206–207
Outdoor grilling, tips about, 287
Oven-Roasted Turkey, 220–221

Parmesan-Lemon Sauce, for vegetables,
    288–289
Parmesan Potato Fans, Easy, 305
Parmesan Potato Wedges, Easy, 310
Parmesan-style chicken, 183–184
Parmesan-style turkey, 224–225
Parmesan-Topped Tomatoes, 325–326
Parsleyed Brown Rice, 240
Parsley and Mint Potatoes, 306
Parsleyed White or Wild Rice, 239–240
Party Cheese Ball—Hawaiian Style, 36
Pasta, 229–231
    Cheese-Stuffed Manicotti, 232–234
    Colorful Shrimp, Pasta, and Vegetable
        Salad, 237–238
    Lean Macaroni and Cheese, 231–232
    Meat-Filled Lasagna Rolls, 236
    Meatless Lasagna Rolls, 235–236
    Salmon (or Tuna) and Macaroni Salad,
        238–239
Pea pods, tips about, 210
Peaches
    Blender Peach Butter, 255

Peaches (cont'd)
    Peach Sorbet, 87
Pear crisps, 69
Peas, tips for microwaving, 258, 332
Peppers, stuffed, 171–172
Pie crusts, 82–84
Pies, 56
    Banana "Cream" Pie, 77
    Blender Chocolate–"Cream" Pie, 78
    Cheddar, Broccoli, and Tortilla Brunch
        Pie, 104–105
    Reduced-Calorie Pumpkin Pie, 81
    Slim Apple Pie, 76
    Strawberry Supreme Pie, 79
Pike, easy crumb-coated, 138
Pita pizza slices, 282–283
Pitas stuffed with cheddar and vegetables,
    281
Pizza Bagelettes, 283
Pizza burgers, 168
Pizza Pie, Fruit, 70–71
Pizza slices made with pita, 282–283
Plastic wrap, venting, 127
Poached chicken, 180–181
Poached Eggs, 90, 96
Poached Salmon Colombard and Vegetables,
    132
Polyunsaturated fats, 22
Pork
    Chinese Pork and Vegetables, 165
    Pork tenderloin, tips about, 165
    Sweet-and-Sour Pork, 166
Postum, 32
Potatoes
    Baked Potatoes, 303
    Boiled Potatoes, 302–303
    "Cream" of Potato Soup (Vichyssoise),
        276–277

Potatoes (*cont'd*)
    Easy Parmesan Potato Fans, 305
    Easy Parmesan Potato Wedges, 310
    Fast Egg and Potato Frittata, 100–101
    German Potato Salad, 308–309
    grilling tips, 287
    Parsley and Mint Potatoes, 306
    Potato and Broccoli Vichyssoise, 277
    Slim Au Gratin Potatoes, 304
    Twice-Baked Potatoes, 306–307
    Yam or Sweet Potato Bake, 311
Poultry Microwaving Time Chart, 178–180
Poultry, tips about microwaving, 177–180.
    See also Chicken; Turkey
Power levels, 13–14
Preserving foods, tips about, 287–288
Protein, 23
Pudding, Lite Chocolate, 74
Pumpkin
    English Pumpkin Pudding Wedges, 80
    Reduced-Calorie Pumpkin Pie, 81

Quiche
    Tofu-Mushroom Quiche, 102–103
    See also Frittatas
Quick breads, tips for microwaving, 41–42
Quick Chow Mein, 210
Quick "Cream" of Mushroom Soup for Two, 260–261
Quick "Cream" of Spinach Soup, 261
Quick "Cream" of Tomato Soup for Two, 261–262
Quick Fish Creole, 137
Quick Mandarin Vegetables and Tofu, 314–315
Quick Saucy Chicken, 190
Quick Spaghetti Meat Sauce, 163–164

Quick Spaghetti Sauce with Meatballs, 164
Quick Vegetable Soup, 279

Ranch dressing, 251
Raspberries
    Blender Red-Raspberry Cheesecake, 61–62
    Chicken and Red Raspberry Salad, 216–217
    Raspberry jam, 254
Ratatouille, 316–317
Redfish, Cajun-style, 112
Red raspberry and chicken salad, 216–217
Red Raspberry Jam, 254
Red snapper, Kiev-style, 135
Reduced-Calorie Pie Crust, 83–84
Reduced-Calorie Pumpkin Pie, 81
Reheating breads, 43
Rice, 229–231
    Chicken and Rice Casserole, 209
    Parsleyed Brown Rice, 240
    Parsleyed White or Wild Rice, 239–240
Roasted chicken stuffed with celery and onion, 182–183
Roast Microwaving Chart, 173
Rolled Red Snapper Kiev, 135
Rolled Roast Microwaving Chart, 173
Roquefort-apple and chicken salad (hot), 215–216
Rotating a dish, 12–13
Roughy, Orange Almondine, 122–123
Round steak
    Company Round Steak, 151
    Low-Calorie Round Steak Royal, 149–150

Salad dressings
    Bleu Cheese Dressing, 246–247
    Diet French Dressing, 252
    Favorite Vinaigrette Dressing, 250–251
    Mock Ranch Dressing, 251
Salads
    Chicken-Mandarin Salad, 213
    Chicken and Red Raspberry Salad, 216–217
    Colorful Shrimp, Pasta, and Vegetable Salad, 237–238
    Curried Chicken Salad, 214
    Egg Salad Deluxe for One, 97
    Garden and Pasta Salad, 291
    Hawaiian Chicken Salad, 218
    Hot Chicken and Roquefort-Apple Salad, 215–216
    Molded Waldorf Salad, 299
    Salmon or Tuna and Macaroni Salad, 238–239
    Summer Fresh Vegetable and Fruit Salad, 289–290
    Waldorf Chicken Salad, 219
Salmon, 132–133
    Lemon Salmon with Cucumber Sauce, 133–134
    Poached Salmon Colombard and Vegetables, 132
    Salmon and Macaroni Salad, 238–239
    Salmon Salad, 239
Salsa, 128
    Shrimp Salsa, 128
Salt substitutes, 244–245
Sandwiches, 258–259
    Fast Pita Pizza Slices, 282–283
    Saucy Cheddar-and-Vegetable-Stuffed Pitas, 281
Saturated fats, 22

Sauces, 241–242
    Burgundy sauce, 146–147
    Cream sauce, 121–122
    Fast Berry Sauce, 64
    Garlic sauce, 196
    Homemade Spaghetti Meat Sauce, 162–163
    Homemade Spaghetti Sauce and Meatballs, 162–163
    Lean Blender Tomato Sauce, 249–250
    Light Gravy or Wine Sauce for Chicken or Vegetables, 248–249
    Mornay sauce, 293
    Orange Sauce, 118
    Parmesan-Lemon Sauce, 288
    Quick Spaghetti Meat Sauce, 163–164
    Quick Spaghetti Sauce and Meatballs, 164
    Sherry-Mushroom Sauce, 174–175
    Shrimp cocktail sauce, 126
    Slim Cheese Sauce, 247–248
    Sugar-Free Cranberry-Apple Sauce, 301
    Sugar-Free Cranberry Sauce, 300
    White sauce, tips about, 247
    See also Cucumber sauces; Lemon sauces; Wine sauces
Saucy Cheddar-and-Vegetable-Stuffed Pitas, 281
Saucy chicken, 190
Saucy Vegetable Fish Fillets, 136
Sausage
    Lean Breakfast Sausage, 176
    Lean Sausage Breakfast Frittata, 98
Scallops, 129–130
    Sautéed Garlic Scallops, 129
    Scallops in Wine Sauce, 130–131
Scrambled eggs, 90, 92–93
Seasoned Bread Crumbs, 243–244

Seasoned Cornflakes, 243–244
Seasoned Salt Substitute #1, 244–245
Seasoned Salt Substitute #2, 245
Seasoning, Italian, tips about, 235
Sensitive foods, 15
Sherry-Mushroom Sauce, for leg of lamb,
    174–175
Shielding, 15–16
Shrimp, 126, 237
    Colorful Shrimp, Pasta, and Vegetable
        Salad, 237–238
    Micro-Steamed Shrimp, 126
    Shrimp Creole, 127
    Shrimp Primavera, 124–125
    Shrimp Salsa, 128
Slim Apple Pie, 76
Slim Au Gratin Potatoes, 304
Slim Cheese Sauce, 247–248
Slim Corn Bread, 52–53
Sloppy Joes, 154
Snapper
    Easy Crumb-Coated Snapper, 138
    Rolled Red Snapper Kiev, 135
Snow peas, tips about, 210
Soaking beans, tips about, 271–272
Sodium, 25
Soft bread crumbs, 325
Sole (lemon), 116
Soluble fiber, 23–24, 45
Sorbets, 84–88
Soups, 257–258
    Blender Cucumber Soup, 264–265
    Broccoli Yogurt Soup, 267
    Chili con Carne, 263–264
    Chilled Watercress Soup, 280
    "Cream" of Asparagus Soup, 270
    "Cream" of Broccoli Soup, 266–267
    "Cream" of Cauliflower Soup, 269–270
    "Cream" of Mushroom Soup, 270–271

Soups (cont'd)
    "Cream" of Potato Soup, 276–277
    Egg Drop Soup, 273
    French Onion Soup, 275–276
    Gazpacho, 274
    Lean and Trim Chicken Soup, 278
    Lean and Trim Turkey or Chicken Broth,
        278
    Lean and Trim Turkey Rice Soup, 278
    Lean and Trim Turkey Soup, 277–278
    Lentil Soup, 272
    Lite Asparagus Soup, 262–263
    Low-Calorie "Cream Soup" Mix or Cream
        Soup Substitute, 259–260
    Navy Bean Soup, 271–272
    New England Clam Chowder, 265–266
    Old-Fashioned Cabbage Soup, 268
    Potato and Broccoli Vichyssoise, 277
    Quick "Cream" of Mushroom Soup for
        Two, 260–261
    Quick "Cream" of Spinach Soup, 261
    Quick "Cream" of Tomato Soup for Two,
        261–262
    Quick Vegetable Soup, 279
    Split Pea Soup, 272
    Trim Blender Vichyssoise, 276–277
    Watercress and Tomato Soup, 280
Sour Cream Substitute, 246
Sour Cream Topping, Mock, 63
Spaghetti. See Pasta
Spaghetti sauces
    Homemade Spaghetti Meat Sauce,
        162–163
    Homemade Spaghetti Sauce and
        Meatballs, 162–163
    Lean Blender Tomato Sauce, 249–250
    Quick Spaghetti Meat Sauce, 163–164
    Quick Spaghetti Sauce and Meatballs,
        164

Spaghetti Squash, 318–320
Sparkling Rosé, 31–32
Spinach
    Cheesy Meat Loaf Florentine (spinach- and
      cheese-stuffed), 158–159
    Spinach Dip in Rye Bread, 38–39
Split Pea Soup, 272
Squash
    Cheese-Topped Zucchini-Tomato
      Casserole, 326–327
    Garden Vegetable and Squash Casserole,
      321–322
    Spaghetti Squash, 318–320
    Summer Squash Medley, 320–321
    Sweet Apple-Filled Squash, 317–318
    Zucchini Boats, 323–324
Standing time, 8
Steak
    Company Round Steak, 151
    Low-Calorie Round Steak Royal,
      149–150
    Marinated Teriyaki Steak, 145–146
Steamed shrimp, 126
Stew, Turkey-Vegetable, 226–227
Stir fry Chinese style, beef and vegetable,
    144–145
Stir Fry Vegetables, 315–316
Strawberries, 79
    Blender Strawberry Cheesecake, 61–62
    Blender Strawberry Sorbet, 86–87
    Fast Strawberry Sauce, 64
    Strawberry Chiffon Boats, 72
    Strawberry–Oat Bran Muffins, 46–47
    Strawberry à l'Orange Sorbet, 87
    Strawberry Supreme Pie, 79
    Strawberry Yogurt Salad, 67
    Sugarless Strawberry Jam, 253
Stuffed Acorn Squash, 318
Stuffed artichokes, 292

Stuffed Chicken Breasts, 211–212
Stuffed Flounder, 114–115
Stuffed Green Peppers, 171–172
Stuffed Mushrooms, California-style, 34
Stuffed Mushrooms, Zucchini-, 39–40
Stuffed pitas with cheddar and vegetables,
    281
Stuffed roasted chicken, 182–183
Stuffed squash with apples, 317–318
Substitutions—In a Pinch, 334
Sugar-Free Cranberry-Apple Sauce, 301
Sugar-Free Cranberry Sauce, 300
Sugarless Strawberry Jam, 253
Sugarless Strawberry Sorbet, 87
Sugar Substitute Equivalency Table, 333
Summer Fresh Vegetable and Fruit Salad,
    289–290
Summer Squash Medley, 320–321
Sunshine Zucchini and Carrots, 327–328
Sunshine Zucchini and Carrots with Orange
    Sauce, 328
Surgeon General, dietary recommendations
    of, 27–28
Sweet Apple-Filled Squash, 317–318
Sweet Potato Bake, 311
Sweet-and-Sour Pork, 166
Swiss Asparagus, 293
Swiss chard, 322
    Garlic and Lemon Swiss Chard, 322–323
Swiss Mushroom Meat Loaf, 159
Swordfish, 123
    Orange-Baked Swordfish Fillets, 123–124

Taco salad, 172–173
Tangy-cheesy cauliflower, 296–297
Temperature probe, 16–17
Teriyaki steak, marinated, 145–146

Thawing frozen foods, tips for
  breads, 43
  fruit, 64, 66, 87
  meat, 139–141
  scallops, 130
  shrimp, 237
Time chart for blanching vegetables, 329
Time charts for microwaving
  defrosting meat, 141
  dried beans, peas, and lentils, 332
  eggs, 90
  fish, 108–109
  fresh vegetables, 330–331
  meat, 142–143
  pasta and rice, 230
  poultry, 178–180
Tofu
  Quick Mandarin Vegetables and Tofu,
    314–315
  Tofu-Mushroom Quiche, 102–103
Tomato cocktail (low-cal), 30
Tomatoes
  Cheese-Topped Zucchini-Tomato
    Casserole, 326–327
  Italian Tomatoes, 325
  Parmesan-Topped Tomatoes, 325–326
Tomato sauce, blender made, 249–250
Tortilla, cheddar, and broccoli brunch pie,
  104–105
Trim Blender Vichyssoise, 276–277
Trim Chicken Cordon Bleu, 186–187
Trim Microwave Meat Loaf or Turkey Loaf,
  156–157
Tuna and Macaroni Salad, 238–239
Turkey, 156, 177–180, 220–221
  Ground meat, tips about, 156
  Lean Breakfast Sausage, 176
  Lean and Trim Turkey Soup, 277–278
  Meat Loaf for One or Two, 155

Turkey (*cont'd*)
  Oven-Roasted Turkey, 220–221
  Sloppy Joes, 153–154
  Trim Microwave Turkey Loaf, 156–157
  Turkey Breast, 222
  Turkey Cutlets with Lemon Sauce,
    223–224
  Turkey Kabobs, 205
  Turkey Parmesan, 224–225
  Turkey Parmigiana, 195
  Turkey-Vegetable Stew, 226–227
Turkey breast, tips about, 222
Turning a dish, 12–13
Twice-Baked Potatoes, 306–307

Unstuffed chicken breasts with broccoli and
  cheese, 211–212
Utensils to use in microwave ovens, 9–11

Variable Power Levels Chart, 13
Veal, tips about, 156
Vegetable recipes
  Chicken and Vegetable Rosemary for
    Two, 200–201
  Chinese Beef and Vegetable Stir Fry,
    144–145
  Chinese Pork and Vegetables, 164–165
  Colorful, Shrimp, Pasta, and Vegetable
    Salad, 237–238
  Fresh Vegetable Medley with Parmesan-
    Lemon Sauce, 288–289
  Lemon Chicken Breasts with Vegetables,
    203
  Light Gravy or Wine Sauce for Chicken or
    Vegetables, 248–249
  Oriental Chicken and Vegetables,
    206–207

Vegetable recipes (*cont'd*)
   Quick Mandarin Vegetables and Tofu, 314–315
   Quick Vegetable Soup, 279
   Saucy Cheddar and Vegetable-Stuffed Pitas, 281
   Saucy Vegetable Fish Fillets, 136
   Summer Fresh Vegetable and Fruit Salad, 289–290
   Vegetable-Turkey Stew, 226–227
   See also specific vegetables
Vegetable tips
   blanching, 328–329
   dehydrating, 244
   Fresh Vegetable Microwaving Time Chart, 330–331
   frozen, 124–125
   microwaving, 285–287
Vented plastic wrap, 127
Vichyssoise, 276–277
Vinaigrette dressing, 250–251

Waldorf Chicken Salad, 219
Waldorf salad, 299
Warm Citrus Appetizer, 33
Watercress, 280
   Watercress and Tomato Soup, 280
White Fish Fillets with Cucumber Sauce, 134
White sauce, tips about, 247
White or Wild Rice, Parsleyed, 239–240

Whole Roasted Chicken Stuffed with Celery and Onion, 182–183
Wine for cooking, tips about, 146
Wine sauces
   for chicken or vegetables, 248–249
   for lemon chicken, 183–184
   for scallops, 130–131

Yams, 311
   Yam or Sweet Potato Bake, 311
Yeast breads, tips for microwaving, 42
Yogurt
   Frozen Blueberry Yogurt, 84–85
   Homemade Yogurt, 85–86
   Strawberry Yogurt Salad, 67
   Yogurt-Baked Flounder, 113
Yogurt makers, about, 85
Yolks (egg), freezing, 92

Zest
   citrus, 256
   lemon, tips about, 203
Zucchini
   Cheese-Topped Zucchini-Tomato Casserole, 326–327
   Sunshine Zucchini and Carrots, 327–328
   Zucchini Boats, 323–324
   Zucchini-Stuffed Mushrooms, 39–40

HARD-TO-FIND MICROWAVE AIDS

For your convenience and in answer to many requests, Micro Shake and Microwave Candy Thermometers may be reordered using the cookbook order form.

WHAT IS MICRO SHAKE?

Micro Shake is an all-natural seasoning developed solely for microwave cooking. It includes a blend of herbs and spices that beautifully browns, tenderizes, seals in juices, and deliciously seasons meats.

Micro Shake contains **NO** MSG, sugar, preservatives, or artificial color yet boasts of only 4 calories per ½ teaspoon.

—A set of 3 shakers includes Natural Fish, Country Fried Chicken, and Meat with Onion and Garlic.

—A salt-free (0 sodium) set of 3 shakers includes Natural Meat, Country Fried Chicken, and Fish.

WHAT IS A MICROWAVE CANDY THERMOMETER?

A microwave candy thermometer is designed to be left in candy, soups, or casseroles while microwaving and can be easily viewed through the oven door. It registers temperatures to 325°, which makes recipe conversion from conventional to microwave very easy. The thermometer has a paddle which may be used for stirring and an adjustable clip to hold the thermometer upright in the cooking utensil. It's a wonderful aid to candy making and may be washed in the dishwasher.

ORDER FORM

Additional copies of *Easy Livin' Low-Calorie Microwave Cooking* may be ordered directly from the publisher by returning the coupon below with check or money order to St. Martin's Press, 175 Fifth Avenue, New York, N.Y. 10010, ATTN: Cash Sales. For information on credit card orders, quantity orders, and discounts, call the St. Martin's Special Sales Department toll-free at (800) 221-7945. In New York State, call (212) 674-5151.

You may also enjoy *Easy Livin' Microwave Cooking,* a primer designed for beginning microwave cooks, and *Easy Livin' Microwave Cooking for the Holidays,* also by Karen Kangas Dwyer.

Please send me _____ copy(ies) of EASY LIVIN' LOW-CALORIE MICRO-
WAVE COOKING (ISBN 0-312-03821-6) @ $14.95 per book $_____

Please send me _____ copy(ies) of EASY LIVIN' MICROWAVE COOKING
(ISBN 0-312-02910-1) @ $10.95 per book $_____

Please send me _____ copy(ies) of EASY LIVIN' MICROWAVE COOKING
FOR THE HOLIDAYS (ISBN 0-312-03480-6) @ $10.95 per book $_____

Postage and handling
($1.50 for first copy + $.75 for each additional book) $_____

Amount enclosed $_____

Name_____

Address_____

City_____ State_____ Zip_____

Any of the products shown on page 355 may be ordered directly from the author by writing: Karen Dwyer, P.O. Box 471, Boystown, Nebraska 68010. Please make check or money order payable to Karen Dwyer.

_____ sets Micro Shake (3-shaker set) @ $8.95 $_____

_____ sets Salt-free Micro Shake (3-shaker set) @ $8.95 $_____

_____ Microwave Candy Thermometer(s) @ $7.95 $_____

Postage and handling are included in the above prices.

Amount enclosed $_____

Send to:

Name_____

Address_____

City_____ State_____ Zip_____

For answers to questions about microwave cooking, send a stamped self-addressed envelope to Karen Dwyer, P.O. Box 471, Boystown, NE 68010.

ABOUT THE AUTHOR

——————— · ❄ · ———————

Karen Kangas Dwyer was graduated from the University of Nebraska with a Bachelor of Science in Home Economics and a Master of Arts in Communication.

In addition to teaching junior and senior high school home economics for eight years, she has worked as a microwave specialist and instructor representing Sharp Microwave Ovens and as a home economist for Litton Microwave Ovens.

Mrs. Dwyer currently gives microwave presentations for television and community organizations and teaches public speaking at the University of Nebraska at Omaha. She is also the author of *Easy Livin' Microwave Cooking* and *Easy Livin' Microwave Cooking for the Holidays*.